Ireland's Traditional
Foods

In Ireland's tranquil Golden Vale, with the Galtee mountains in the background.

Ireland's Traditional Foods

An exploration of Irish local and typical foods and drinks

Prepared for GEIE/Euroterroirs
by
Cathal Cowan & Regina Sexton

Published by Teagasc,
The National Food Centre

The National Food Centre
Dunsinea
Castleknock
Dublin 15
Ireland

The National Food Centre wish to thank An Bord Bia
(The Irish Food Board) for its generous support to-
wards the publication of this volume.
First published 1997

ISBN 1 901138 04 6

Designed and produced by
A. & A. Farmar
Beech House
78 Ranelagh Village
Dublin 6

Drawings by Catherine MacConville
Photography by Hugh MacConville
Copy editing by Patricia Carroll
Printed and bound by Betaprint

Contents

Meats and Meat-based Products

Fish and Shellfish

Confectionery

Drinks

Foreword
by Alexandre Lazareff

Alexandre Lazareff is Directeur General du Conseil National des Arts Culinaires, gérant d'Euroterroirs

When the Conseil National des Arts Culinaires tried to find an Irish member for 'Euroterroirs', we got the warmest welcome from The National Food Centre as a research body with recognised expertise in Irish food products.

This European inventory was a bet that proved to be a success. We wanted to check that each of the member states of the European Community, from North to South, from the Anglo-Saxon countries to the Latin ones, had a complete range of quality products. We had previously launched an 'Inventaire du patrimoine culinaire' in each of the French regions but we did not want to claim that we were the only ones in Europe to have a culinary identity.

The National Food Centre believed in our project from the beginning, like the other members of Euroterroirs. The European Commission provided the finance for this project to commence. Thanks to this support, and the work of Cathal Cowan, Regina Sexton and the many people in Ireland who helped them, we are happy to welcome the publication of this unique description of traditional food products.

May I also congratulate The National Food Centre of Teagasc Agriculture and Food Development Authority. The publication of the Irish edition is the first of all the European publications, to be followed by the French, the Spanish, the Portuguese, the Italian and others, all in their national languages. So, congratulations and . . . Bon appétit !

Introduction
by Cathal Cowan and Regina Sexton

Over time, a substantial number of the typical and local foods of Ireland, while not unique or indigenous to the island, have become part of the cultural fabric of Irish life. They are important items, in terms of consumption and reputation, in the Irish diet. Internationally, many are closely associated with the country and identified with the Irish food scene. Items which hold such a special position in Irish foodways include the potato, whiskey, stout, tea, smoked salmon and shellfish. In addition, a number of unexpected products have also been recognised as traditionally Irish. In this group non-native items such as spiced beef, gingerbread, simnel cake, plum pudding and marmalade have, through outside influence, been established as popular or occasional foods in Ireland. In many cases the methods of preparation and production originated with the influx of outside settlers and colonisers through time, and within this area the influence of English food traditions in Ireland is of particular relevance.

A small number of products are uniquely Irish in origin. Of these, items such as drisheen and buttered eggs are produced and enjoy popularity only within the country, while others, notably soda bread, now enjoy a limited international reputation as an original Irish product. In addition commercial products like Jacob's Biscuits and Cream Crackers, and Iced Caramels, though Irish in origin, are now manufactured both at home and in Britain.

Specific regional foods and dishes include Waterford blaa, Dingle mutton pie, Cork drisheen and potato dishes such as boxty and potato cakes, which are particularly associated with northern Irish counties.

Changing food trends and tastes are, however, threatening the production and consumption rates of certain products. In particular, meat derived products such as drisheen, tripe, salted pork bodice, and salted stockfish like ling are declining in popularity and must be recognised as foods under threat. We are happy, therefore, that these declining traditional foods have been recognised and documented.

Over the last few years, The National Food Centre has documented typical and local foods of Ireland, as part of an EU project called *Euroterroirs*. The project sought to identify and describe foods and drinks of local origin in each region of the EU member states and has now been completed.

The co-ordinator of this EU-funded project (within the framework of the EAGGF, 8th article, EU Commission DGVI) was GEIE (Groupement Europeén d'Intérêt Economique) Euroterroirs. GEIE Euroterroirs is an overall management group or association, with members from all the participating EU states and is chaired by the French partner.

We completed the main part of our work for the EU on the Euroterroirs project in 1995. Regina concentrated on the history of the foods and Cathal covered the other aspects, particularly technique and producers. We forwarded a draft report with information on the 100 foods and drinks to GEIE Euroterroirs. They are publishing a shortened version, including foods from all the countries of Europe, in French.

We wrote to many companies to seek their assistance. We undertook many telephone interviews and visited a number of companies. We compiled a list of products associated with Ireland or regions of Ireland. Besides typical and local food and drink, products more recently introduced, so-called 'emerging products', could be included if they have a strong local association (historical, geographical, cultural). Both regions of Ireland, North and South, were covered by the brief for the project. We owe a debt of gratitude to the many people who provided information and any deficiencies in conveying information provided are our own. Without their help this publication would not have been possible. A select bibliography of the books and sources we found most helpful is included.

We have made an attempt to include any product with a strong local association or tradition. Information on the techniques used as well as the history of the product, a product description and composition and use is documented. This section obviously could not include commercially sensitive information. To some extent the element of chance decided which producers we talked to and we hope anyone not mentioned will not feel too aggrieved by this. As our brief required us to identify commercial producers, we included commercial examples of products which are mainly made at home, such as plum pudding. We have taken the approach of including general type entries such as pork sausage rather than any particular brand of sausages. Some products are exceptions to this, in view of their long history and uniqueness. For this project the emphasis was on food products that involved some processing. Some fresh products such as the potato are included, although they are not processed, because they are such important foods in the Irish tradition; GEIE Euroterroirs were in agreement with this approach.

We hope the publication is not only of academic interest but will stimulate food companies to develop their marketing of many of our local and typical foods.

We think we have covered all the most suitable products and the book includes a full contents page which allows the reader to see at a glance the products covered. However, this publication will without doubt unearth some more interesting food products; for example, there are many more black puddings and sausages which are of interest.

GEIE Euroterroirs did not accept some of our entries in their report to the EU as they argued that some of the products have no tradition, or no specific tradition in Ireland that is different from other countries. The former was argued for farmhouse cheeses (processes not old enough) and the latter for cabbage, onions, apples, tea and butter. We have decided to leave these entries in our book as such an approach is helpful to the ongoing debate on protection.

In recent years the EU introduced regulations for protection of designations of origin (PDO) and geographical indications (PGI) for agricultural products and foodstuffs (No. 2081/92) and on certificates of special character (CSC) for agricultural products and foodstuffs (No. 2081/92). The regulation on certificates of special character was amended in 1994. This regulation deals with proper use of the EU symbol (No. 2515/94).

Just one Irish product had been submitted for such protection by the time we had completed our report. In terms of meeting the more rigorous criteria for labels of origin or geographic designations many of our selections may not be suitable, for various reasons, but we feel our work gives the Irish food industry valuable information for those interested in seeking these labels.

Some food interests have asked us for suggestions on how the food industry could take advantage of these EU regulations. Despite the rigorous criteria we feel Ireland needs to test the waters, as it were. The industry itself must take the initiative and in this way we will establish whether we have a case for recognition of any of our foods.

Indeed the EU has recently launched a campaign in all the member states on the EU labels of protection for foods of specific character. In Ireland interested food producers should contact the Food Division of the Department of Agriculture, Food and Forestry.

In conclusion, Teagasc would like to acknowledge EU Commission support in undertaking this research and the assistance of Bord Bia towards the cost of publication.

Meats and Meat-Based Products

Tripe and drisheen on sale in Cork City (Covered Market).

Dry-cured Bacon and Ham

Ireland's traditional breakfast

Also Traditional cure, Limerick ham, Belfast bacon, Irish roll, Ulster cure, Irish dry cure

Variant: Hard-cured country bacon.

Special feature: Dry salt cure with added secret ingredients. Traditional cures in other parts of Ireland were also usually dry salt cures. Although some are probably a higher salt cure than wet cures, the Limerick cure was a mild cure.

Composition: Pork, cured. In the case of an Irish roll, the back of the bacon is boned out and rolled. The original Limerick cure contained salt, water and saltpetre. Nowadays prepared saltpetre-substitute products are used to give preservation and colour. The ingredients are pork, salt, saltpetre or saltpetre substitute.

History: Traditionally bacon and ham were dry-cured at home. One family method was as follows:

When you take your hams out of the pickle, and have rubbed them dry with a coarse cloth, hang them in the chimney, and make a fire of oak shavings, and . . . over it horses litter and one pound of juniper berries. Keep the fire smothered down for 2 or 3 days and hang them up to dry.

From about 1750 the commercial salting of pork and bacon grew rapidly in southern Ireland. In 1820 Henry Denny began operating in Waterford and developed several production methods for bacon, which he patented. Lipton opened his first shop in Glasgow in 1871 and 'initially he specialised in ham, bacon, eggs, butter and cheese which he imported direct from producers in Ireland'.

Bacon-curing became a very important industry in Limerick City. One company in the business indicated that cooked hams were originally developed in Limerick by an English farmer from Cumberland. Mattersons, the first Limerick bacon factory, was established in 1839 and in Cork somewhat later. Eventually, four large factories were set up— Mattersons, Denny's, O'Mara's and Shaws. The emergence of tank cures in the 1920s and 1930s made dry cures uncompetitive, as yields improved with tanking. Irish bacon was the brand leader. Indeed in 1894 Denny acquired a plant in Denmark and introduced Irish techniques to the Danish industry. O'Mara's set up bacon-curing facilities in Russia in 1891.

Thus, apart from the domestic production of salted bacon and ham, Ireland from the late eighteenth century developed an extensive export trade in bacon and ham. Bacon was exported to England, whilst hams were delivered to

Parisian, Indian, and North and South American markets. The method of curing was by sandwiches of salt and pork laid many feet deep on a curing floor. However, in 1862 the method of injecting strong brine into the meat by means of a pickling pump was invented and was immediately adopted by the Irish bacon-curers. This period also saw a concerted effort by the commercial Irish bacon industry to improve the quality of bacon destined for the export market. In 1887 the Bacon Curers' Pig Improvement Association was formed and successfully introduced the Large White Ulster into most districts by the turn of the century. This breed provided suitable raw material for the production of 'Wiltshire' bacon.

Failure to modernise led to the decline of bacon production in Limerick in the 1960s and all four factories closed down. The Limerick cure appears to have originated by chance, as a Department of Agriculture document from 1902 states:

> 1880 . . . Limerick producers were short of money . . . they produced what was considered meat in a half cured condition. The unintentional cure proved extremely popular and others followed suit. By the turn of the century the mild cure procedure was brought to such perfection that meat could . . . [be] sent to tropical climates for consumption within a reasonable time.

Different industry contacts disagree about whether the typical Limerick product is produced or not nowadays.

Belfast was also an important place for bacon and Irish roll is popular in Northern Ireland. Today the only product identified in the dry cure tradition is from Sprott's of Portadown, Northern Ireland.

Use: Hams are particularly popular at Christmas. Otherwise all types of bacon are used throughout the year. Bacon rashers are popular for breakfast and boiled bacon and cabbage is a traditional Irish dish. Dry-cured products can have a long shelf life and Limerick ham has a shelf life of six months at ambient temperatures.

Technique: Bacon and hams were treated somewhat differently, with additional flavourings used for the ham. Farmers originally cured their own bacon. They rubbed the fat pork with crude rock salt and well water. The meat often assumed a pink colour, due to nitrates in the salt and well water. The meat's keeping quality was extended by storing the cured meat dry. In some cases the bacon was stored in the farmhouse chimney, where it was dried and smoked. An Ulster cure is a dry cure in the traditional way. The pigmeat was laid out and salt shovelled on the sides. They were taken and wrapped in a roll with cords. For dry cures in other parts of the country the salt was put on and the bacon was stacked in a cold room on large wooden shelves.

In Limerick long cut hams were used, cut a further 5 cm below the oyster bone than other hams. They were also shaped after curing. The hams were put in water, or steeped for a night, then taken out and laid on pallets, after which they were dry salted. Saltpetre was used to extract the moisture, and sometimes sugar and other flavourings were added. The process took three weeks, with the hams being turned from time to time. This process is a dry cure. The hams are then carefully piled for maturation.

For a mild cure less salt is used than for other dry cures. There are conflicting views on whether juniper was used at all, despite the association of Limerick ham with juniper. Others say some juniper may have been used, but it was not that important and juniper was not exclusive to Limerick. In Limerick, following maturation, the hams were washed and placed in a drying oven for several hours. They were then removed, refrigerated overnight and trimmed and prepared for drying and smoking. The final yield of the ham is about 75% of its original weight. Historically, the smoking was done by the wholesalers who bought the hams.

For smoked bacon, the side must be slowly dried out. The traditional method of smoking was to have a large brick stove with a cement floor and a simple ventilating system with a draught from the bottom. Sawdust was spread evenly on the floor to a depth of 10–15 cm. Hot ash was spread across the sawdust and allowed to smoulder until it burnt out. Oak and deal sawdust are mostly used nowadays. The temperature is about 32°C. In Limerick the hams were heavily smoked and were therefore very dry.

Belfast hams were dry salt cured and produced in factories. The ham was cut in a rounder shape than other hams. After curing and maturing they were washed, dried and the meat side trimmed and rubbed with vegetable oil, giving a bright lean appearance. The shank was sawn off short, giving a thick, compact look. Most were smoked but some were pale dried. The dry salt cure ensured a firmer fat and meat. Today the only product identified in the dry cure tradition is from Sprott's of Portadown. Portadown is often a pale ham but it may also be smoked.

Traditionally pork flitches destined for domestic consumption were wet or dry (hard) cured. If the dry cure process was used, the pork was well rubbed and covered with salt and saltpetre, and then barrelled between layers of coarse salt and left to cure for two to three weeks. In old-style hard-cured country bacon, fat pork is layered into a barrel in salt (about 7–8 kg of collar and other pieces are layered into the barrel) and is left for 6–8 weeks in the barrel, where the red colour develops of its own accord. The bottom half turns into liquid and the bacon is dry cured. This bacon hanging in shops is called a 'flitch'.

Producers: William Sprott, Edward Street, Portadown, are traditional producers of dry-cured Ulster cooked ham. Hard-cure country bacon is produced by some butchers such as O'Connor's in Limerick and is still quite popular. Shannon Vale Meats produced Limerick ham at Christmas until recent years but no longer do so and nobody is producing it in the traditional way nowadays.

Season: Dry cure bacon tends to be produced only at Christmas.

Packaging: Both loose and prepacked.

References: Northern Ireland Pork and Bacon Forum and Morrow, personal communications. Michael O'Mara, Limerick, personal communication.

Useful address: William Sprott (Portadown) Ltd, Edward Street, Portadown, Northern Ireland. Tel 01762-332-157.

Wet-cured Bacon and Ham

Special feature: Most Irish bacon is wet cured nowadays.

Composition: Uncooked bacon pieces vary in size and weight from 1 to 3 kg. Rashers are thin slices of bacon; pieces of ham vary in weight. The cooked product, known as 'cooked ham', is also available. Cooked hams vary in size and shape, with a weight of between 4 and 6 kg. Hams are available with rind on or off, with bone in or bone out, and flat or round in shape. The ingredients are pork, cured, uncooked or cooked. Most brines used in Irish cures today contain water, salt, sodium nitrate, sodium nitrite and sodium phosphate. Regulations govern the amount of these ingredients. Cooked hams can be smoked or fully cooked.

History: The pig features prominently in the story of Irish traditional food, and bacon and ham are amongst the oldest of all Irish foods. There is substantial evidence for the consumption of pigmeat in the prehistoric period and there can be no doubt that much of this was salted down and smoked. For example, there is evidence of consumption of wild boar as early as 7000 BC from the Mesolithic site of Mount Sandel in Co. Derry.

In the early medieval period bacon and ham were considered important items in the diet of all classes. These meats are mentioned frequently throughout the corpus of early Irish literature. Salted bacon appears continuously in the seventh- and eighth-century Brehon Laws as a food item and as a food rent demanded by lords from their clients. In addition, bacon and ham are included in the list of luxury foodstuffs referred to in the eleventh-century *Aislinge meic Conglinne*.

That bacon and ham continued as important constituents of the later medieval diet is evidenced in the continual regulations passed regarding the keeping of large numbers of pigs on the streets of cities and towns. In 1382, for example, it was agreed by the citizens of Waterford that any pigs found wandering on the streets were to be killed immediately by specifically appointed pig wardens.

Numerous foreign visitors to Ireland also comment on the popularity of bacon in the diet of the Irish. Payne, writing in his late-sixteenth-century work, *A Briefe Description of Ireland* 1589, states:

> *butter, cheese, bacon, beef and tallow were very cheap.*

John Dunton also points to the prevalence of bacon; in his 1698 *Letters from Ireland* he describes a typical Irish dinner as follows:

> *Dinner now came in, we had salt fish and eggs, hen and bacon, and rabbits, but our liquor was very ordinary.*

Similarly, Amhlaoibh Uí Shúileabháin of Callan, Co. Kilkenny, dined frequently on bacon and other choice meats. In his diary entry for 5 October 1828 he writes:

> *we had a splendid dinner at the parish priest's . . . we had a leg a mutton, bacon, chickens and white cabbage . . .*

In all, however, meat was a luxury item in the diet of the Irish and when meat did appear on the table it was most usually in the form of bacon. Until the early twentieth century most Irish rural households kept a small number of pigs. Tradition dictated that one pig was slaughtered on St Patrick's Day and one or two more were killed in October or November. This small pig-keeping was encouraged by the use of potatoes, which were not considered a commercial crop, in the fattening of the animals.

The history of the Irish bacon-processing industry is contained in the section on Irish dry-cured bacon and ham.

Use: Large hams are important at Christmas. Otherwise all types of bacon and ham are used throughout the year. Cooked ham is mainly used in sandwiches or in salads, but is also used as an added ingredient in other dishes. It has a shelf life of about 40 days, depending on the brine and cooking method used. The product is kept refrigerated at all times and, once sliced, should be consumed in a day or two.

Technique: In the traditional wet cure the meat was rubbed with salt and placed in brine for three weeks. After curing, the salted meat was wrapped in brown paper and placed in the chimney to smoke. Nowadays bacon is multi-needle-injected and tank-cured. This process takes at most 9–10 days for the wet cures used in Ireland, compared to 6–8 weeks for dry curing. The period of tanking is about 3–4 days followed by a period of maturation, with the amount of brine measured automatically for each side. The injection represents about 8–10% of the side weight. Before putting sides in a brine tank, they are sprinkled with salt. Sides are stacked and battened down. The brine contains salt (sodium chloride), sodium nitrate and sodium nitrite. After brining, sides are stacked and allowed to mature. While tanking used to be considered essential, with the introduction of phosphate cures in recent years it is now possible to inject only and not to tank.

After curing, the meat may be smoked and the final yield is higher than the original—about 110% of the original pork leg for a ham. The product can also be cooked for cooked hams and then vacuum packed. Nowadays many hams are cooked in steel pots with a defined mould shape. Low-fat, low-salt and phosphate-free hams have become more popular in recent years.

Producers: All the major bacon factories produce bacon by injecting and tanking. Many thousands of tonnes are produced annually for both the home and export markets. Cooked hams are produced by a number of companies. The product is usually vacuum packed with a label or packed in greaseproof paper, if crumbed.

Packaging: Both loose and prepacked.

Reference: Michael O'Mara, Limerick, personal communication.

Useful address: Galtee Meats, Mitchelstown, Co. Cork. Tel 025-84227.

Pork Sausage

Special feature: Irish pork sausage is a typical product of Ireland and has its own particular composition. The inclusion of relatively large quantities of rusk is found only in Irish and British sausages.

Composition: Sausages are cylindrical in shape, usually 7.5–10 cm long and about 1 cm wide. Standard-size sausages are sold loose or packed. Packs contain 8 or 16 sausages in 227 g or 454 g packs. Larger sausages are packed 8 to 10 in a 454 g pack. Smaller sausages are called cocktail sausages and a 454 g pack contains 32 sausages. The colour is light pink but can vary due to variations in pigmeat colour. The softness of the sausage depends on whether frozen or fresh ingredients are used.

In general, sausages contain approximately 65% (minimum 55%) pork meat, 22% water and 11% rusk. Forequarter meat (shoulder) and bellies are used as well as some fat, and loin and leg trimmings. Some producers use some skin. Rusk includes seasonings, salt, spices, herbs, antioxidants, polyphosphates and preservatives. Recipes vary from producer to producer; for example, one producer uses forequarter and bellies as well as loin and leg trimmings but no head or gel meat. For one factory the composition is pork, water, rusk, soya protein, mixed spices, salt, SO_2 and colour E128. Per 100 g there are 12 g protein, 22 g fat and 9 g carbohydrate. Each producer has their own special formulation which ensures great variation in flavour. In most cases the natural casings used are from sheep gut. Casings from the gut of pigs are thicker and less used today. Synthetic collagen casings are also widely used.

History: Given the socio-economic importance of the pig in Ireland since at least the prehistoric period, it is reasonable to assume that pork sausages were an important component of the Irish diet from this period onwards. Sausages are mentioned regularly in the eleventh-century tale *Aislinge meic Conglinne*: in the visionary land of plenty, the gate to a fortress is described thus:

> *there was a gate of tallow to it, whereon was a bolt of sausage.*

Sausages and fat puddings are also mentioned in the Middle English poem 'The Land of Cokaygne':

> *the pinnes beth fat puddings rich met to princes and kinges.*

The popularity of the sausage is well illustrated in Charles Read's humorous description of Peg Woffington, an eighteenth-century Irish actress who rose to prominence after playing the role of Polly in John Gay's *Beggar's Opera*:

> *she [Peg] wrenched from her brow a diamond and eyed it with contempt, took from her pocket a sausage and contemplated it with respect and affection.*

In rural areas the consumption of sausages was connected with periods of pig slaughter. Andrew Kettle, a prosperous Dublin farmer, outlined his diet in the years preceding the Famine of 1845–8 as follows:

the food is nearly all home-made; whole-meal bread, oaten meal flour . . . no tea, not much butcher's meat unless at Christmas and Easter, but plenty of pork steaks and the best of pig's puddings and sausages.

The commonality of sausages following the killing of a pig must surely have been a long-established culinary tradition in rural Ireland, even well before the nineteenth century. The establishment of the commercial bacon-curing industry in the late nineteenth century brought sausages such as Denny's to the tables of a growing urban population. Indeed Denny's sausages are described with relish by James Joyce in *Ulysses* (1922):

He halted before Dlugacz's window, staring at the hanks of sausages . . . Fifty multiplied by . . . The shiny links packed with forcemeat fed his gaze and he breathed in tranquilly the lukewarm breath of cooked spicy pig's blood . . . And a pound and a half of Denny's sausages . . . The ferreteyed porkbutcher folded the sausages he had snipped off with blotchy fingers, sausagepink.

In Dublin most of the well-known sausage makers developed their businesses early in the twentieth century. Byrnes, for example, were established about 1875 and were producing pork sausages before the Second World War, but sausages were not a big seller until the 1940s.

Use: At any meal, but particularly breakfast, as part of the traditional Irish breakfast. Sausages are grilled or fried, and are used in a traditional Dublin dish, Dublin Coddle. Fresh sausages must be kept refrigerated and used within a few days of purchase.

Technique: Originally fresh and cured pork trimmings were simply mixed with water, breadcrumbs and spices and packed into pork casings. Today considerable variation in preparation may occur, but generally ground pork meat is mixed with rusk and seasonings, formed to size and shape and filled into casings. Casings may be natural or synthetic.

Pork meat is derinded, skins taken off, boned out and chopped in a bowl chopper (60 cm diameter) with ice and seasonings. Oleo-resins are often used instead of natural seasonings. Oils from the spices are pressed out of kernels by suppliers of seasonings, bagged and the same amount added to each bowl of choppings. This increases the shelf life of the product as ordinary ground spices are likely to have a higher bacterial count. Belly pork is then added to the bowl. The fat helps ensure a soft texture. Breadcrumbs, chilled water and possibly more ice are added. Some mixing may be done by hand, turning the mix to ensure proper blending of the ingredients. The skill of the operative is important in judging the degree of mixing. The mixing can be stopped once the mixture comes off the edge of the bowl. The product is then put into the filler and filled into casings. Natural casings are used for loose sausages and some packed sausages, and synthetic casings for packed sausages. Nowadays the sausage production process can be highly automated, particularly by some of the larger plants who started processing sausages in more recent years.

Producers: Many butchers and small manufacturers as well as major co-ops produce pork sausages. Well-known brands include Byrnes, Denny, Olhausen, Galtee, Mallons, Granby and Kearns.

Season: Sausages are produced and used throughout the year.

Packaging: Sold loose or in trays and in overwrap film packs of 8 or 16. Some packs are gas flushed.

Reference: Kevin Byrne, Byrnes (Chatham Street), personal communication.

Useful addresses: John Brennan, Secretary, Irish Butchers' Association. Tel 0902-75326. Byrnes (Chatham Street) Ltd, 14A Fade Street, Dublin. Tel 01-677-2819.

Black Pudding

Variants: Small local producers use their own name.

Special feature: Black pudding is a typical pigmeat product found everywhere in Ireland. The recipe varies from producer to producer but all contain animal bloods and pork meat.

Composition: Black pudding is black in colour with white flecks. It is a long cylindrical sausage shape, about 2.5 cm thick and two-thirds of a metre long in the traditional ring form. Pieces of 198g in weight are typical from large-scale producers. Newer products can have different shapes, such as flat pieces or pudding cakes.

The traditional ingredients of black pudding are blood, pork skin and seasonings. While original recipes contained pig blood, most producers use beef blood. Pigskin with fat on is important to bind the ingredients and gives a white fleck to a pudding. Denny's black pudding is made from animal bloods, pork, cured pork, barley, oatmeal, rusks, starch, onion, caseinate, salt, spices and cereal extract. Rudd's is made from fresh blood, barley, rice, pork fat, water and spices. It contains no additives. Casings are usually from beef gut.

History: Despite the popularity of black pudding in the diet of the Irish, there are few direct references to the product. A variety of puddings is mentioned throughout the eleventh-century tale

Aislinge meic Conglinne, but the contents of these are not specified. Similar puddings are mentioned in the early fourteenth-century poem 'The Land of Cokaygne', which may have been written in the east of Ireland:

> Flour cakes are the shingles all
> Of church and cloister, bower and hall.
> The pinnacles are fat puddings,
> Rich meats of princes and of kings.

While there is a paucity of reference to black pudding in the historical texts, the Irish folklore record of the nineteenth and twentieth centuries abounds with reference to puddings and their preparation. One such account, from Ring in Co. Waterford, recounts traditional preparation techniques:

> Long ago when they killed pigs they kept the intestines to make puddings. They washed them clear in a running stream and they were left to soak in spring water overnight. The casings were cut into fifteen inch lengths, tied at one end. Salt, lard, oatmeal, finely chopped onions, spices, peppers and cloves, together with a cup of flour were mixed with the pig's blood which had been collected in a bucket. Each pudding was three-quarters filled and tied at the end. It was dropped into a pot half-filled with water which had been brought to simmering point, cooked for about an hour, then taken up, allowed to cool, and divided amongst the neighbours. This was always done. When needed for use puddings were fried in a pan.

Indeed the widespread preparation of black puddings in a domestic setting continued well into the mid-twentieth century.

The increase in commercially produced black pudding in the late nineteenth and twentieth centuries is evident in James Joyce's 1922 *Ulysses*:

> In Youkstetter's, the porkbutcher's father Conmee observed pig's puddings, white and black and red, lying neatly curled in tubes.

It is only in this century that the major dairy/meat co-ops started to produce black puddings; local butchers made their own for centuries. Each producer has developed his or her own recipe.

Use: The product must be kept refrigerated. It is sliced in 12 mm slices, which can be either grilled or fried. Typically used as part of the traditional Irish breakfast, it is used nowadays at other meals and is sometimes found on restaurant menus as a starter with an apple sauce. It can be served at any meal with bacon and sausage.

Technique: As for white pudding, farmers originally used pork pigmeat trimmings with the additional ingredient of blood. The product is cooked until no blood oozes out and may be filled into natural or synthetic casings.

Beef blood is used, as it solidifies quickly in boiling water. Lamb blood does not solidify enough, while pig blood may be used if enough beef blood is not available. For example, one typical producer mixes the blood with the fat and some cooked rind as well as oats, pearl barley and seasoning. The rind helps to bind the ingredients together. Natural spices are used, and the product is cooked in a boiler until firm. This ensures that bacteria are killed and the blood is cooked. In fact the product could be eaten without further cooking by the consumer. After cooking, it is filled into natural beef gut casings. Nowadays large food companies producing black pudding have automated plants.

Producers: Produced by large dairy and meat companies, independent butchers or by other small-scale producers. Black pudding is widely available in all supermarkets and butchers' shops.

Season: Black pudding is produced and used throughout the year.

Packaging: Sold in sausage-type casing with labelling information on the casing. Puddings are often vacuum packed by cylinder machine in pre-printed film by large producers.

References: Kevin Byrne, Byrnes (Chatham Street) Ltd., Dublin 2, personal communication. Galtee Meats, Mitchelstown, Co. Cork, personal communication.

Useful addresses: Kerry Foods, 66 Cookstown Industrial Estate, Dublin 24. Tel 01-451-1833. P. and D. Rudd Ltd, Busherstown, Moneygall, Co. Offaly. Curran's Victuallers, Green Street, Dingle, Co. Kerry. Tel 066-51398.

Drisheen

Variant: A pudding called 'packet' is manufactured in Limerick.

Special feature: A unique preparation of animal bloods, made only in Cork and surrounding counties. The exact quantity of each blood used is critical, as the product will be too light and fragile if too much sheep blood is used and too heavy if too much beef blood is used. In Cork, it is sometimes served with tansy sauce and, as it is rather tasteless, drisheen depends on sauce for flavour. It is recommended as a highly nutritious dish for the elderly and for pregnant women.

Composition: A specialised type of blood pudding found in Cork with possible variants in parts of Kerry, Limerick and Clare, drisheen is found mainly in these regions. Its shape resembles an inflated bicycle tube; the colour is a brownish-grey and it has a distinctive blancmange-like texture. It is composed of serum, which forms after the coagulation and settling of a mixture of sheep and beef blood, mixed with salt and boiled in beef casings. Until the 1950s tansy was occasionally used as a flavouring. Today no additives or flavourings are used.

History: Sexton suggests that drisheen may be alluded to in the eleventh-century tale *Aislinge meic Conglinne*, which focuses on the monastery of Cork. A rudimentary form of the dish receives frequent mention between the fifteenth and nineteenth centuries. During this period a succession of antiquarian visitors to Ireland recorded that the Irish engaged in the practice of blood letting for food. The earliest reference is a native one, occurring in the fifteenth-century tale 'Forbais Droma Damgaire' in the *Book of Lismore*. The earliest reference in English is by Edmund Campion writing in 1571, who states:

Theire kyne they lett bloode, which growen to gelly they bake and overspreadd with butter, and soe eate yt in lumpes.

The tradition of blood consumption was endorsed by the commercial developments of Cork City between 1680 and 1825, when it became the largest and most important port in Ireland and Britain for the export of salted beef. The best beef cuts were exported to England, Europe and America and as a by-product the city's slaughter-houses were producing large quantities of beef blood. It is highly likely that the blood was used in the manufacture of the pure blood pudding of Cork.

Traditionally three varieties of drisheen were manufactured in Cork: sheep drisheen, beef drisheen and tansy drisheen. Sheep casings were considered too fatty and troublesome to clean, while the attraction of tansy-flavoured drisheen waned with the general decline in the product. Beef drisheen is the only variety now available.

Use: In Cork drisheen is traditionally served with tripe. The drisheen and tripe are almost invariably served with a rich buttery white sauce which is seasoned with plenty of pepper. Drisheen can also be sliced and fried lightly in butter and is usually eaten with a thick slice of heavily buttered white bread.

Drisheen is claimed to be very good for people with stomach complaints as it is very digestible, and in the past has been used in St Finbarr's Hospital in Cork.

Technique: The beef and sheep bloods are blended in a tank and a little salt added. The mixture is left to solidify and, once coagulated, the blood is scored with a knife and left overnight. By morning the mixture has separated into blood serum and coagulated blood residue, the original blood mixture rendering about one-fifth of its original volume in usable serum. The serum is drawn off and carefully poured into prepared beef casings. The puddings are then boiled for about five minutes and are ready for sale, needing no further cooking. The drisheen is delivered to city stalls and shops and must be kept under water. It is very perishable and is not suitable for freezing.

Producer: There is one commercial producer, in Cork. Demand is good and all production is sold readily. The producer also retails the product, selling to local butchers, hospitals and hotels.

Season: Drisheen is produced throughout the year.

Packaging: Sold loose and cut to order.

Reference: Stephen O'Reilly, personal communication.

Useful address: A. O'Reilly and Sons, The Tripe and Drisheen Stall, 1, 2 & 10 Grand Parade Market (English Market), off Patrick Street, Cork. Tel 021-966397.

Clonakilty Black Pudding

Special feature: An original local product with a very workable loose and rough texture. The pudding is particularly suited for use in a number of mixed food dishes.

Composition: The pudding, which is dark brown, is a long cylindrical sausage shape and is sold in rings which vary in weight from 0.5 to 0.75 kg. Its ingredients are beef blood, pinhead oatmeal, minced meats, onions, spices and beef casings.

History: Philip Harrington opened a butcher's shop at 16 Sovereign Street (now Pearse Street) in Clonakilty, in West Cork, in the 1880s. He manufactured black pudding to his own recipe and sold it in his shop. In 1976 Edward Twomey purchased the butcher's shop and inherited the secret black pudding recipe. He continued to produce the black pudding and after some time began selling it to other shops in the area.

By 1983, responding to a growing interest in black pudding, Edward Twomey decided to brand the product. The result was Clonakilty Black Pudding made with Harrington's Original Recipe.

Use: The pudding can be used at all meals but is particularly associated with the traditional Irish breakfast. In recent years Clonakilty pudding has appeared on the menus of some of the country's most prestigious restaurants.

Technique: Pinhead oatmeal is soaked in beef blood overnight. The following morning the remaining ingredients are minced together and blended into the blood mixture. The beef casings are filled with the mixture and boiled in water for 20 to 25 minutes. The mixing of the ingredients and their ratio differentiate Clonakilty pudding. After boiling they are hung in racks and rolled through a cooling tunnel. They travel through a second cooling tunnel and are then boxed for distribution.

Producer: Edward Twomey of Clonakilty is the only commercial producer and the product is available in shops and supermarkets nationwide.

Packaging: The puddings are sold in loose rings. There is a label attached to the casing which bears an illustration of a ring of pudding. Inside the ring are the words 'Original Harrington Recipe'. 'Clonakilty Black Pudding' is printed on the upper section of the logo.

Reference: Edward Twomey, personal communication.

Useful address: Edward Twomey, 16 Pearse Street, Clonakilty, West Cork. Tel 023-33733.

Staunton's Black Pudding

Special feature: An original local West Cork product. The Stauntons slaughter their own pigs and therefore all the raw ingredients for the puddings are 'in-house products' emanating from a single source.

Composition: The pudding, which is dark brown, is a long cylindrical sausage shape, and is made of pig blood, cereal, fresh onions, seasonings and spices, pork fat and beef casings. Each pudding varies in weight between 0.75 and 1 kg. Stauntons also produce a black-coloured pudding which is identical to the brown pudding in terms of ingredients but has a characteristic jet black casing. This colour is obtained by dyeing the casing with natural dyestuffs.

History: In 1954 Michael Staunton opened a butcher's shop in the small town of Timoleague in West Cork. He was also engaged in retailing pork, beef and lamb. With the opening of the shop in 1954 Mr Staunton also began production of loose linked sausages and home-made pork puddings. The puddings, based on a family recipe, soon gained popularity in the locality. In the early 1980s the butcher's shop closed but his sons, Michael and Fachtna, continued the retail business, specialising in the production of pork puddings. Today the Stauntons slaughter 200 pigs a week on their premises in Timoleague and the by-products are used directly in the preparation of the puddings. At the time of writing the Stauntons were in the process of constructing a new purpose-built factory for the slaughter of animals and the manufacture of puddings, with a budget of approximately IR£2 million.

Use: Black pudding can be used at all meals but is particularly associated with the traditional Irish breakfast of bacon, sausage, eggs and mushrooms.

Technique: Pig blood is soaked in a cereal binder the night before the puddings are prepared. The following morning the remaining ingredients are minced together in a large chopping bowl. The minced ingredients are blended into the blood mixture and placed in the beef casings via a vacuum filler. Once filled, the puddings are boiled in water for fifteen minutes. After boiling they are taken out and left to cool. The cooked pudding rings are delivered to shops in approximately 2, 4 and 7 kg (5, 10 and 15 lb) weights. These are cut into various weights by the individual shop owners.

Producer: Stauntons of Timoleague are the only commercial producers and the product is available in many shops and supermarkets in Ireland.

Packaging: The puddings are sold in loose rings with an information label attached to the casing. The label is red and green and is rectangular in shape, with an illustration of a pig inserted in its upper section. Staunton's also vacuum pack puddings destined for sale in larger shops and supermarkets.

Reference: Anthony Staunton, personal communication.

Useful address: Michael Staunton and Sons, Main Street, Timoleague, Co. Cork. Tel 023-46128.

White Pudding

In Irish Putóga bána

Many producers prefix white pudding with their own name, e.g. Denny White Pudding and Rudd's White Pudding.

Special feature: White pudding is a typical Irish food, made from cooked pigmeat and cereals.

Composition: Made in a long round cylindrical piece about 25 mm thick and up to 30–60 cm long in a ring, it is off-white in colour with a varying weight. The full ring is over 400 g in weight, while a typical piece is 198–9 g. The ingredients are pork, water, cured pork, barley, oatmeal, rusks, starch, onion, caseinate, salt, spices and cereal extract. The ingredients for white pudding from one factory are pork, water, barley, rusk, soya protein, onion, salt, seasoning, emulsifier, sodium phosphate, flavour enhancer (monosodium glutamate) and preservative (sodium nitrite, sodium nitrate, sodium sulphite). One home-made white pudding contains fresh pork, bacon, pork liver, water, barley, rice, oatmeal, cornflour, onion, eggs and spices. It contains no additives. While the colour is off-white, the more traditional puddings are darker, as they contain liver. Some of the pigmeat has to be salted. The casing is usually beef gut.

History: The preparation of white pudding was intrinsically associated with the killing and butchering of the pig on Irish country farms. Once the stocks of pig blood were depleted in the making of rich black puddings, the remaining offal pieces were used to make a variant, the white pudding.

It is probable that white puddings are referred to in the eleventh-century tale *Aislinge meic Conglinne*. The tale mentions 'full fat puddings' and in the visionary land of plenty Mac Conglinne encounters a food-filled house with

puddings fresh boiled
They were its thatch rods.

Until the early twentieth century the pig was one of the most important economic assets for the Irish farmer and particularly for the Irish peasantry. White puddings were, therefore, a regular item in the diet. In the diaries of Amhlaoibh Uí Shúileabháin from Callan in Co. Kilkenny there is a reference to a festive meal on Easter Sunday 1827 which consisted of

delicious mutton, whitish pudding, and
a drop of whiskey.

In addition, Florence Irwin, in her 1937 publication *Irish Country Recipes*, refers to white puddings (also called drisheen) made with a mixture of unrendered lard, onion, salt and pepper packed into prepared pork casings. In rural areas, domestic production of white pudding continued until well into the mid-twentieth century and it was customary to distribute the surplus puddings to neighbouring farms.

Commercial puddings have been made by butchers for many years and nowadays they are produced at these enterprises.

Use: The product must be kept refrigerated before cooking. Sliced in 12 mm slices and grilled or fried, it is usually served hot with bacon rashers and sausages. White pudding is a standard part of a traditional Irish breakfast.

Technique: There are almost as many recipes as there are butchers. The most traditional product was made from pigs' lung, heart and liver as well as oatmeal and seasonings. Traditionally, pigs' liver, lights, heart, stomach and gristle pieces were boiled until tender. These were then minced and boiled again together with a mixture of allspice, thyme, cayenne pepper, pepper and onions. Subsequent to the second boiling, the flavoured mincemeat was mixed with breadcrumbs and boiled rice, and the dry mixture was packed into prepared pig casings. It was usual to use the large intestine in the preparation of white puddings. Natural casings are still often used in loosely sold products but synthetic skins are more widely used nowadays.

One typical producer uses liver, pigs' head and lung. The ingredients are cooked in a boiler, the meat is taken off the bone, put in a chopper and chopped into pieces, the seasonings are added and it is mixed. It is cooked again, left overnight in water and then put into a filler and into casings.

Producers: Widely produced by large meat processors, smaller sausage makers and individual butchers.

Season: White pudding is produced throughout the year.

Packaging: Sold loose or encased. Rudd's is loose in a transparent plastic wrapper with a stick-on label.

Reference: Kevin Byrne, Byrnes (Chatham Street) Ltd, personal communication.

Useful address: Byrnes (Chatham Street) Ltd, 14A Fade Street, Dublin 2. Tel 01-677-2819.

Brawn

Brawn was an established Irish dish by at least the early nineteenth century.

Also Collared head, pigs' head cheese

Special features: Cured and cooked pigmeat pieces in a gelatine.

Composition: Made of cooked pigmeat pieces in its own gelatine (jelly), brawn looks like a firm jelly with chopped pieces of meat throughout. Sections are shaped in an oval or rectangular container, or as a roll: 0.3 by 1.2 by 1.5 metres or 1.8 by 1.2 by 0.9 metres would be typical. A piece may weigh 1–3 kg. The colour can be pinkish, depending on whether dye has been used, and the amount and type.

One Dublin-based producer uses cured pigs' cheeks, ham shanks and pork skins, aspic or jelly. Another producer uses cured heads and hock, some ribs, leftovers and collars. In some cases added flavours such as nutmeg or lemon juice are used. Occasionally some vinegar may be added.

History: Given the importance and prevalence of pork in the Irish diet, it was necessary to employ a convenient method of preserving the perishable pig offal pieces of the head, feet and tongues. Brawn was therefore an established Irish dish by at least the early nineteenth century. The dish is noted in an 1801 Co. Waterford manuscript recipe book where brawn is termed 'a pretty collar'.

The preparation of collared head is also detailed in Mary Carbery's *The Farm by Lough Gur,* recalling life in late nineteenth-century Co. Limerick:

> From pigs' heads she made brawn or collared head, . . . We little girls helped — or hindered—her as she went about her preparations. We—and mother—made collared head by boiling part of the head almost to jelly, then chopped the meat very small and spiced it with pepper, allspice and finely ground nutmeg. After that we put it in a mould which opened on a hinge and was kept shut with a skewer. When it was set and turned out of the shape it made a dish fit for a King.

Naturally the traditional ingredients of brawn vary, with some including only pressed pig's head (referred to in Florence Irwin's *Irish Country Recipes* as 'pig's head gelatine'); other recipes call for the pressing of 'pig's cheek' and feet; while others include pig's head, feet and sheeps' tongues.

Brawn is also mentioned in Oliver St John Gogarty's 1939 book, *Tumbling in the Hay*:

> I stole a glance at Mercedes and ordered a helping of collared head.

With the establishment of a large bacon-curing industry in the latter half of the nineteenth century, brawn began to be produced on a commercial basis. During this period, 'tinned brawn' was produced for both the home and overseas market.

Brawn has been made in Dublin for over a century. Associated with poorer areas of the city, it is no longer manufactured by some of the original producers. There are still a number of producers in Dublin—Capranis of Bray and Byrnes of Chatham Street have been producing brawn for over sixty years. Pork butchers became increasingly important in the second half of the nineteenth century in Dublin and brawn was one of the products that was prepared. It is a particular tradition in the Summerhill area of Dublin.

Use: Brawn is regarded as a food eaten by the less well-off. Slices are used cold as part of a midday or evening meal.

Technique: Cast iron boilers were used in the past, but these have given way to aluminium or stainless steel boilers. The cast iron boiler gave a more gentle 'cook', giving greater tenderness and better flavour.

At one of the present-day production plants, pigs' cheeks and ham shanks are cooked in the boiler. The amount of salting affects the final flavour. Pickling is usually done by single injection needle or by steeping in a liquid pickle. Some pigs' feet or skins of pork are included to get gelatine into the water. The cooked meat is lifted out of the boiler, and the water is strained off. The meat is taken off the bones and put in a chopper bowl and chopped into pieces. In order to get a fleck of fat some rind and the meat are mixed in the boiler. The original water with the gelatine from the bones is added until the mixture is sufficiently thick but not too runny. Seasonings and gelatine (to ensure proper setting) are added and the mixture is brought to the boil. Dye is added by some producers.

The hot liquid product, which is nearly at boiling temperature to ensure it is almost sterile, is then poured into containers. These containers, which vary in size, can be deep trays or smaller containers about 10–12 cm deep. The product is then left to cool as it hardens on top, and must be stirred every half hour to ensure uniform cooling and thickening. Producers need to do this to ensure that it settles properly and meat pieces are uniformly distributed in the aspic rather than rising to the top. It is then refrigerated overnight and is set by the following morning. In summer it is made early in the morning, but in winter it can be made later in the day. It is kept in containers until taken out for sale in retail outlets.

If the cooking is not done sufficiently quickly the product can go sour. Soft lard at the top of the container acts as a seal. Traditionally, galvanised tin containers were used. While rectangular and oval shapes were usual, bowls were also used. The moulds used by current producers are also about 11 cm deep.

Producers: Brawn is produced by a number of pork butchers in Ireland. One producer makes about 200 kg daily, while another makes 50 kg at a time and sells half of this in a week. Shelf life is about three weeks in the container, but this reduces to a week or less if taken out of the container. If it is produced in larger shapes and then cut and wrapped it will not keep as long. Brawn is also produced by factories and is available in supermarkets as well as butchers and other grocers.

Season: Brawn is produced and consumed throughout the year.

Packaging: Taken out of containers and sold loose in slices. The thickness of slice is varied to customer requirements. Customers usually buy between 0.1 and 0.25 kg at a time.

References: Kevin Byrne, Byrnes (Chatham Street) Ltd, personal communication. Conor Caprani, personal communication.

Useful addresses: Byrnes (Chatham Street) Ltd, 14A Fade Street, Dublin 2. Tel 01-677-2819. Capranis, 6 Main Street, Bray. Tel 01-286-2044. Hick's Butchers, Wood Park, Sallynoggin, Co. Dublin. Tel 01-285-4430.

Crubeens

Also Pig's feet, pig's trotters

Special feature: Traditional Irish product.

Composition: Pig's feet.

History: The prevalence of the pig in Ireland, together with the self-sufficient nature of the Irish rural economy, ensured a careful utilisation of all pig offal parts. Pigs' feet/crubeens have always been a popular dish, particularly amongst the poorer sectors of Irish society.

One of the earliest references to the consumption of crubeens is found in the early ninth-century tale, *Scéla Mucce meic Dathó*:

> Conall then began to carve the pig . . . He did leave the foretrotters to the Connachta.

The crubeens are given by Conall to his enemies the Connaughta in a gesture of disrespect and insult, which results in a wild outbreak of violence and slaughter. It is clear that in the earliest documentary evidence crubeens had a very low status as a food. This observation is reaffirmed in another tale, 'The Settling of the Manor of Tara', which contains a reference to the pig's trotters being thrown in the course of the feast to 'the jugglers and the rabble and the common people'. The distinct association with the poor may well explain the general paucity of reference to crubeens in the documentary record throughout the late medieval and early modern periods.

There is frequent reference to pigs' feet by nineteenth-century travellers in Ireland. William Makepeace Thackeray, for example, who made a tour of Ireland in 1842, comes across crubeens frequently and refers to 'Open Pigfoot Stalls' in town streets. With the establishment of the commercial bacon industries in the latter half of the nineteenth century, crubeens became abundantly available, particularly in the large cities attached to the curing factories: Cork, Waterford, Limerick, Dublin, Belfast. In these cities, up to the 1940s it was commonplace for women to sell baskets of cooked crubeens in the open streets. Up to this period, crubeen-eating was also strongly associated with public houses and the many illegal drinking establishments (shebeens).

Use: Boiled until tender. Traditionally, they were a popular tea-time dish or snack food. They are particularly associated with stout-drinking and large social get-togethers, such as wakes, evening refreshment following a wedding, or sporting occasions when large

groups of supporters bring their own sustenance. Today, some publicans serve salty crubeens, but this is now more a novelty than an adherence to the tradition referred to earlier. Nowadays they are very popular at stag parties.

Technique: Pigs' feet are properly scalded, and cleaned, all hooves and skin removed. They are then pickled and sold raw. They are brined in a tank for 8–10 hours by some butchers. In the past they were cooked only if they were not quickly sold raw. Nowadays they are boiled and crumbed and sold cooked.

Producers: Available in Cork Covered Market and at butchers' shops in the Meath Street area of Dublin.

Season: Crubeens are sold throughout the year.

Packaging: Sold loose.

Reference: Clarkes Butcher Shop, Meath Street, Dublin, personal communication.

Useful address: Clarkes Butcher Shop, Meath Street, Dublin. Tel 01-454-0275.

Skirts and Kidneys

Special feature: The dish of skirts and kidneys is uniquely Irish. The skirt and kidney are boiled together and served as a dinner dish.

Composition: A pork skirt is the diaphragm of the animal, a long flat piece of meat varying in length and width in accordance with the individual animal. The kidney is also from the pig.

History: Given the socio-economic importance of the pig in Ireland since at least the prehistoric period, it is reasonable to assume that pork skirts and kidneys were an important component of the Irish diet from this period onwards. A dish of skirts and kidneys was traditionally a prized meal that followed immediately after the killing of a pig in rural areas. The dish was considered special because the meat was consumed fresh, unlike most of the pig which was salted down for later consumption. In urban regions the tremendous popularity of the dish is directly attributable to the establishment of the export trade in provisions of salted beef and bacon from the eighteenth century onwards. Indeed from this time skirts were consumed at home, mostly by the poor, but they were also exported abroad, as is evident in the following account from Cork in the mid eighteenth century. Lord Chief Baron Edward Willes, writing of the city in 1757–62, says:

> *Hearts and skirts—salted and ship'd in bulk for Scotland. This is a trade lately found out at which the poor are very angry.*

The establishment of the commercial bacon-curing industry in the nineteenth century also made the product abundantly available. Limerick, Cork and Waterford became areas where skirts and kidneys were popular food items. In recent years, however, the popularity of the dish has been steadily falling due to the decline in offal consumption. Today skirts and kidneys are probably consumed mostly by the older generation.

Use: A dinner or tea-time dish.

Technique: The diaphragm flap of meat is butchered from the pig's rib cage. The diaphragm is skinned and larger ones

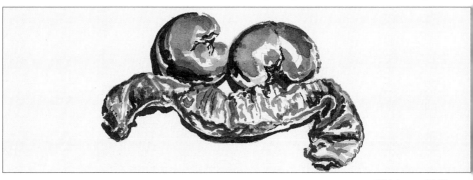

Skirts and kidneys

are split lengthways. The kidney is removed from the loin, the surrounding fat is removed and it is then scored and cleaned to remove urine.

Producers: Many of the large commercial bacon-curing factories butcher the skirts and kidneys and distribute them to shops and market stalls.

Packaging: At market stalls the skirts and kidneys are sold loose. In supermarkets they are sold in trays and in overwrap film packs.

References: Ahern's Fresh Meat Stall, Cork Covered Market, Cork, personal communication. Anthony Staunton, Timoleague, Co. Cork, personal communication.

Useful addresses: Ahern's Fresh Meat Stall, Cork Covered Market, Cork. Stauntons Meat Retailers, Timoleague, Co. Cork. Tel 023-46128.

Bodice

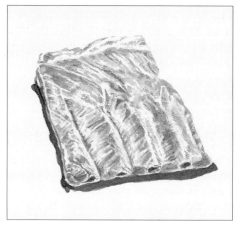

Traditionally bodice was consumed mostly by the poor and it formed the main meal for many large families.

Also Pork ribs, bacon ribs

Special feature: Corned pork ribs are associated with urban areas that have a history of extensive commercial pork butchering.

Composition: Called 'bodice' in Cork, the ribs have a pinkish-grey colour and are sold in rib sheets of between one and a half to two pounds in weight. The ribs can also be cut from the sheet and sold in any weight desired by the customer. The ingredients are pork ribs, salt, brown sugar, water, nitrates and nitrites.

History: Since at least the early medieval period Ireland has had an extensive pig economy and consequently pig meat and offals have been commonplace in the diets of both urban and rural dwellers. Historically, fresh offals have had a weak association with rural areas. Offal spoils quickly and in country areas the off-cuts were generally used in preparation of preservable foodstuffs such as sausages and black puddings. In contrast, the city's large bacon-curing industries afforded a year-long supply of offal produce. In particular, the establishment of large bacon-curing factories in Cork, Limerick and Waterford in the latter half of the nineteenth century resulted in the availability of a wide variety of offal cuts, and corned bodice was one of the more popular and enduring items. Traditionally bodice was consumed mostly by the poor and it formed the main meal for

many large families. In Verdon's *Old Cork Remembered* Maisie Flynn recalls childhood meals served in poorer households in the city during the 1920s and 1930s:

> Sunday it would be corned beef and cabbage. Monday was leftovers because it was wash day. Tuesday, tripe and drisheen. Wednesday, steak and chops and onions. Thursday, [corned] ribs and cabbage . . . Friday battenburg [battleboard] fish.

Today corned ribs are a popular, though declining, foodstuff.

Use: Corned ribs are used as part of main meals. Pre-cooked ribs are also a popular snack food for those going fishing or hunting.

Technique: The rib cage is butchered from the bacon loin or the streaky belly. It is then cut into individual sheets which are soaked in brine for up to four or five days. Traditionally the ribs were heavily cured and soaked in a pickle for one to two weeks. However, nowadays, a shorter pickling period is used. The ribs are pickled by the retail meat companies but they can also be pickled by the shop retailers on their own premises according to their own recipes. In recent years a number of prepared pickling recipes have come on the market and are used increasingly to make up the pickling brine. The convenience of these branded mixtures has discouraged many retailers from preparing their own individual brines.

Producers: Cured ribs are produced by a number of retail meat suppliers such as Stauntons of West Cork. Fresh ribs are also cured by many meat shops such as Mulcahy's in the Cork Covered Market. Ribs are also prepared by many butchers in Dublin and other parts of Ireland.

Packaging: The ribs are sold loose in shops and market stalls, where they are cut to the individual requirements of customers.

Reference: Michael Staunton, personal communication.

Useful addresses: Mulcahy's Meat Stall, Old English Market, Cork. Michael Staunton, Main Street, Timoleague, Co. Cork. Tel 023-46128.

Irish Beef

Irish beef, for sale on the local market, was traditionally cut differently from meat in other European countries. Nowadays few butchers cut traditionally. Generally heifer meat is sold on the home market. The forequarter consists of shin on the bone, brisket, rib of beef, top rib (roast or shoulder steaks), traditional rib steak and neck. The hindquarter consists of flank steak, sirloin and ham (round) of beef.

Composition: Fresh heifer meat.

History: Beef-eating is a long-established feature of the Irish diet. One of Ireland's oldest historical sources, the seventh- and eighth-century Brehon Laws, testifies to the prevalence of beef-eating, especially among the aristocratic classes. In these texts beef is demanded as a substantial portion of the annual food rents extracted by lords from their clients. The association of beef with the aristocratic class is highlighted in the ninth-century tale *Fled Bricrenn*. Here beef is the centre piece for a great banquet:

> *a lordly cow that is also seven years old, and, since it was a calf, it has eaten nothing but heather and twigs and fresh milk and herbs and meadow grass and corn.*

A range of beef cuts and varieties is listed in the eleventh-century tale *Aislinge meic Conglinne*, including rump pieces and corned beef. Specific meat cuts are also mentioned in the eighteenth-century *Shapland Carew Papers*— for example, sirloin steak was regularly delivered to the Wexford estate of the wealthy Carew family throughout the second half of the eighteenth century.

Overall, however, the historical evidence indicates that for the general population beef was a rarity and consumed only on festivals, holy days and at weddings and wakes. When John Dunton visited the O'Flagherties in Iarconaught in the west of Ireland, he was presented with beef 'boyled and roasted' as a mark of hospitality to their guest.

The lack of meat in the diet of the general population is related to the immense economic value of cattle in society. Until the seventeenth century cattle were an indication of wealth and social status and valued highly for their dairy produce, and were rarely killed for their meat outside aristocratic circles. The seventeenth-century *Advertisements for Ireland 1623* highlight this widespread reluctance:

> besides the common sort never kill any [cattle] for their own use, being contented to feed all the year round upon milk, butter and the like. (Lucas)

However, from the late seventeenth century an extensive beef export industry was established in Ireland. Between 1685 and 1825 Cork became one of the largest ports exporting beef to Britain, Europe and America.

For many years Irish butchers cut meat in the form outlined below, but since the 1970s consumers have demanded new cuts and the traditional way of cutting is now a rarity. Changes in consumer preferences and the use of different breeds have led to major changes. There are few butchers now cutting in the traditional style, but one who does is Martin & Joyce in Benburb Street, Dublin.

Use: Beef is widely used in various dishes, usually as a main component of the meal. Popular uses include grilling, roasting and stews. Details of the cuts for each use are given in the section on technique.

Technique: The main processes in cutting a heifer carcass are as follows:

A. Forequarter, including shin, brisket, rib and neck

1. *Shin.* Shin was taken off and sold off the bone.

2. *Brisket.* The whole piece of brisket was pickled and sold on the bone as corned beef. It was hand pumped with saltpetre pickle. There are three parts to the brisket: button end, high brisket and plate end.

3. *Rib.* Of the remaining part of the fore end, a piece with six or seven ribs was cut. It was cut into three or four pieces and each of these pieces could be further divided in two. The chine bone was broken so that each double rib piece could be cooked. Each piece was cut to allow it to be folded. Since the late 1960s this part has been boned and rolled. The remaining piece is cut into three: top rib, traditional rib and neck. Top rib was usually used for top rib roast or housekeeper's cut, with the round bone piece used for stewing beef. Alternatively this piece was used as steak for frying, called 'shoulder steaks'. Traditional rib steak or chuck steak was cut with a hand saw, yielding 12–15 steaks. It was hung up with

the bone on. Today cutting is done with a band saw.

4. *Neck.* The neck was used for stewing beef or mince.

B. Hindquarter

There are three main parts: flank, sirloin and ham. The udders were left on and there was considerable dug fat. The kidney was also left. Beef kidney suet was made for customers and surplus dug fat was rendered down (boiled and strained) for dripping. This is not done today.

1. *Flank.* The flank steak was cut off and generally minced. Nowadays it is rolled.

2. *Sirloin.* The sirloin piece, including the diamond bone and fillet, was cut into 12–15 steaks (bone in sirloin). Today the fillet is removed and sold separately and the sirloin is boned out. The rest was the T-bone and was usually sold as steaks but also as a T-bone joint. Boned out, it is called 'strip loin' today. The remaining piece, the wing end, was prepared similarly to rib on the bone. It was sold as a piece for roasting on the bone.

3. *Ham.* From the ham the aitch bone piece was sold fresh for roasting or else with the bone in, pumped with pickle, and sold as corned beef (tail end corned beef). The bone was removed if the customer so wished. The next piece is the round. It is cut in one of two ways, first, for ball of the round, as two pieces each about 1.4–1.6 kg or more (sold more trimmed today), and, second, traditional round steak. In this case the top end was for frying, the bottom end for stewing. Sometimes customers bought the whole piece, sometimes they bought top end or bottom end. In total between 12 and 15 pieces of round steak were cut on the bone. Today the round is seamed, i.e. cut down the seam rather than across. Finally, the last piece of the ham is the hind shin or leg beef. This was sold, like the shin, on the bone for stewing or boiling for soup.

Producers: There is huge production of meat in Ireland. While most is exported, the domestic market also consumes large amounts.

Season: Produced and consumed throughout the year, with higher seasonal production in the autumn.

Packaging: Meat is sold loosely and wrapped to order. It may also be prepacked for supermarket sales.

References: John Byrne, personal communication. John Cosgrave, personal communication.

Useful addresses: Cosgrave Bros Butchers, 104 The Square, Tallaght Town Centre, Dublin 24. Tel 01-459-6961. Martin & Joyce, Victuallers, 74 Benburb Street, Dublin. Tel 01-677-2002.

Tripe

In Irish Tríopas

Special feature: Tripe is easy to digest and is therefore recommended as a nourishing dish for those with stomach disorders. In Cork it is traditionally eaten with drisheen, the city's blood pudding.

Composition: Beef paunches, washed and bleached in a peroxide solution. The paunches weigh about 7 kg. Tripe is hard—like leather in the raw state. Beef paunches are stomach tissue from the first and second stomachs of cattle.

History: Tripe is often mentioned in the eleventh-century tale *Aislinge meic Conglinne*. Caulfield points out that it was a common and regularly available commodity in the shops of Cork City in 1649, and it also featured as a regular and important item in the diet of the community of Franciscan friars in Cork throughout the eighteenth century.

Traditionally the stomach tissue of all cud-chewing animals, in addition to that of the pig, was consumed. However, by the mid-twentieth century the sale of sheep and pig tripe was abandoned by offal vendors. Today all tripe is invariably beef tripe. The most abundantly available comes from the first stomach or rumen and is termed 'plain' or 'blanket' tripe. More popular, but not always available, is the 'honeycomb' which comes from the second stomach or reticulum. It is given its name because of its characteristic honeycombed texture and is preferred by some Irish people.

Clarkes of Meath Street, Dublin, have been selling tripe since 1937. Street fighters in Dublin in the 1930s and later decades consumed it, as it was good for absorbing alcohol.

Use: Tripe is an everyday dinner dish and is also served as a Saturday night tea-time dish. It is a very bland foodstuff and relies almost exclusively on its accompanying sauce for flavour. The tripe is usually cut into small pieces about 2.5 cm square and requires at least one full hour of boiling. When cooked, it is reheated in a mixture of milk and previously cooked onion, which can be left thin or thickened with some flour and butter. Tripe was a popular remedy for an excess of alcohol.

Technique: After slaughtering, the animal stomachs are removed and cleaned with spray rods. The cleaned paunches are chilled before delivery to the tripe dressers. At the triperies the enveloping stomach membranes and fat are removed in a 'washing machine'. The fat may also be scraped off with a skin patter. After washing, the tripe is boiled in a large vat and bleached in a weak peroxide solution. It is simmered for a number of hours—at least three. The exact preparation process is kept secret by some companies. The tripe receives a final trimming or dressing before being sent to stalls and shops for sale.

Producers: Available at many butchers' shops in Dublin and throughout the country. Salmons of Finglas, Dublin, supply many shops. Tripe is also available widely throughout Cork City and county. It is sold in the Cork Covered Market and by a number of butchers' shops. O'Reilly's open-air stall in the market is dedicated exclusively to the sale of tripe and drisheen. Tripe is also widely available in Limerick and Dublin.

Season: Demand varies with the seasons and is greater in the winter.

Packaging: Dressed tripe is kept moist and sold loose in butchers' shops and stalls. It is cut to order, wrapped separately for each customer and sells at £2 per kg.

Reference: Stephen O'Reilly, personal communication.

Useful addresses: A. O'Reilly and Sons, The Tripe and Drisheen Stall 1, 2 & 10 Grand Parade Market (Old English Market), off Patrick Street, Cork. Tel 021-966-397. Clarkes Butchers, Meath Street, Dublin 8. Tel 01-454-0275.

Corned Beef

Also Salt beef, pickled beef, hung beef

Special feature: A traditional Irish product, salted beef served with cabbage is one of the most famous Irish dishes.

Composition: Traditionally the ingredients of salted beef are beef, salt and saltpetre. Modern products contain sodium ascorbate. Most butchers use silverside or topside, which is lean, though brisket (breast), which is fatty, may also be used. Brisket is very popular in some parts of Dublin. Joints are between 1 and 3 kg in weight.

History: Corned beef has a long history in the Irish diet. It is listed as a 'delicious prodigious viand' in the eleventh-century text *Aislinge meic Conglinne*:

many wonderful provisions,
pieces of every palatable food,
. . . full without fault,
perpetual joints of corned beef.

In the eighteenth century it was commonplace for large aristocratic households to salt their own beef after slaughter for later consumption. Daniel Corkery illustrates this practice in his work *The Hidden Ireland*, referring to the wealthy Martin family who killed a bullock once a month. Any beef that was not consumed fresh was pickled down in large stone troughs.

Salt beef appeared frequently on the menus of the aristocratic classes, and if those not so well-off were fortunate enough to eat beef, it was also of the salted variety. In all, therefore, beef was most frequently consumed salted/corned, with fresh beef a rare and luxurious treat for all classes; as Cullen points out:

> As farmers could scarcely afford to kill more than a single cow, the bulk of beef consumed by the population at large, even by the larger farmers was salted.

Hung or salt beef was a popular item at town and city markets throughout the nineteenth century: Lieutenant Joseph Archer, in his *Statistical Survey of Dublin* in 1801, records that hung beef was on sale in the Dublin market at 11d per pound.

Corned beef has a distinctive regional association with Cork City. Between the late 1600s and 1825 the beef-corning industry was very important in the city and county. In this period, Cork exported corned beef to England, much of Europe and as far away as Newfoundland and the West Indies. In 1776, for example, Cork exported 109,052 barrels of salt beef to the British Empire, Europe and America. During the Napoleonic Wars corned beef exports from Cork were at an all-time high and the British Army was principally supplied with corned beef from Cork. In the eighteenth and nineteenth centuries the tradition of corned beef travelled with the Irish emigrants to America. Today vast quantities are consumed on St Patrick's Day by the extensive Irish-American population. Downey's of Dublin have been producing corned beef for over a century.

Use: Among the feasts it was particularly associated with are Halloween,

Christmas, St Patrick's Day, Easter Sunday and other festive occasions such as weddings. Special joints were kept for festive occasions. The salted joint is soaked overnight and brought to the boil in fresh water, then simmered for a period, usually about an hour to a kilogram and a little more, depending on the weight and cut. Some vegetables and herbs are usually added to the cooking pot. Corned beef is served hot, in slices, usually with cabbage and potatoes.

Technique: Traditionally the most effective means of preserving beef after the slaughter was to corn beef pieces in a simple wet pickle of salt, sugar, saltpetre and water. Charles Étienne Coquebert de Montbret, who described the city of Cork in 1790, maintained that the use of saltpetre in the preservation of beef was a Jamaican innovation and remarks:

> but not insisted upon until a short time ago.

Today meat is rubbed with salt and then put in a prepared salt pickle for a number of days. In some cases it may be pumped and left for a night only in the pickle. Needle injection may be used for the tail end, while a vein pump may be used for the brisket. Although mostly sold uncooked, some butchers cook the product and sell it at delicatessen counters. In the 1940s Hicks boiled the meat in an open boiler like a huge saucepan containing 40–50 gallons of water. Today low temperatures and controlled cooking in a steam oven are used so the product loses less weight.

Producers: Joints are produced by many butchers. Supermarkets also buy in the beef and cure it.

Season: Prepared and consumed throughout the year.

Packaging: Joints are sold either loose or packed in butchers and supermarkets. Downeys (Connoisseur Meats) use a multi-coloured stick-on label with cooking instructions.

References: John Downey, Connoisseur Meats and Game Ltd, personal communication.

Useful address: Downeys (Connoisseur Meats and Game Ltd), 97 Terenure Road East, Dublin 6. Tel 01-490-9239.

Spiced Beef

Special features: Salt beef with special spices and herbs.

Composition: Beef marinated and cured with spices and herbs. The outside is dark brown, while the meat is red in colour due to spices and curing. The cut used is topside or silverside. Each piece weighs about 5–6 kg. The ingredients are beef, spices such as pimento, cinnamon, ginger, salt and water. Nowadays other ingredients such as cider, wine and Guinness may be used in a marinade as well as brown sugar and treacle.

History: Traditionally it was a special and novel treat at Christmas time, as beef was most frequently consumed salted during the rest of the year. The exotic spiced flavours of the Christmas joint therefore made a welcome change from mundane salt beef.

An early reference to spiced beef occurs in the fourteenth-century poem 'The Land of Cokaygne', which is thought to have been written somewhere in the east of Ireland. A modern rendering of the Middle English text reads:

> *The meat is spiced, the drink is clear,*
> *No raisin-wine or dull slops there.*

Whether this is clear evidence of spiced beef in Ireland in the fourteenth century or simply the voicing of a poetic ideal is difficult to substantiate. Nevertheless, what is certain is that following 1169 and the Anglo-Norman invasion, there was a dramatic increase in imports of spices to Ireland. The Anglo-Norman taste for spiced foods must surely have influenced native Gaelic culinary practice and it is likely that the spicing of beef was an Anglo-Norman innovation. The difficulty and, more important, the expense of procuring the different spices ensured that spiced beef was a luxury of the rich. Reference to it become more frequent in the nineteenth century: an 1850 manuscript recipe book from Cork details the spicing of beef in a domestic setting.

Spiced beef was one of the many dainties served at dinner for 'Little Woman's Christmas' by Aunt Kate in James Joyce's short story 'The Dead':

While Gabriel and Miss Daly exchanged plates of goose and plates of ham and spiced beef . . .

Originally prepared at home, spiced beef is nowadays mostly commercially produced. There are a number of companies and butchers who have been preparing spiced beef for generations. Downeys of Dublin, for example, have been preparing spiced beef to the same recipe for 160 years.

Use: It is particularly associated with St Stephen's Day, the day after Christmas, but used throughout the year. Spiced beef is soaked overnight and then boiled in the same water. It is cooked for about an hour and a half per kilogram. It may be served hot or cold, cut in thin slices—hot spiced beef is often served with cabbage. If served cold, it is allowed to cool in its liquid. Used as part of a main meal or in sandwiches, spiced beef can be kept for several weeks and the longer it is spiced the

longer it will last.

Technique: One traditional producer uses beef, topside and tail-end or silverside. The meat is put in a barrel and soaked in salt water with spices and herb marinade for one to three months. The product is then taken out of the barrel and wrapped in salt and spices which preserve it. Spices and flavourings used can include allspice (pimento or Jamaican pepper), nutmeg, cinnamon and ginger. Garlic is added at Christmas. Other producers may not marinate for as long, or use different recipes. Supermarkets prepare spiced beef for Christmas. They buy in the silversides and marinate them for a few weeks. A standard brine and marinade are made up separately, then mixed. The beef is pumped and marinated, spiced for a few days, then vacuum packed, which allows the flavour to soak in. Downeys marinade the beef in cider casks, and have used English West Country cider for over a century. Commercial factories may use allspice only. Other recipes include brown sugar, black peppercorns, juniper berries, powdered cloves and mace.

Producers: Spiced beef has been sold in Cork for over two hundred years. There are a small number of traditional producers with stands in Cork Covered Market. A number of meat factories also produce spiced beef and sell the product to supermarkets. Spiced beef is also produced by butchers in Dublin such as Downeys and F. X. Buckley and supermarkets such as Superquinn. In the home, corned beef may be spiced to give a spiced beef.

Season: Spiced beef is mainly produced for Christmas and some producers prepare it only for the Christmas market.

Packaging: Sold loose, in pieces between 1 and 2 kg, cut to customer requirements in Cork Covered Market. The supermarket product is vacuum packed. The large vacuum packs are opened, the beef is cut into pieces of 1 to 2 kg and vacuum packed again for sale to the consumer. Cooking instructions are usually on the bag.

References: Paul Boyling, Best Meats, Cork Covered Market, personal communication. John Downey, Connoisseur Meats and Game Ltd, company leaflet and personal communication.

Useful addresses: Best Meats, Cork Covered Market. Tel 021-294098. 'Downeys Connoisseur Meats and Game Ltd', 97 Terenure Road East, Dublin 6. Tel 01-490-9239.

Tongue

Also Ox tongue, pickled ox tongue

Variant: Spiced ox tongue.

Special feature: The tongue is salted and sometimes pressed.

Composition: Tongues from cows, heifers and steers. Each tongue weighs 2–4 kg. It is made from tongue, brine and gelatine, and pressed.

History: Traditionally tongue was one of the few offal dishes considered appropriate for inclusion in the diet of the wealthier sectors of Irish society. It appears frequently in the estate accounts of the Carew family from Castleboro in Co. Wexford throughout the eighteenth century. For example, on 20 June 1774 tongue is purchased along with other luxury foodstuffs such as veal, rump steak and sirloin steak.

Salted tongues were an important item of export throughout the eighteenth century. Lord Chief Baron Edward Willes, writing of Ireland between 1757 and 1762, refers to the export of salted tongues from the port of Cork which were destined for the tables of British military officers.

Tongue is regularly mentioned in a variety of nineteenth-century historical documents. The diaries of Amhlaoibh Uí Shúileabháin from Callan in Co. Kilkenny refer to the purchase of 'six neat's tongues' on Shrove Tuesday 1831 to preserve for Easter. An 1850 manuscript cookbook from Co. Cork also includes a recipe for salted tongue.

Spiced tongue was also a common nineteenth-century dish. It was spiced with allspice, ground ginger and ground cloves and flavoured with onion, thyme, parsley, salt and pepper. Today spiced tongues are available for sale in the Cork Covered Market, where they are particularly popular during the Christmas season.

Use: If unpressed tongue is bought, the consumer will do their own pressing. Ox tongue is soaked overnight, or alternatively the first boiling is thrown off to remove the excess salt. It is simmered for 1–1.5 hours. The skin is removed and the tongue is pressed in a bowl under a weight or between two plates. The tongue is best consumed cold. Pressed tongue is usually served as a cold meat with other cold meats and salads.

Technique: In the past the tongues were dry salted. The extent of preparation varies. In some cases the tongues are cured by butchers by needle injection or at processing plants and sold raw to the consumer. Larkins in Meath Street, Dublin, use needle injection and soak the tongues for two days. Another producer injects and soaks for 24 hours. They are sold with the skin on. In other cases the skin is removed and pressing is also undertaken.

Some local butchers may press tongues if they can get a supply, but this is rare nowadays. When they do, the tongues are allowed to soak for about three days in a typical salt solution. The tongues are then cooked, the skin is removed, and they are packed into containers, cans, casings or moulds. Sinews which are high in gelatine are also cooked and minced and almost liquefied. This is added to the container and fills it out. The can is sealed and sterilised—Downeys Connoisseur Foods, for example, cook and press between two and four tongues, depending on the size of the press. Iron or aluminium presses are used, but pressed tongue is prepared only to order. These processors tend to use the tongue's own juices and juice from pigs' feet instead of gelatine. This helps to bind the product. Christmas is the most popular time for spiced tongue. West Country cider is used in the marinade, plus around fourteen spices. No additives are used and the tongues are bedded in cloves for two days, then finished with ordinary spices. The recipe is claimed to be an old Dublin recipe from the last century.

A chopped tongue product is also available.

Producers: Cured uncooked ox tongues are prepared by some butchers' shops, such as Larkins in Meath Street, Dublin. Pressed tongue is rarely produced nowadays due to the export of most tongues to France from export licensed plants. The product available in many supermarkets and delicatessens is usually imported. There is, however, some pressed tongue available from time to time from local butchers, such as Downeys in Dublin.

Packaging: Cured unpressed tongue is sold loose. Pressed tongue is sliced to order and sold loose wrapped.

Reference: John Downey, Connoisseur Foods, personal communication.

Useful address: Bresnans Butchers, Cork Covered Market, Cork.

Irish Stew

In Irish Struisín gaelach

Special feature: Traditional and famous Irish food dish, made with mutton chops and vegetables, which originated as a peasant dish made with readily available cheap ingredients. Mutton was the only fresh meat available throughout the year.

Composition: A stew made from mutton pieces, potatoes and onions. Lamb is usually used today instead of mutton. The traditional composition of the dish is a matter of dispute among purists, but Irish stew is usually made from mutton or lamb chops or stewing lamb, bacon, onions, potatoes, salt, mustard, pepper and water. Many use stewing beef instead of mutton or lamb and still call it Irish stew, although it is debatable whether this is authentic. The inclusion of carrots, or not, is an area of particular debate. Purists maintain that the only acceptable ingredients are neck mutton chops, potatoes, onions and water. Other additions include carrots, turnips and pearl barley, but Fitzgibbon maintains that these spoil the true flavour of the dish. Mahon observes that in country areas pork ribs and griskins were added at pig-time. Sexton notes that in urban areas, where pig abattoirs were located, the poor had a constant supply of pig offal and bones, and inferior cuts of pork or bacon replaced the mutton.

Shannon Meats' Irish stew contains both mutton and beef. The ingredient list for this commercial product is vegetables (potatoes, carrots and peas), meat (mutton, beef), water, starch, salt, stock, onion salt, monosodium glutamate and pepper. Mutton rather than lamb is always used by Shannon.

History: Although the exact historical origin of the dish is uncertain, Sexton maintains that a rudimentary form of Irish stew was current as early as the seventh century. The seventh- and eighth-century Brehon Laws recount that old dressed wethers (castrated male sheep) were rendered as rents and taxes to the nobility. These were boiled together with the available cereal and vegetable produce, thus rendering an Irish stew (albeit with cereal rather than potatoes). Old wethers are also listed as a foodstuff in the eleventh-century tale *Aislinge meic Conglinne*. Dunton's observations of Ireland in the 1690s affirm that boiled mutton was a very common dish.

The boiling of mutton over the open fire in a large iron pot continued as the normal cooking method from early historic times until well into the twentieth century, and it is likely that the dish known as Irish stew has its origins in this tradition. The adoption of the potato as a staple food by the Irish peasantry from the late sixteenth century onwards ensured that it became a major ingredient in the dish. Any seasonally available vegetables and herbs would also have been added to the boiling pot. Today, Irish stew is a very popular dish prepared extensively in Irish homes during the winter months. It is a dish described affectionately by Samuel Beckett in his 1948 novel *Molloy*:

I peered into the pots. Irish Stew. A nour-

*ishing and economical dish, if a little in-
digestible. All honour to the land that
has brought it before the world.* (O'Mara
and O'Reilly)

Use: Cooked over a slow heat and thickened with potatoes. Nowadays home-
produced Irish stew is cooked in a cas-
serole in the oven. Shannon Irish stew
is emptied into a saucepan, brought to
the boil, simmered for two minutes and
then served. The stew is served hot as a
main course. Connery indicates that in
some localities, Irish stew was traditionally served with mushroom ketchup or
pickled cabbage and accompanied by a
bottle of stout.

Technique: The Shannon product is
precooked. The recipe used by Shannon
is confidential but is based on old-style
recipes. The boneless mutton is
trimmed and minced. Vegetables and a
gravy sauce are prepared. The mix is
put into a can and cooked at a specified
temperature in the can. The Shannon
product keeps for three years in the tin.

Producers: The main commercial producer identified is Shannon Meats, who
have been producing Irish Stew for
thirty-five years. Their product is
canned in a 369 g can. Irish stew is also
produced in domestic kitchens and sold
at local markets.

Season: Available throughout the year.

Packaging: Round cylindrical-shaped
can with a wrap-round label showing a
ready meal and a picture of chunks of
meat, carrot and potato pieces and peas.
Also sold loose at country markets.

Useful address: Shannon Meats,
Rathkeale, Co. Limerick. Tel 069-64111.

Connemara Lamb

Also Other local mountain lamb

Special features: Lamb has long been
produced in Ireland and today large
quantities are exported. Connemara
mountain lamb is descended from a
Scottish breed and has a stronger flavour due to its mountain habitat and
its diet of mountain heathers and
grasses. Traditional methods of cutting
and preparing Irish lamb, including
Connemara lamb, are different from
those of other countries.

Composition: The carcasses are smaller
than other lambs, weighing about 10 kg
compared to 25 kg for lowland lambs.
Connemara lamb is very close to being
an organic food and has a darker colour and strong flavour. The meat is also
leaner.

History: Lamb has a long history in Ireland. From earliest times until the twentieth century sheep were kept predominantly for their milk and wool and
therefore appeared on the table only as
old and tough mutton. Lamb was,
therefore, a rare treat and was not a
commonplace feature in the Irish diet
until well into the twentieth century.

The consumption of dressed wethers
is mentioned in the seventh- and eighth-
century Brehon Laws, while a 'full-
fleshed wether' appears among a list of
luxury foodstuffs in the eleventh-century tale *Aislinge meic Conglinne*:

> *And he called for juicy old bacon, and ten-
> der corned-beef and full fleshed wether.*

The prevalence of mutton as opposed to lamb continued in Ireland, as is clear in a number of nineteenth-century sources. Amhlaoibh Uí Shúileabháin, for example, regularly partook of mutton in the early nineteenth century. In his diary entry for 5 October 1828 he is presented with a leg of mutton for dinner at the parish priest's house.

Outside rural areas mutton seems to have been a common item for sale at city and town markets. In Lieutenant Joseph Archer's *Statistical Survey of the County of Dublin*, mutton was on sale at Dublin Market on 7 April 1801 for 10d per pound along with other goods such as cereals, potatoes, fish, veal and beef. In James Joyce's *Ulysses* (1922) there is also a reference to a 'tanner lunch' of

> *boiled mutton, carrots and turnips, bottle of Allsop.*

In general, therefore, lamb was eaten only in the aftermath of a culling of young male lambs, which were economically useless in terms of milk production; or when an animal died or was injured through misadventure. Such an occurrence is described in Mary Carbery's *The Farm by Lough Gur*, which details rural life in nineteenth-century Co. Limerick:

> 'The crayther! fallin' from the rocks the way it did to break its neck, and it neither a lamb nor a sheep.'
> 'With mint sauce, it is lamb' I said firmly. 'Make a good fire and have it on the spit in plenty of time.'

The exception to this lamb-eating pattern occurs in the case of Connemara lamb, consumption of which dates to the mid nineteenth century. Initially some Scottish-bred stock were brought in by landlords. Their main characteristic was their ability to forage better than other breeds. They were hardy and agile and could climb to the top of mountains. Over 150 years they have evolved into a distinctive strain, and have been adapted and selected to suit the rugged conditions of Connemara. They are different to hill sheep in other parts of Ireland, such as Kerry. They are a lighter breed and smaller in body weight.

Use: Connemara lamb is regarded as a quality product and is served as such in restaurants. In general lamb is used for grilling, roasting and stews (see the section on technique).

Technique: Connemara lambs live on mountain grass, heathers and herbs and are usually not dipped. Traditionally they stay out all year, but in recent years some producers have housed them for part of the year. The rams are let out on 20 November and the lambs are born around mid-April at a time when the growth of herbs and grasses on the hills is vigorous. They come on the home market in August and the 15th of August is the traditional day for the first sale of Connemara lambs. There is no difference in the slaughter and preparation of Connemara lamb from that of any other lamb. The traditional method of cutting, rarely used today is described below. The carcass weight is about 10 kg, much lighter than other breeds of sheep.

Connemara and other lamb carcasses in Ireland are cut into two sides. Each side has three main parts—fore end, full loin and leg. The fore end is the piece forward from the fourth or fifth rib, including the neck. There are three main parts to the fore end—neck, back gigot and shoulder. The neck can be boned out and is sold in pieces or as a piece for stew. The gigot is cut into chops for stewing; the shoulder is usually sold as a piece for roasting or boiling. The shank bone is taken out in a roasting piece. Sometimes the whole forequarter can be cut into chops.

The full loin is from the fourth or fifth rib to the leg bone. It is cut into two pieces—the top end with ribs is called the fair end and the rest is the loin. The fair end may be cut into cutlets or disjointed and sold as joints to hotels or restaurants for roasting (like a rack). The loin is usually cut into side loin (wide end nearer the leg) and centre loin chops (narrower and nearer ribs). The remaining piece of the centre part is the lap, which can be boned out or stuffed or sliced into strips for stew. The leg can be cut into fillet (top end) and shank or sold whole. All pieces are for roasting.

In the case of Connemara lamb, because it is much smaller than lowland lambs, the full carcass is sometimes divided into just four quarters.

Producers: The mountain lambs are not born as early as hill and lowland lambs. They are born in April, whereas other lambs may be born from Christmas onwards. Connemara lamb is available from about August to November, and is sold at butchers' shops. Some younger Connemara lambs are slaughtered at 10–11 weeks for export to Portugal and Italy, where markets require a whiter meat.

Packaging: Much Connemara lamb is sold to butchers for selling on to hotels and restaurants. At butchers' shops it is sold loose packed for each customer or in prepacks.

Reference: David Callinan, Teagasc, Galway, personal communication.

Useful addresses: Sean Loughnane, Butcher, Foster Court, Galway. Tel 091-564437. Teagasc, Galway Offices. Tel 091-62101.

Wicklow Lamb

Also Other local hill lamb

Special features: Mutton and, to a lesser extent, lamb have been produced in Ireland for many centuries and today lamb exports are very important. Wicklow lambs are Cheviot on Cheviot, a late-finishing lamb which is leaner than other lamb. Traditional methods of cutting and preparing Irish lamb, including Wicklow lamb, are different from those of other countries.

Composition: The carcasses weigh about 18 kg compared to 25 kg for lowland lambs. The meat is also leaner. The Wicklow Mountain environment, combined with skilful breeding, has evolved the Wicklow Mountain breed. This breed possesses in a marked degree a number of very valuable characteristics, such as extreme hardiness and freedom from foot rot and other diseases to which sheep are generally subject; and the ewes, as well as being prolific, are particularly good nurses.

History: Mutton has a long history in Ireland, as documented under Connemara lamb. McGrath summarises:

The date of origin of the Wicklow Mountain Sheep can only be guessed at, but may be associated with the woollen industry and the general history of the country. There is evidence to show that, in the middle of the fifteenth century, a breed of fine woolled sheep existed in the Wicklow Mountains, which was distinct in appearance and character from any breed then in existence in these islands. At this time the Wicklow Mountain Sheep were contributing to the reputation of Irish woollens, not only in the spun-wool markets of Holland and the manufactured-woollen markets of Flanders, but also in the markets for both these commodities in England . . .

Isolated attempts were made during the last century by various breeders to improve the native breed. The most suitable breed for crossing was found to be the Scotch Cheviot, and they were first introduced by the Barton family of Glendalough and the Kemmis family of Ballinacor. Many of the smaller mountain breeders failed to introduce fresh blood, and haphazard methods of breeding, and want of a proper ideal on the part of the owners, resulted in the breed becoming mixed and lacking in character and uniformity . . . many breeders realised that they were not reaping the same benefits as would accrue if the breed bore the hall marks of a pure breed, namely, individuality, uniformity and definite character. Accordingly in 1926, a number of interested and leading sheep breeders, with the co-operation of the Department of Agriculture and the Wicklow Committee of Agriculture, established the Wicklow Mountain Sheep Breeders' Society, with a view to giving encouragement to the breeding improvement, development and maintenance of the native sheep as a pure breed. The best flock owners throughout the county joined the Society. Annual inspections of ewes and rams were held at various centres and those which reached the required standard of excellence were entered in the Flock Book.

For some twenty years annual flock inspections were conducted by competent judges who were keen breeders and at present registered flock owners have attained in large measure uniformity of type and that most essential attribute, breed character.

The Society holds an annual Sale of Registered Rams in September, where approximately six hundred rams are exhibited.

Wicklow Mountain ewes are sought after by lowland farmers throughout Ireland . . . Direct crossing with the Suffolk is the commonest practice when Wicklow ewes are purchased by lowland farmers . . . The pure-bred Wicklow lamb, although not as early to mature, when finished, has the carcass most sought after for the Continental trade.

Use: Wicklow lamb is regarded as a quality product when served in restaurants. In general lamb is used for grilling, roasting and stews (see section on technique).

Technique: Wicklow lambs live their early life on mountain grass, heathers and herbs and they are a late-finishing lamb. Very few are finished on the hills; this is traditionally done on the lowlands in Kildare. There are large lamb sales in places such as Aughrim and Roundwood in mid-August, September or October at which Wicklow hill lambs are sold. The ewe lambs may be bought for breeding and the wether lambs as stores for fattening. Rams are let out in the late autumn. The hill lambs are born in March and April at a time when the growth of herbs and grasses on the hills

is vigorous whereas other lambs may be born from Christmas onwards. The traditional Wicklow lamb is Cheviot on Cheviot but the Cheviot ewe may also be crossed with the Suffolk. There is no difference in the slaughter and preparation of Wicklow lamb from any other lamb. The carcass weight is about 18 kg, and the main procedure for cutting Wicklow and other lamb carcasses in Ireland in the traditional way is described under Connemara lamb.

Producers: Wicklow lamb is generally exported to France. Factories buying Wicklow lamb include Doyle's in Bray, Fenlon's in Newtownmountkennedy, Slaney Meats in Bunclody, Anglo Irish Meat Packers and Kepak. Wicklow lamb is available in December and January.

Packaging: Much Wicklow lamb is sold to breeders in the autumn for fattening on arable farms. Finished lambs are generally exported to France, with smaller amounts sold on the home market. At butchers' shops it is sold loose packed for each customer or in prepacks.

References: Peter McGrath, leaflet and personal communication. Nick Molloy, Teagasc, Wicklow, personal communication.

Useful addresses: Peter McGrath, Hon. Secretary, Wicklow Mountain Sheep Breeders' Society, Thessaly, Ballymore Eustace, Co. Kildare. Tel 045-864138. Teagasc, Wicklow Offices. Tel 0404-67315.

Dingle Mutton Pie

Also Kerry pies

Special feature: Unique local product, which is traditionally served in a mutton broth.

Composition: A round mutton shortcrust-type pastry pie. The ingredients are mutton, flour, fat, shortening agent, salt and pepper.

A recipe from Allen has the following ingredients: lamb or mutton, onions, carrots, flour, mutton or lamb stock, parsley, thyme and ground pepper. The pastry is made from white flour, salt, butter, water and an egg.

History: In the mountainous coastal regions of Co. Kerry, sheep-rearing was and still is of great economic importance to the local community. Consequently mutton dishes form a substantial part of the county's traditional fare. William Makepeace Thackeray, who travelled through Ireland in the 1840s, makes specific reference to Kerry mutton in his work *The Irish Sketch Book*:

> Dirty as the place was, this was no reason why it should not produce an exuberant dinner of trouts and Kerry mutton.

By at least the nineteenth century the small fishing town of Dingle, Co. Kerry, had developed a distinctive regional dish, the 'Dingle Mutton Pie'. At this time the town boasted no less than four 'Pie Houses' where the only commodity available was 'Mutton Pies'. While the houses catered for the local inhabitants, they were designed specially for animal drovers who congregated in the town on fair and market days. It was commonplace for the drovers to rise in the small hours of the morning before the fair and commence the long arduous journey to Dingle. The early morning start not only ensured that the animals arrived in good time for the fair, but that their drovers had an appetite on arrival. Thus, the mutton pie was developed to satisfy the needs of the animal drover.

The last surviving pie house was run by Mary Ellen and Lizzy Begley. Ms Begley continued to produce mutton pies until 1983/4. She died in 1986 and the business was taken over by Edna Ní Chinnéide. Edna still produces the pies and they are available in her restaurant and Bed and Breakfast, 'An Dreoilín'. Eileen McCarthy also produces pies and these are supplied for sale in De Barra's public house. The pies are celebrated in a song written by Paul Creightin, a Dubliner now living in Dingle:

> They look so neat,
> they're packed with meat,
> They surely are the best,
> They'd warm the cockles of your
>   heart,
> And put hair upon your chest.
> The poor ole vegetarians,
> They can't believe their eyes,
> At the crowds outside De Barra's
> Waiting for her mutton pies.

The pies are regularly produced in a domestic setting and home recipes travelled to America in the late nineteenth and early twentieth centuries with the Irish emigrants.

The dramatist and novelist John B. Keane recounts the nature of the pies in his novel *Durango*:

The pies . . . were a local delicacy made from finely chopped lap of mutton encased in saucer-sized discs of dough and baked to a light brown. The pies would be made in their thousands for several days before the fair and preserved in air-tight tins and boxes until required. Many of the pubs as well as the pie shops and restaurants served the popular and savoury offerings from morning till night. Once removed from their air-tight surrounds the pies were allowed to cook for several minutes in pots of mutton broth and were then served in dishes or soup plates brimming with the steaming hot broth in which they had been simmering. Most countrymen would eat several throughout the duration of the fair. Apart from their celebrated palatability they were also renowned for keeping drunkenness and hunger at bay. At a total cost of 1/- the customer was provided with pie and soup and for good measure one half of a baker's tile, known in the countryside as shop bread.

Use: Traditionally the pies were eaten on fair (e.g. Puck Fair in Killorglin) and market days. They were served hot or cold with an accompanying mutton broth. They are also traditionally served on St Stephen's Day (26 December) and St Patrick's Day (17 March).

Technique: Mutton is cut from the bone and chopped into small pieces. Care is taken in finely chopping the mutton: it is sometimes cut with a scissors. The mutton is seasoned to taste with salt and pepper. Afterwards, the shortcrust pastry is prepared, with butter or margarine, plain flour and milk or water. Traditionally mutton fat was used in the preparation of the pastry. The pastry has a high flour content and this floury pastry is rolled out in rounds. The seasoned mutton is heaped in one round and covered with another to form a small pie. The pies are baked on floured baking trays or in individual pie dishes for one hour at 218°C. An accompanying broth is also prepared: mutton bones seasoned with salt and pepper are brought to the boil and left to simmer for an hour. When ready for serving the cold pies are reheated in the broth and a quantity of broth is served with the pie.

Producer: Produced by Eileen McCarthy, who supplies De Barra's pub.

Season: Produced occasionally.

Packaging: Sold loose.

References: Máire De Barra, De Barra's Pub, The Pier, Dingle, Co. Kerry, personal communication. Edna Ní Chinnéide, An Dreoilín Restaurant, Dingle, Co. Kerry, personal communication.

Useful address: De Barra's Pub, The Pier, Dingle, Co. Kerry. Tel 066-51215.

Fish and Shellfish

Irish waters contain an abundance of fine quality fish.

Salted Ling

Also Battleboard

A salted fish which was in widespread use in the past in Ireland, it is a flat white fish, a member of the cod family.

Composition: Fish, salt.

History: Dry salted ling must be viewed as one of the major players in the story of traditional food in Ireland. Its prominent place is conditioned by two main factors: first, for inland communities, fresh fish was an expensive rarity and if fish did appear on the menu, it was invariably of the preserved salted variety. Second, salted fish was a necessary and important addition to the diet on Fridays and during Lent, when the consumption of meat was forbidden by the Church.

Traditionally salted ling has had an association with the southern and western coastal regions of Ireland. Here the fish was the main part of the winter diet. O'Neill points out that in the fourteenth century the Bishop of Cloyne, in Co. Cork, was supplied with ling, cod and haddock by his tenants in the coastal region of Ballycotton, Co. Cork, in part payment for their rents. It is evident that by the later medieval period a significant export trade in salted fish had developed in Ireland. In 1479–80 Ireland exported over £122 worth of salted fish to Bristol, while O'Neill again notes that a consignment of ling and cod valued at 52s arrived at Poole, in Dorset, from Youghal in Co. Cork in 1504.

At home the fish was consumed widely: for example the Franciscan friars in Cork City purchased half a hundredweight of dried ling on 12 February 1794, while in February 1773 the wealthy Carew family of Castleboro in Co. Wexford paid 11s 2d for ling and cod for the castle. The prevalence of dried ling in the Irish diet, particularly during Lent and winter, meant that it was considered undesirable by many. Amhlaoibh Uí Shúileabháin expresses such a sentiment in his diary entry on 2 April 1831:

I do not like salt fish, and fresh fish was not to be had, except too dear and seldom.

Until well into the twentieth century salt ling stewed in milk was usually eaten with boiled potatoes in many households. Florence Irwin, in her 1937 publication *Irish Country Recipes*, details the traditional cooking method, whereby the ling and potatoes were stewed together in water in the one cooking pot. In many regions the fish is called 'battleboard', possibly because the drying and salting process renders the fish rock hard.

Use: Traditionally salt ling was a staple food of the poor during Lent and winter, and served as a substitute for cod. It was also eaten as a supper dish on Christmas Eve. Nowadays ling is not widely eaten, there is a noticeable decline in the popularity of salt ling, and its consumption is limited to the older generation.

Technique: As Mahon states, 'for centuries . . . dried ling and salted cod' were prepared in Ireland. With cod and other white fish the ling was salted and hung in the rafters from a piece of string, until needed. The fish were gutted and split and then dried pegged to a line, or from a hoof or on hedges or bushes. Large and flat, they looked like a stiff shirt. At night they were brought inside and after one to two weeks they were stiff and could be stored for a year. They were stacked in piles of ten, with the flesh side up and salt put between each fish. This helped the drying process and gave a stronger flavour. The same basic processes are used today. The fish are gutted, split, salted and hung.

Producers: Ling is no longer widely available except for a few places in the south-west and in Cork Covered Market.

Packaging: Loose.

Useful address: Cork Covered Market, off Patrick Street, Cork City.

Kippers

Also Smoked or salted filleted herring with many local types and brands such as Woodcock

Variant: Red herring (whole salted herring)

Kippers are herring that have been lightly salted and then smoked. Sometimes they are sold on the bone, sometimes filleted, such as Carrowkeel smoked kipper fillets. Traditional kippering involves hand filleting. Many 'kipper' producers use fillets from processing for roe extraction, and if these are overwashed they do not produce the same quality as the hand-filleted fish on the bone. Smoked herring is variable in colour and size; dye is sometimes used.

Composition: Herring, salt, smoke.

History: The herring featured prominently in the diet of the Irish from the medieval period through to the early twentieth century. The fish was an indispensable item for two main reasons: first, although it could be eaten fresh, it preserved well and proved a most valuable food item for winter and early spring. Second, it was linked with the numerous Christian days of fast and abstinence. The documentary record indicates that by the fourteenth century herring was an integral and prevalent item in the Irish diet. In 1306 Scottish fishing fleets were trading in herring, destined for sale in the Dublin and Drogheda fish shambles, while in 1403

John Slene of Rush exported 4,000 salted herring to England.

The mid-fifteenth century saw a marked increase in the consumption of herring by both the noble and peasant classes, as migrating herring from the Baltic appeared in increased numbers in the North Sea, the Irish Sea and off the southern and western coasts of Ireland. Irish fishing fleets exploited these new developments to supply home and foreign markets. The developing urban area of the Pale—around Dublin—consumed particularly large quantities of the fish from the nearby ports of Howth, Rush and Malahide.

Throughout the sixteenth century the availability and consumption of herring remained high. Irish fishermen and merchants continued to sell their stock on a large scale to England, which at times must have deprived the home market. The extent of herring fishing in Ireland is demonstrated by reference to the presence of no less than six hundred English fishing boats operating from Carlingford in 1535.

Its popularity as a foodstuff endured through the eighteenth and nineteenth centuries. Arthur Young, writing in the 1770s, notes that the poor of Wexford eat 'herrings and potatoes', while of the Limavady region he writes: 'the poor live on potatoes, milk and oatmeal with many herrings and salmon'. In the same period Jonathan Swift records the colourful cries of Dublin's fishmongers:

Be not sparing
Leave off swearing
Buy my herrings
Fresh from Malahide
Better was never tried
Come eat 'em with pure fresh butter and
mustard
Their bellies are soft and as white as
custard.

Large quantities were exported from Donegal in the late eighteenth century. During the eighteenth and nineteenth centuries the bland Irish diet of potatoes and buttermilk welcomed the salty smoked flavour of herring. A popular dish at this time was a stew made of chopped herrings, milk and unpeeled potatoes. The commonplace nature of the fish ensured that it featured in much folk custom and tradition: in Belfast in 1850, for example, young girls threw fatty pieces of herring against the wall of the house in an effort to determine the character of their future husbands.

Until the early twentieth century herring was an important part of Easter Sunday festivities. In a number of towns the butchers, who had little sale for their meat during Lent, celebrated the arrival of Easter by holding a funeral-like procession of a herring, the staple of the church-going community during the forty days of Lent. Danaher refers to Henry Morris's description of the custom as it took place in Dundalk in 1902:

They [the butchers] got big long rods and walked through the town . . . beating the poor herring until hardly a fin was left. On reaching the bridge they hurled the horrid herring into the water with insult, and hung up a quarter of lamb decorated with ribbons and flowers in its place.

Use: Herrings were probably the fish most eaten by Irish people in the eighteenth and nineteenth centuries. They can be served hot or cold, and are used at breakfast or as a starter for other meals.

As they are high in fat, they are grilled dry. They may be soaked overnight in water before cooking, or may be eaten in raw marinated form. Herring in oatmeal is a traditional dish, with the oatmeal giving a crisp coating. Nowadays they are most often lightly smoked. They are more expensive now as stocks have been depleted.

Technique: Vast quantities were salted for winter use. Traditionally, they were preserved by closely packing them in barrels between layers of salt. During the eighteenth and nineteenth centuries barrels of pickled herrings were commonplace in wealthy households, while in the homes of the poor a number of gutted and salted herrings were hung from the rafters as 'winter kitchen'. On a dry, warm day the fish were placed outside on the thatched roof of the house where the sun and wind assisted in their drying. At commercial premises Dunns of Dublin have been smoking herring since the 1930s. The details of the process are the same as for smoked salmon. A shorter time is needed for kippers, and dyes are used to give colours suited to different markets. Nolans also do a tra-

ditional-style kipper, a boneless fillet, lightly salted, cured and smoked. The smoking process takes about four hours.

Today the preparation involves filleting, salting, rinsing/drying, smoking and vacuum packing.

Producers: Produced by a number of fish companies, for example, Woodcock, a group of six small producers in the West Cork area. They are widely available in fish shops and supermarkets as well as delicatessens, and are also sold to restaurants and hotels.

Packaging: Loosely or in plastic bags with a label. Carrowkeel smoked kipper fillets come in a 227 g pack.

References: George Nolan, H. J. Nolan, Dublin, personal communication. Woodcock Smokery, Gortbreac, Castletownshend, Skibbereen, Co. Cork, personal communication.

Useful addresses: Woodcock Smokery, Gortbreac, Castletownshend, Skibbereen, Co. Cork. Tel 028-36232. Dunns Seafare Ltd, 95 Manor Street, Dublin 7. Tel 01-677-3156. H. J. Nolan, Rathdown Road, Dublin 7. Tel 01-838-1431.

Smoked Salmon

Also Salted salmon

Irish smoked salmon is different to Scottish, as the Irish product is more smoked. However, there is less of a difference today than in the past, as Irish producers are smoking the fish less. Sugar is generally used in Irish cures, but not in Scottish. Both farmed and wild salmon are produced. Undyed wild salmon sides vary widely in size and weight, but the average weight is about 1 kg. The product is fresh, but can be frozen out of season, and is sold both as a whole side and in slices. Pack sizes vary, but a typical pack of a whole side weighs about 0.5 kg, while the sliced version comes in 100 g or 200 g packs. Forty-gram packs are aimed at single-person households.

Composition: Salmon, salt, hardwood smoke (spices), sugar. Nolans (Murphys label) use oak, Chamco use beechwood, and Ben Eadair use oak.

History: As with trout, it is believed that the southern Irish waterways were colonised by migratory salmonids as early as 35,000 years ago. The historical evidence is littered with references to salmon: the fish is mentioned in the eleventh-century Irish tale *Aislinge meic Conglinne*. In fact salmon is an integral part of both the mythological and folklore traditions of Ireland. The fish was also historically an important commodity in the Irish export trade from the later medieval period onwards.

Salmon is mentioned as a luxury food in the tenth-century life of St Finian of Clonard, but it also appears that salmon was enjoyed by both the peasants and wealthy alike. For example, Arthur Young, in detailing the diet of the poor of Wexford in the late eighteenth century, notes:

> *the poor live on potatoes, milk and oatmeal with many herrings and salmon.*

The abundance of the fish also saw the development of a lively salmon export trade as early as the fourteenth century, with the Bann and Galway fisheries supplying much of this foreign market. O'Neill points out that two citizens of Waterford were licensed to ship eight casks of salmon from either Wexford or Waterford in 1338–9. Indeed between 1400 and 1416 almost thirty licences were issued to Bristol merchants who were permitted to import old wine, salt and cloth and afterwards return home with salmon and Irish goods. At this time most of the fish destined for the English market entered via the port of Bristol. The export trade continued and during the eighteenth century large quantities of salted salmon were exported to Italy and France, where there was a great demand for the fish in the monasteries, particularly during Lent.

At home the demand for salmon was also high during Lent and Christian days of fast and abstinence. This, together with the large export trade, necessitated the development of reliable preservation techniques. Salmon pickled in old wine or brine is mentioned often in the historical evidence. For example, pickled salmon was one of the items for sale in 'The Sheaf' provision store in Cork City in the 1680s, and pickled salmon served as a breakfast dish is mentioned in the 1897 publication *The Sportsman in Ireland.*

It is also reasonable to suppose that smoking evolved at an early date as a variant preservation technique. In a domestic setting salted salmon left hanging in the chimney or rafters of a cottage or cabin was unavoidably smoked from the dense turf or wood smoke of the open fire. Smoked salmon is mentioned in the diaries of Amhlaoibh Uí Shúileabháin from Callan in Co. Wexford. On 17 March (St Patrick's Day) 1829 he records:

we had for dinner . . . salt ling softened by steeping, smoke dried salmon and fresh trout.

In 1822 John Dunn turned his pub in Moore Street, Dublin, into a fish shop. The retail shop moved to D'Olier Street in 1895. Dunns have been smoking salmon since the late 1930s or early 1940s from a smoke house in the basement of their premises in D'Olier Street. In 1966 Peter Dunn moved to Baggot Street and set up a wholesaling business in Manor Street where four smoking kilns were installed.

Nolans of Dublin, who own Murphys of Dublin, have also been selling fish for nearly a century. They claim to have been smoking salmon since the late 1920s or early 1930s, but only on a small scale. When buyers put smoked salmon on the supermarket shelves in the 1970s, demand exploded, and since then smoked salmon has been a more important food not only at Christmas but throughout the year.

Use: Traditionally salmon was popular during Lent and on days of fast and abstinence. In folk medicine salmon gall was used as a remedy for blindness or defective vision. Today smoked salmon enjoys a high reputation as a quality foodstuff served as a first or main course. Smoked Irish salmon has a shelf life of three weeks to a month. It can be kept in the deep freeze for three to four months. With the old traditional processes the salmon could keep for 90 days.

Technique: Dunns used an open fire system from the 1930s until 1965. Only larger salmon were smoked. The fish, always at least 5.44 kg (12 lb) in weight, was dry salted, washed, and hung to dry. An open fire with wood chippings, and sawdust to stop too much flaming from the chippings, was used for smoking. No particular wood was used. There was no humidity or temperature control, and if the chippings got too hot water was used to damp them down.

Nolans used a similar method. Only larger salmon were smoked, and after curing the salt content was as much as 25%. The salmon were hung in the chimney and chippings were lit underneath. As chippings varied in quality and there were no temperature or humidity controls, quality was very variable. The process took two to three days, and resulted in a product that was very dry, didn't need refrigeration and would keep indefinitely.

Today filleting, salting, rinsing/drying, smoking and vacuum packing are the main processes involved. Curing is much milder so that the salt content is only 3–4%. Generally the fish is filleted, salted and cold smoked at temperatures in the low twenties. One smoker uses a temperature of 28°C, another 25°C. Modern kilns with microprocessors are now being introduced by many processors, which allow more control over humidity, and weight loss is kept to between 11% and 15%. They allow for up to a hundred different smoking recipes so that the product can be prepared to customer requirements. Time varies from six to twelve hours—for example, Nolans smoke for about 6.5 hours. Smoke content can vary from 1% to 4%. Different woods are used. Dunns use oak, and Nolans also use oak for their Murphys traditional whole side of smoked salmon. Today's smokes are milder and not so strong or pungent as some of the older smokes. Continental customers want a milder smoke, so smoked salmon for both the home and export markets is less heavily smoked than in the past.

Smoked salmon is a large-scale seller on home and export markets.

Producers: Most salmon is supplied from farms in the Atlantic. The main producers of smoked salmon are Clayton Love, H. J. Nolan and Chamco. Others include Dunns, Irish Sea Spray, Burren Fisheries as well as Woodcock, who use only wild salmon. Ben Eadair produce smoked salmon slices. Some processors use farmed salmon and dyes.

The Woodcock product is sold to delicatessens, quality restaurants, hotels and selected local shops. There is also some mail order business.

Packaging: A plastic bag with a label and vacuum packing are standard. In the past parchment and greaseproof paper were used.

References: S. Carthy, Chamco Foods, personal communication. P. Curtin, Burren Fish Products Ltd, Kincora Road, Lisdoonvarna, Co. Clare, personal communication. Peter Dunn, Dunns of Dublin, company leaflets and personal communication. George Nolan, personal communication. Woodcock Smokery, Gortbreac, Castletownshend, Skibbereen, Co. Cork, personal communication.

Useful addresses: Burren Fish Products Ltd, Kincora Road, Lisdoonvarna, Co. Clare. Tel 065-74432. Chamco Foods, Chamco House, Shankill, Co. Dublin. Tel 01-282-3688. Dunns Seafare Ltd, 95 Manor Street, Dublin 7. Tel 01-677-3156. Woodcock Smokery, Gortbreac, Castletownshend, Skibbereen, Co. Cork. Tel 028-36232. H. J. Nolan, Rathdown Road, Dublin 7. Tel 01-838-1431.

Smoked Eel

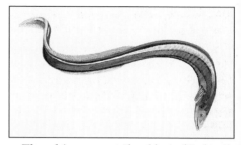

The eel is amongst the oldest of Ireland's traditional foods.

In Irish Eascann

One of the oldest foods in Ireland, prepared by traditional methods of salting and smoking. In folk belief eel fat was considered a cure for rheumatism and the skin was a charm against rheumatic pains. The oil produced by burying a live eel in a bottle in a dung-hill was used as a cure for baldness. Size and weight vary, with individual fish from 500 g to 1.5 kg live. Adults are usually black, greenish-black or grey-brown on the back and sides, and yellowish below. The sides and belly become bright silver when the eel reaches sexual maturity. They are not skinned, and the whole smoked gutted product is 700–800 g.

Composition: Fish, salt, smoke (spices).

History: The eel is amongst the oldest of Ireland's traditional foodstuffs. The country's extensive internal waterways have always been rich in eels, a feature noted in the twelth century by the Welsh historian Giraldus Cambrensis. Their popularity as a food throughout the prehistoric period is evident from the discovery of numerous eel spears and eel rakes from a number of archaeological sites. In the historic era the eel featured predominantly in the diet of both the aristocracy and ordinary people. In 1338, for example, during a particularly severe winter in Dublin the River Liffey froze over and the people made a fire of timber and turf on the ice on which they roasted eels. A list of purchases made in Kilkenny by the Earl of Ormond around 1400 includes a quantity of eels and other fish. Mary Carbery's account of life in late-nineteenth-century Co. Limerick indicates that eels were still an important, though declining, dish in both urban and rural areas.

The popularity of the eel can be attributed to the fact that it was an important source of fresh food, but it also preserved excellently by salting or smoking. Traditionally eels could be kept alive for long periods in suitable boxes provided with fresh water until required for consumption. Until the nineteenth century large quantities were smoked and salted down for winter and early spring, when they were used in place of herrings. However, in the post-Famine period (the 1850s onwards) the consumption of eels declined steadily, as they became increasingly associated with famine and poverty and were thus despised widely and eventually abandoned.

Use: Until the Famine eel, both fresh and salted or smoked, was a popular food, mostly in winter. Nowadays, although used all year round, volumes are small and smoked eel is not popular. Mostly served in mixed seafood platters.

Technique: Up to the mid-twentieth century methods of eel fishing had changed little from prehistoric practices. Evans states that as late as the 1950s pronged eel rakes and spears, popular since the Bronze Age, were still employed by fishermen along the River Bann. Today extensive eel fisheries are located on the River Bann and Lough Neagh. The products are destined mainly for the foreign market. However, most of these fish are exported fresh and smoked abroad. At home they are not skinned, but are gutted and whole smoked. Small amounts of fish are also filleted, salted and smoked in 24 hours by various smokers. It is only in the last ten years that many smokers started smoking eel.

Producers: The eel fisheries on the River Bann and Lough Neagh are the most important in Western Europe. There are about 25 commercial smokehouses in Ireland and some of these produce smoked eel. Producers include Dunns, Nolans, The Olde Village Smokehouse and Burren Fish Products. Today most eel is exported to other European countries, particularly the Netherlands. Small amounts are sold to hotels in Ireland.

Packaging: Smoked fish are usually vacuum packed in transparent packs.

References: Peter Curtin, Burren Fish Products Ltd, Kincora Road, Lisdoonvarna, Co. Clare, personal communication. Peter Dunn, Dunns of Dublin, company leaflets and personal communication. George Nolan, H. J. Nolan, Dublin, personal communication.

Useful addresses: Burren Fish Products Ltd, Kincora Road, Lisdoonvarna, Co. Clare. Tel 065-74432. H. J. Nolan, Rathdown Road, Dublin 7. Tel 01-838-1431. The Olde Village Smokehouse, Douras, Woodford, Co. Galway. Tel 0509-49064.

Smoked Mackerel

Smoked mackerel is a fatty, oily fish with firm flesh. Its size and weight vary with the individual fish. Traditional methods are used for salting and smoking. Nowadays the mackerel are often hot smoked. Whole fish and slices are sold. The flavour is similar to trout and is often called the 'poor man's trout'. Peppered mackerel is available from Ben Eadair, Chamco and Eagle Seafoods. The Chamco pack with two fillets is 227 g, the Eagle pack 200 g. Herbed mackerel fillets are also available.

Composition: Fish, salt, smoke (spices). Annatto, a natural colouring, is used by Ben Eadair in mackerel slices. No artificial colouring or preservative is used; the fish is oak smoked.

History: Mackerel is found in abundance around the Irish coast, yet historical references remain remarkably scarce prior to the seventeenth century. From this period onwards, Irish mackerel shoals were fished intensively by French fishing fleets, particularly off the southwestern coast. In 1671, for example, Robert Southwell of Kinsale, who had an interest in pilchard fishing, wrote to the Lord Lieutenant complaining of the activities of French mackerel fishing fleets around the south coast. Similarly, in 1757, a Cork City newspaper reported the presence of fifty French mackerel fishing vessels fishing near Bantry Bay in Co. Cork, 'without interruption from revenue cutters'.

By at least the eighteenth century

mackerel was a frequent item in the native Irish diet; writing in *A Tour in Ireland 1776–79*, Arthur Young remarks:

> her [Ireland's] coasts and innumerable creeks and rivers' mouths are the resort of vast shoals of herring, cod, hake, mackerel &c.

While of Killala, Co. Mayo, Young notes:

> fish very plentiful; I partook of three gurnet, two mackerel and one whiting at the bishop's table.

An eighteenth-century manuscript detailing the activities of the Franciscan friars of Cork City reveals that in 1797 mackerel, along with herrings, sole and plaice, appeared regularly in the diet of the friars. In 1842, William Makepeace Thackeray, visiting the town of Dunmanway, stated:

> There is a little, miserable, old market house; where a few women were selling buttermilk . . . another had dried mackerel on a board.

Throughout the eighteenth and nineteenth centuries there was a considerable export trade in pickled and sometimes smoked mackerel. Writing in 1758, Richard Pococke detailed Irish exports of mackerel to America, and he said of the Sherkin Island (Co. Cork) fishermen:

> they salt and barrel up the Mackrel and Herring. The Mackrel sell well, as they give only half a Mackrel to the Negroes (on the American Plantations) which they call the fish with one eye.

However, it was between 1887 and 1901 that the trade in mackerel to America reached its peak. During this period, the Autumn Mackerel Fishery, which lasted in good seasons from August to Christmas, was destined for the American market. This extensive trade between Ireland and America gave an economic boost to many west of Ireland communities. In 1892, for example, the Congested Districts Board established the Spring Mackerel Fishery on the Aran Islands. The shoals were fished with seine nets and this method of fishing continued almost to the present day.

After a decline in the 1920s recent years have shown some recovery, although new problems such as overfishing have emerged.

Use: Used all year round. Often served with a sauce that cuts through the taste, traditionally gooseberry, rhubarb or creamed horseradish. The product must be kept refrigerated and eaten within two days of purchase.

Technique: As it deteriorates rapidly because of its oiliness, mackerel is filleted, salted and smoked as soon as possible after catching, and can be either cold or hot smoked. Ben Eadair mackerel is hot smoked. Hot smoking means that the product cooks as it smokes. This is usually done at a temperature of about 160°C and gives a longer shelf life to the product. Nolans use a beech and oak combination for smoking.

Producers: There are many commercial smokehouses in Ireland. Producers include Dunns, H. J. Nolan, Ben Eadair, Chamco and Eagle Seafoods.

Packaging: Vacuum-packed, transparent plastic, with stick-on label. Chamco sell Irish smoked mackerel fillets with two fillets per pack.

References: George Nolan, H. J. Nolan, Dublin, personal communication. Peter Dunn, Dunns of Dublin, company leaflets and personal communication.

Useful addresses: Ben Eadair, West Pier, Howth, Co. Dublin. Tel 01-839-2419. Eagle Seafoods, Ballygomartin Industrial Park, Belfast BT13 3NH. H. J. Nolan, Rathdown Road, Dublin 7. Tel 01-838-1431. Dunns Seafare Ltd, 95 Manor Street, Dublin 7. Tel 01-677-3156.

Smoked Trout

The smoked sea trout is a large fish, similar to salmon, but the size and weight vary with the individual fish. The rainbow trout is much whiter, and, like the brown trout, which is a smaller indigenous fish, is found in most rivers and lakes throughout the country. Chamco produce smoked Irish Atlantic farmed sea trout. Six slices weigh 0.1 kg.

Composition: Fish, salt, smoke (spices). IDAS in Co. Wicklow use an oak smoke, Chamco a beech smoke.

History: Scholarly opinion suggests that southern Irish waters were colonised by migratory salmonids as early as 35,000 years ago. However, as the ice sheets receded, roughly about 10,000 years ago, sub-groups of the early salmonids lost their migratory instinct and became resident in Irish waters. Today Irish trout is mainly composed of resident stocks, although sea trout and brown sea trout do appear in coastal streams and in maritime coastal lakes.

The abundance of the fish in Irish waters is a feature noted in a variety of historical accounts; for example, in the twelfth-century tale *Acallam na Senórach* trout is listed as one of the Irish bounties:

forth from thy banks, thy trouts are to be seen, thy wild swine in thy wilderness.

Arthur Young, in his *Tour of Ireland*, which was compiled between 1776 and 1779, comments on the abundance of fish in general in Irish waters; he notes in particular the fine trout specimens:

beside perch, there is a pike upwards of five foot long, bream, trench, trout of 10 lb [4 kg] and as red as a salmon.

'Stewed Troutes' formed part of the supper menu in Castlemartyr House on 3 July 1679.

Dunns of Dublin have been smoking trout on a commercial basis since the 1930s. Today they continue to distribute smoked trout for one of the country's major fish processors.

Use: Used all year round as part of a starter or as a main course.

Technique: Traditionally, large trout were preserved by pickling and smoking. Turf and wood smoking were variously employed depending on the availability of materials. Today the fish is filleted, salted and smoked in 24 hours, with each smoker having their own specialised approach. For example, one company uses beechwood chips. At another company, after gutting and brine salting, including steeping for a time, rainbow trout is smoked whole. The smoke is a hot smoke with a temperature of 70°C. The trout is filleted but not sliced and sold as a ready-to-eat skin-off product. Sea trout are filleted, dry salted and then cold smoked at 25°C, a process which takes 8–10 hours with varying temperature and humidity.

Producers: Most sea trout are farmed on the west coast. There are a number of commercial smokehouses in Ireland. The major producers are Chamco (Carrowkeel brand) and IDAS, Woodenbridge, Arklow, Co. Wicklow. Other producers include Burren Fish

Products.

References: P. Curtin, Burren Fish Products Ltd, Kincora Road, Lisdoonvarna, Co. Clare, personal communication. S. Carthy, Chamco Foods, personal communication.

Useful addresses: Chamco Foods, Chamco House, Shankill, Co. Dublin. Tel 01-282-3688. Burren Fish Products Ltd, Kincora Road, Lisdoonvarna, Co. Clare. Tel 065-74432.

Mussels, Fresh, Cooked and Smoked

The native Irish mussel is *Mulilus edulis*. The Irish mussel has a blue shell and a distinct flavour. Irish mussels from Carrowkeel are cooked and ready to eat. The smoked product is from farmed mussels from Roaringwater Bay in west Cork. Smoked mussels are vacuum packed and chilled.

Composition: Mussels. Garlic butter sauce is sold with the Carrowkeel pack. No artificial colours or preservatives are used. Smoked mussels are hardwood smoked.

History: Mussels have a long and established pedigree in the Irish diet. There is a lovely *seanfhocal* (or proverb) in Irish which runs:

> Rí 'sea diúilicíní ach bia tulaigh 'sea báirnigh.
> Mussels are the food of kings, limpets are the food of peasants.

Archaeologically, they are well represented in both prehistoric and historic sites. Evidence from the excavation of early historic deposits at the site of Rathmullan ringfort, Co. Down, for example, revealed substantial quantities of mussel shell.

The papers of the French consul Coquebert de Montbret contain the following colourful account of the cooking and eating of mussels towards the end of the eighteenth century. In 1790

Coquebert made a visit to the Old Head of Kinsale in Co. Cork, where he encountered an Irish family living near the base of the lighthouse. He recounts that the family spent their day fishing and in the evening sat down to a meal of grilled mackerel and a pot of mussels which had been prepared over the open fire.

The folklorist E. Estyn Evans, in his book *Irish Folkways,* recounts how the abundance of mussels in many regions led to their use in fertilising the soil. He details how, in south Donegal, boatloads of mussels were scraped off the rocks with spades and distributed in creels for spreading on the potato ridges. In Dundalk Bay, a Mr H. G. Tempest related to Evans that mussels were harvested both for the table and as fishing bait.

Following the popularity of the Galway Guinness and Oyster Festival, Murphy's Stout teamed up with the mussel producers in Bantry, Co. Cork, to create the Murphy's Stout Bantry Mussel Festival.

Use: First course. Mussels are cooked in a saucepan for five minutes, with occasional shaking. They are served with crusty bread. In coastal regions in the past mussels were the most common accompaniment and relish to the non-meat potato meal observed through Lent. Connery maintains that saffron was widely used throughout the eighteenth century to add colour to mussel soup.

Technique: Traditionally spring was the period associated with collecting mussels and shellfish in general. Mussels were harvested wild but nowadays are mostly farmed. Evans credits the technique for this to a Corkman called Walton, shipwrecked off La Rochelle, in France, in 1235. He invented a net, attached to long poles, sunk into the mudflats. The mussels grew on the poles. Today mussels are grown on ropes suspended from rafts. After harvesting, they are cooked and vacuum packed. They must be kept refrigerated. In the case of the smoked product, cooked mussels are bought in and then salted, oiled, smoked and vacuum packed.

Producers: Widely produced on mussel farms—Woodcock, for example, are produced by six small producers in the West Cork area. Mussels are sold in fish shops and stalls, in supermarkets and delicatessens, and to restaurants and hotels. Cooked brands include Carrowkeel, while smoked are from Woodcock.

Packaging: The Carrowkeel pack is a 500 g vacuum pack and is transparent. Woodcock pack mussels in a plastic bag with a label.

Reference: Woodcock Smokery, Gortbreac, Castletownshend, Skibbereen, Co. Cork, personal communication.

Useful address: Woodcock Smokery, Gortbreac, Castletownshend, Skibbereen, Co. Cork. Tel 028-36232.

Oysters

Oysters are particularly associated with areas such as Galway and Bantry and Rossmore in Co. Cork. They were once widely available around the coast, particularly the west coast. Galway has always been a major centre for oysters and an oyster festival is held there each September.

The native Irish oyster is *Ostrea edulis*. It is a soft-bodied mollusc, enclosed by two flattened pear-shaped shells, 'valves', which are dark grey in colour. They are hinged at the end by an elastic ligament. A number of grades are offered for sale to ensure maximum uniformity in size. The grades are: Royals, No. 1s, Small 1s, No. 2s, Small 2s, No. 3s, Small 3s, No. 4s, Buttons.

Composition: Shellfish.

History: Oyster is one of the oldest foods in Ireland: there is archaeological evidence for the extensive exploitation of oysters from the Later Mesolithic period (Middle Stone Age from *c.* 5500 BC onwards). One of the earliest sites is Curran Point at Larne Harbour, Co. Antrim. In addition, exploration and excavation around Cork Harbour have uncovered at least twenty major 'Shell Middens', which include substantial quantities of oyster, most likely prehistoric. In turn, there is evidence of a substantial shell midden associated with Cork City at Grattan Street, dated to the thirteenth century.

During the later medieval period (fourteenth and fifteenth centuries) oysters were popular fare amongst all social classes, appearing regularly for sale at the Dublin, Limerick, Galway and Cork markets. The prevalence and commonplace nature of oysters in the diet of the Irish were noted by a host of foreign observers: one of these, in the mid-seventeenth century, was Dr Massari, secretary to Archbishop Rinuccini, who noted the huge size and abundance of oysters in Irish waters. He remarks:

we bought pilchard and oyster very cheaply indeed.

In the same period, John Dunton recounts, in his letters from Ireland in 1698, his journey to Malahide, Co. Dublin:

I began the sally upon my first Ramble to Malahide to eat oysters, where they may be dredged out of the sea almost at any time.

An attorney visiting the Rosses in Co. Donegal in 1753–4 noted that the oysters there were of 'gargantuan size', which 'made every meal a feast'. He also recorded how the locals gathered the oysters:

when the tide was out, the young women waded into the sea where they knew the beds of such fish lay; some of them naked; others having stripped off their petticoats, went in with their gown tucked up about their waist; and, by armfulls, brought to shore, whatever number of scollops and oysters they thought requisite.

Throughout the nineteenth century the Irish oyster beds were continuously overfished: as early as the 1840s a dredge rope was in operation in Clew

Bay in Co. Mayo for the systematic harvesting of the large oysters which grow in that region.

In the nineteenth century the oyster beds were overfished in Co. Cork but commercial oyster farming was revived, in the inlet of Rossmore, six miles from the open sea, in 1969. The Rossmore oyster farm is now the largest in Ireland.

Use: As a first course or part of a main meal. They should only be bought alive. They can be stored for a number of days in a refrigerator or in ice. Oysters are eaten in the raw state from the deep part of the shell, which retains the juices, with a squeeze of lemon. In Galway they are eaten in the flat part of the shell and often accompanied by a pint of stout.

Technique: At one modern farm eight years of research were needed to develop the technology for breeding native oysters in large sea-water ponds. There are 22 ponds, covering 4 hectares, and millions of sprat are transferred to the oyster beds each year. They grow for three to four years to reach market size. By 1986 over 30 acres were under intensive cultivation and the oysters are marketed in almost every country in Europe. The product is air freighted to destinations to ensure freshness. They are delivered anywhere in Ireland within 24 hours of ordering. Tens of thousands of seed oysters, or spat, are produced from each spawning oyster, where only one or two would have survived in the wild. Modern technology is used to clean and grade the oysters so they are ready to serve without further cleaning. All the shellfish are put through an ultra-violet purification system.

Producers: There are a number of oyster farms in Cork and other parts of the country, particularly in Galway and Co. Down in Northern Ireland.

Season: Oysters are in plentiful supply from September to April.

Packaging: Packed in leakproof, polythene-lined boxes, tightly strapped. A display card and carrier bags with full instructions for home storage and opening are provided.

Reference: Atlantic Shellfish, Rossmore, Co. Cork, personal communication.

Useful addresses: Atlantic Shellfish Ltd, Rossmore, Carrigtwohill, Co. Cork. Tel 021-883-248/883-168. Cuan Sea Fisheries, Whiterock Bay, Northern Ireland. Tel 01238-541-461.

Cockles

Cockles and mussels, alive, alive, O!

Cockles are particularly associated with Dublin and the legendary character Molly Malone. The native cockle is a white bivalve shellfish, with a shell about 2.5 cm in diameter.

Composition: The body of the cockle is enclosed in two hinged, brittle, heart-shaped shells. It is very fleshy.

History: There is archaeological evidence for the consumption of cockles from the early historic sites of Oughtymore, Co. Derry, Park Cave, Co. Antrim, and Potters Cave, Co. Antrim. Excavation of ninth- and tenth-century Viking Dublin also confirms the popularity of cockles in the diet of the medieval Irish population.

The historical evidence suggests that cockles were prevalent in the diet of all social classes by at least the eighteenth century. In the *Shapland Carew Papers*, which detail the transactions of the estate of the Carew family of Castleboro, Co. Wexford, cockles appear as part of the family diet. For example, on 1 April 1772 cockles are purchased by the family and again on 16 June 1773 fish and cockles are bought for the castle kitchens.

Throughout the nineteenth century considerable quantities of cockles were sold at city and town markets: in 1837 the *Ordnance Survey Memoirs for the Parishes of Co. Antrim* indicate that cockles were for sale at Blaris Parish Market, Lisburn, Co. Antrim. In Dublin the sale of cockles is inextricably linked with Molly Malone, whose activities are celebrated in song in the city's anthem 'Molly Malone':

As she wheeled her wheelbarrow
Through streets broad and narrow,
Crying cockles and mussels
Alive, alive, O!

Cockles formed the mainstay of the peasant diet along coastal regions throughout periods of famine and poor potato harvest. The gathering of cockles was particularly prevalent during the Famine of 1845: *The Congested District Board Records* tell how cockle-gathering was widespread around Donegal on the eve of the famine. However, many perished, having eaten dead or improperly prepared cockles.

Florence Irwin's 1937 publication, *Irish Country Recipes,* includes several cockle recipes. In Dublin, Sandymount Strand was a traditional cockle-gathering location.

Use: As an entrée, usually cooked for three to five minutes until the shells have opened. They are eaten from the shell with melted butter, pepper and salt. They can also be extracted from the shell with a pin and eaten. A favourite Dublin supper dish, cockles are also used in the preparation of cockle soup and cocklety pie.

In the past they were sometimes eaten raw but usually taken home, washed, boiled, and eaten with oatcake. Cockles were often part of the Good Friday menu.

Technique: Cockles live near the tideline, just below the surface of the sand. Traditionally they are picked by hand when the tide goes out.

Producers: Collected on beaches. Sold at fish shops and at seaside stalls in summer.

Packaging: Sold loosely and wrapped to order.

Sea Vegetables

Harvesting seaweed at low tide

Dillisk

In Irish duileasc.

Also Dilisk, dillesk and delish, dillisk (*Rhodymenia palmata*) is called dulse (dolse) in Northern Ireland. Also called sea grass and *creathnach* in Ireland.

An edible seaweed collected and dried for centuries in Ireland, dillisk is eaten with dried fish, butter and potatoes. A natural food, dillisk (*Palmaria palmata*) is an edible perennial seaweed, 20–40 cm tall, reddish-brown in colour, disc-shaped with fine thin elastic long dark strands at the water's edge and with shorter strands known as *creathnach* in deeper water. The fronds sprout from the tiny disc shells, and lobed segments make the plant appear hand-shaped. The taste is salty and nutlike.

Composition: Dillisk contains carrageenan gel, is high in protein and vitamin A, iodine and phosphorus. It also contains sugar, starch, vitamin B6, vitamin B12, vitamin C, soluble nitrogen, yeast and minerals, including iron, potassium, magnesium, sulphur, calcium and sodium as well as trace elements.

History: One of the oldest historical references to dillisk is found in the seventh- and eighth-century Brehon Laws. *Críth Gablach* (the law of status and franchise) stipulates that, in accordance with the rules of hospitality, the prosperous farmer is entitled to the condiments of dillisk, onions and salt, should he visit the house of an acquaintance.

Dillisk is also listed as desirable in the eleventh-century tale *Aislinge meic Conglinne*:

> Then I saw the doorkeeper . . . his steed of bacon under him, with its four legs of custard, with its tail of dulse, from which seven handfuls were pulled every ordinary day.

Historical evidence indicates that consumption of dillisk was associated predominantly with coastal regions, as evidenced in George Scott's *Ordnance Survey Memoirs* for the parish of Lisburn in Co. Antrim. Dillisk and cockles are mentioned as some of the commodities listed for sale at Lisburn market in May 1837. The strong northern association with dillisk is clearly demonstrated in the traditional rhyme celebrating the famous Lammas Fair of Ballycastle in Co. Antrim:

> Did you treat your Mary Anne to dulce and yallaman
> At the auld Lammas Fair of Ballycastle, oh?

However, by at least the early twentieth century dillisk had become established fare sold in urban centres. P. W. Joyce, in his 1903 publication *A Social History of Ancient Ireland*, states:

> you may see it in Dublin hawked about in baskets by women: it is dry and people eat it in small quantities raw, like salad.

Today dillisk is a rare commodity in the Irish diet and is sold predominantly in health food outlets. Carabay has been commercially producing dried dillisk since 1956 and they distribute the product worldwide.

Use: Often eaten like sweets or with a bowl of periwinkles, dillisk can be chewed straight from the bag as a snack. Sun-dried plants can be eaten as a relish with potatoes or boiled milk. It is also added to soda bread which is then eaten with cheese. In Antrim use of dillisk is associated with the Lammas Fair (see history). Dillisk can be added to fish or vegetable soup but requires long slow cooking, it can be served chopped and mixed in boiled mashed potatoes, or added to stews, or toasted and served with eggs or bacon.

Technique: Plants are found at mid-tide to low-tide mark, particularly on the north-eastern and western coasts. Generally harvested by cutting from the rocks at low tide, the plants are washed in sea water and dried outdoors in the sun and wind after harvesting to prevent mould. This process takes six hours, during which time the plants turn black before turning red. Fresh plants may also be dried like hay, compressed in barrels and kept for several months.

Producers: Carabay Dillisk is sold by Seaweed Ltd. It is mainly collected between late spring and mid-autumn. Carabay of Connemara markets in Ireland, Europe and North America. Locally the product is sold through a wholesaler, but most sales are to health food shops in England. The product is available by mail order worldwide. Other producers include Melvins Sea Weed and Kelkin which collect from the Atlantic Ocean. Melvin's dillisk is sold mainly in health food shops throughout the country. Kelkin's dillisk is available in retail outlets, chemists, local markets and fish stalls.

Packaging: Carabay is packed in a plastic bag in a yellow-coloured rectangular box with a weight of 28 g. The pack gives recipes for dillisk meso soup, dillisk crisps and dillisk sauté. Melvin's dillisk is packed in small plastic bags with 'Harvested in the North West of Ireland' on the label.

Reference: B. Casburn, Carabay (Seaweed Ltd), personal communication.

Useful addresses: Carabay (Seaweed Ltd), Kylebroughlan, Moycullen, Co. Galway. Tel 091-85112. Kelkin Naturproducts Ltd, Tallaght Business Park, Whitestown, Tallaght, Dublin 24. Tel 01-452-0377. Carraig Fhada Seaweed, Cabra, Rathlee, Easkey, Co. Sligo. Tel 096-49042.

Carrageen Moss

Also Carrigeen, Irish moss or Sea moss, pearl moss, sea pearl moss, jelly moss

Carrageen moss has been collected for centuries in Ireland. It has long been regarded as having recuperative properties and is found in old Irish folk remedies for many ailments, for example colds, flu and chest complaints.

A natural food, Carrageen moss (*Chondrus crispus*) is a perennial seaweed that grows along the Irish coastline. *Carraígin* means 'little rock' in Irish. It is tangled, and ranges in colour from a yellow-green to a khaki purple-brown colour. It is 7 to 8 cm in length. Its disc-shaped part adheres to rocks and it branches into as many as twenty fronds. A plant reaches maturity in three to five years.

Composition: Carrageen moss contains vitamin A, iodine, protein, sugar, starch, fat, vitamin B, mineral and trace elements (sodium, iodine, calcium and magnesium) and natural gelatine.

History: Traditionally carrageen was valued as an effective remedy in the treatment of coughs and colds. It was also gathered for export in coastal regions, supplementing an otherwise meagre income. In Donegal, in the nineteenth and early twentieth centuries, freshly gathered carrageen moss was washed and boiled in water and given to calves to supplement their food.

Whilst the historical references to the seaweed are comparatively late, they most likely reflect an antiquity of consumption and use in folk medicine. For example, on 25 June 1830 Amhlaoibh Uí Shúileabháin made the following diary entry:

> *I see a plant like edible seaweed which they call carrageen moss. It is largely used by cooks as an ingredient for second course to give it substance.*

In the early twentieth century, John Millington Synge described the gathering of carrigeen by inhabitants off the west coast of Kerry:

> *I could see nothing but the strip of brilliant sea below me, thronged with girls and men up to their waists in the water, with a hamper in one hand and a stick in the other, gathering the moss, and talking and laughing loudly as they worked . . . When the tide began to come in I went down one of the passes to the sea, and met many parties of girls and old men and women coming up with what they had gathered . . .*

The seaweed was traditionally gathered on Good Friday, as a condiment to bulk out a meatless diet. Carrageen moss can still be seen today spread on rocks to dry. Carabay, one of the modern commercial producers, has been in production for nearly forty years.

Use: Palatable only when cooked, it has a cartilaginous, bony texture when fresh. Carrageen is used for cooking blancmange-style puddings, to make aspic dishes and jellies, and to thicken soups. As a remedy, the weeds are soaked and brewed in water, strained and mixed with honey and lemon juice. It can also be drunk with a little whiskey added. It is widely used in the manufacture of ice cream, beer and medicines.

Technique: Traditionally two sorts of moss were gathered at low tide between late spring and late summer. *Gigartina stellata* and the more common, smaller *Chondus crispus* are harvested by rake or by hand at low tide from small boats. Moss is also harvested by wading out into the water and cutting the weed from the rocks. The moss, which is brown, is spread out on the ground for the rain and dew to wash the salt out. It is then left to dry and bleach in the sun and wind, which prevents it from rotting. The drying process can take up to ten days and this period sees a remarkable series of colour changes in the weed. It goes from brown to green to pink, to orange and finally a beige colour. Today it can also be mechanically dried in heated drum dryers. Stalks are trimmed before storing.

Producers: Found near the low-tide mark in pools and rocks in temperate waters on both sides of the Atlantic. Producers include Seaweed Ltd, Melvins Sea Weed and Kelkin Carrageen. (See dillisk for distribution.)

Season: The main harvesting season is late spring to late summer, but the moss is available in shops at most times of the year.

Packaging: Carabay, the brand of Seaweed Ltd, sells in 71 g rectangular, yellow-coloured boxes. The moss is sold as a natural product and as a health food from the waters of the Atlantic coast and the shores of Connemara. Recipes for

Carrageen moss has been collected for centuries in Ireland.

blancmange, jelly and a carrageen drink are given. Melvins' moss is packed in small plastic bags with 'Harvested in the North West of Ireland' on the label. Kelkin Carrageen is packed in a rectangular orange and white box decorated with an Atlantic seashore scene. Its net weight is also 71 g. Recipes for blancmange, chowder and jelly are given on the pack. Carrageen may also be bought in bulk.

References: B. Casburn, Carabay (Seaweed Ltd), personal communication. C. Southern, Kelkin Naturproducts Ltd, personal communication.

Useful addresses: Carabay (Seaweed Ltd), Kylebroughlan, Moycullen, Co. Galway. Tel 091-85112. Kelkin Naturproducts Ltd, Tallaght Business Park, Whitestown, Tallaght, Dublin 24. Tel 01-452-0377. Melvins Seaweed or Carraig Fada Seaweeds, Cabra, Rathlee, Easkey, Co. Sligo. Tel 096-49042.

Sloke

In Irish Sleabhcán
Also Laver (in Wales), Nori (in Japan)
Sloke (*Porphyra umbilicalis*) is a seaweed
with long local usage in the Waterford
area. This seaweed is very slimy, with
thin fronds; purple-green in colour, it is
also translucent.

Composition: Sea vegetable high in minerals including iodine. Green Laver, for
example, contains protein, calcium, iron
and vitamins A, C and B.

History: Shoreline food gathering of
shellfish and sea vegetables has a long
historical pedigree in Ireland. After
dulse, sloke is mentioned most frequently in the historical record. For example, Thomas Dineley, writing in his
1681 *Observations in a Voyage through the
Kingdom of Ireland*, states that the 'vulgar Irish' living near the shore eat 'dillisk
and slugane' (dulse and sloke). However, the consumption of sloke was not
confined to the 'vulgar Irish', as is demonstrated in the *Shapland Carew Papers*
of the wealthy Carew family of
Castleboro in Co. Wexford. The family's household accounts illustrate that
sloke was an item that also appeared on
the tables of the aristocracy. On 18 February 1773 the Carews paid out 6 shil-
lings

for cockles and sloak at severall times.

John Keogh, writing in his 1735 publication *Botanalogia Universalis Hibernica*,
indicates that sloke was valuable for
both its culinary and medicinal proper-

ties. He writes:

*it is good against boils and gout, and
when boiled and dressed, it is esteemed
by some as a delicate dish.*

By at least the early twentieth century
the popularity of sloke had extended to
an urban population and sloke dressed
with pepper and vinegar was sold in
many cities' fish shops. Florence Irwin
confirms the practice in her 1937 publication *Irish Country Recipes*:

*When sold in the fishmonger's it is al-
ready stewed and only requires to be
dressed.*

Throughout the nineteenth and early
twentieth centuries sloke was an important addition to the diet during Lent and
black fast days, particularly in coastal
regions. Danaher points out that on
these occasions, when dairy produce
was prohibited, seaweed and shellfish
were considered tasty condiments for
potato meals.

Use: In the past sloke was used extensively by coastal inhabitants, particularly during Christian periods of fast
and abstinence. It was also considered
a popular supper dish, although it is an
acquired taste, partly because it demanded slow stewing for three to five
hours before it was ready for the table.
Traditionally it was taken as a relish
with oatcakes, mutton and potatoes.
Sloke cakes were also popular. For this
dish sloke was dressed with butter and
cream, mixed with oatmeal and fried on
the pan.
It is used on toasted bread in Waterford, covered with black pepper.

Technique: Sloke grows on rocks along

the coastline. It is collected and has to be washed for 16 hours to get the salt out. It never dries out fully. After boiling for 4 to 5 hours it is strained and put in jars. Traditionally it was believed that the best time for sloke gathering was after a spell of frost. It may be crumbled into a powder and added as a condiment to a variety of dishes.

Producer: Gathered and produced locally in many places such as Waterford. Green Laver and Green Nori are available from Carraig Fhada in Sligo.

Packaging: Packed in glass jars.

References: Carraig Fhada Seaweed, leaflet on sea vegetables. Eddie Wymberry, Waterford, personal communication.

Useful address: Carraig Fhada Seaweed, Cabra, Rathlee, Co. Sligo. Tel 096-49042.

Kelp

A seaweed harvested for centuries in Ireland, kelp (*Laminaria digitata* and *Laminaria saccharina*) is one of the best sources of iodine, iron, potassium and chlorine. A brown seaweed that grows on the Atlantic coast, kelp is more than 30 cm long. It is available today in powder and tablet form. The powder is soft and brown.

Composition: Seaweed containing many minerals. These include aluminium, barium, bismuth, boron, calcium, chlorine, chromium, gallium, iodine, magnesium, manganese, molybdenum, phosphorus and many others. The ground powder has a high iron content.

History: Kelp has been taken from the sea for centuries and used as a remedy for many human ailments; for example, it is claimed to be successful in relieving glandular disturbances. Today it is mostly used as a fertiliser.

Use: Kelp tablets may be chewed. One manufacturer recommends four tablets per day. Powdered kelp is used as a flavouring agent for soups, meats, baked dishes and other dishes. It can also be sprinkled over food in the same way as pepper and salt and can be added to sandwiches and salads.

Technique: In the past kelp, washed up on the shore, was used as a source of potassium and iodine compounds. The kelp was dried and burnt and the ashes were rinsed to remove the mineral salts. Today kelp is harvested from deep-sea waters. It is usually dug out and cut into lengths of 10–12 cm, dried naturally and crushed into a powder.

Producer: Kelp grows in masses along the sea coast. Harvested from the Atlantic Ocean, it is prepared by Carabay Seaweed Ltd, Kylebroughlan, Moycullen, Co. Galway. Mostly exported to health food shops in England, it is distributed in Ireland through Munster Wholefoods. The product is available by mail order world-wide. It is also harvested by Melvins in Sligo and sold to supermarkets and health food shops.

Packaging: It is possible to buy the seaweed in bulk. The powder is sold in small glass jars, weight 57 g net. Shelf life is about a year.

Kelp is a good source of iodine.

Reference: B. Casburn, Carabay (Seaweed Ltd), personal communication.

Useful address: Carabay Seaweed Ltd, Kylebroughlan, Moycullen, Co. Galway. Tel 091-85112.

Fruit, Vegetables and Related Products

Ireland has the highest potato consumption per head of population in the EU.

Potato

Uncooked potatoes are firm tubers which may be round or oval-shaped. Their size varies from 40 mm to over 80 mm diameter for marketable potatoes, with skin colour varying from white to yellow to red. The flesh colour varies from white to yellow. Potatoes are particularly associated with Ireland and this association is linked with the Irish Famine in the mid-nineteenth century, a traumatic period. Today the potato remains important and the Irish people are the highest per capita consumers of potatoes in the EU. A number of modern varieties, such as Cara and Rooster, are Irish-bred.

Cara is a late maincrop variety. The tubers are short oval to round in shape, and the skin is creamy white/pink particoloured, the flesh cream, the eyes shallow. Cara's eating quality is suited for consumers who prefer a low dry matter. Rooster is a maincrop variety. The tubers are oval to short oval, the skin is deep pink/red, the flesh is yellow and the eyes are shallow. The dry matter is higher than Cara.

Composition: Potatoes are high in carbohydrate, low in fat, and have a moderate energy content. They are an important source of vitamin C.

History: There is some controversy as to when and by whom the potato was introduced into Ireland. Legend has it that Sir Walter Raleigh, or rather his gardener, planted the first potato in Ireland on his estate, Myrtle Grove, in Youghal, Co. Cork, in 1586.

It has also been suggested that, in the days following the wreck of the Spanish Armada, the ship's stocks of potatoes were cast on to Irish shores and thereafter the crop was cultivated by the Irish. Whatever its origin, the potato was certainly in Ireland by the close of the sixteenth century. Of course, the potato had already made its way to Europe and England at an earlier date. Viewed as a botanical curiosity for some time, it was slowly embraced as a new and novel food. By contrast, in Ireland the potato gained phenomenal popularity, so much so that on the eve of the Great Famine in 1845 over one-third of the Irish population relied almost exclusively on the potato for their sustenance.

The reasons for the widespread acceptance of the potato in Ireland are many and varied. To begin with, the potato is ideally suited to Irish climatic conditions. The crop thrives in a cool, damp environment and, given that some regions have over 80 mm of rainfall per annum, Ireland was a very suitable place to grow it. In terms of cultivation, potato-growing, when compared to cereal husbandry, was less laborious and more rewarding.

The most common varieties of potato cultivated in Ireland during this period included Blacks, Apples, Cups and Lumpers.

Essentially, therefore, the potato, being relatively trouble-free and giving good yields, brought for the first time a sense of food security in Ireland and was increasingly viewed as a weapon against famine.

Increased reliance is evident in the late-seventeenth-century *Political Anatomy of Ireland*, which notes the dominant position of the potato in the diet of the Irish:

their food is bread and cakes; whereof a peny serves a week for each: potatoes from August 'till May . . . As for flesh they seldom eat it.

Both palatability and ease of preparation additionally facilitated widespread reliance on the potato. Oatcakes were quickly usurped in favour of the superior taste and texture of potatoes laced with buttermilk and melting butter. Such was the taste for potatoes that, in pre-Famine Ireland, the average cottier or landless labourer consumed anything between 3 and 6 kg (7–14 lb) of potatoes per day. Arthur Young, writing in the late eighteenth century, makes the following observation:

six people, a man, his wife and four children, will eat eighteen stone of potatoes a week or 252 lb.

The evidence strongly suggests that ease of food supply provided by the potato facilitated the staggering expansion of the Irish population between the late eighteenth century and the 1840s. In 1780 the population was around 4 million, but by the 1841 Census the figure had risen to almost 8.2 million.

On the eve of the Great Famine nearly 3 million of the Irish population relied almost exclusively on a potato diet. However, it is important to point out that some sectors of society, in particular prosperous farmers and more affluent classes, also enjoyed the potato, but only as an additional item in an otherwise varied diet.

However, by the end of the eighteenth century the dangers of relying on a single foodstuff and, more importantly, the folly of an increased reliance on one potato variety, the Lumper, became all too apparent. (The Lumper was the main variety at the time of the Famine and Indian and English reds were also important.) They were grown on the lazy bed system. Localised potato failures were common, bringing distress to an already impoverished society. By the early nineteenth century the demands of a growing population, soil exhaustion and years of severe frost resulted in poor potato yields and severe food shortages.

Therefore by 1845 people were accustomed to recurrent crop failures and, when one-third of the crop was lost in that year, it was viewed as just another bad harvest. Recognising the impending crisis, Sir Robert Peel, the British Prime Minister, purchased £100,000 worth of maize in the autumn of 1845. The corn went on sale in March 1846 and those who could afford it purchased it for a penny a pound.

However, the presence of the fungal disease *phytophthora infestans*, which destroyed much of the crop in 1845, was to deliver its worst blow in 1846. By September 1846 over two-thirds of the entire crop were lost.

The change of government in England in 1846 exacerbated the crisis at home and Lord John Russell's policy of government non-interference meant the end of the food relief scheme. Continued bad harvests in 1847 and 1848 saw famine and disease sweep through the labouring and poorer classes. Deprived of their sole means of existence, the peasantry was forced to exploit the food resources of the wild. Starving bands, if they had the energy to do so, migrated to coastal regions and picked the shores bare of shellfish and edible seaweeds.

In 1847 the Temporary Relief Act or 'Soup Kitchen Act' saved many from death and starvation, but was ill equipped to cope with the enormous numbers of distressed and destitute. By the 1851 Census the population of Ireland was reduced to 6 million. Over 1 million died as a direct result of famine and fever and a further 2 million were forced to emigrate throughout the late nineteenth century.

Despite the tragedy of the Famine, the Irish people returned to the potato as a staple food in the latter half of the nineteenth century. From this period onwards the crop was made secure with the introduction of spraying against potato blight. This agricultural practice was universal by 1914. Today the potato is still of paramount importance in the diet of the Irish and in many households the potato is served daily with main meals.

Use: The potato is an important part of the main meal of the day in most Irish households. Traditionally, it is also used in the preparation of boxty, colcannon and potato cakes. It is also an indispensable ingredient in the preparation of Irish stew. In the past (and perhaps to a lesser extent today) vast quantities of potatoes were used in the manufacture of the illegal alcoholic beverage called 'poteen'.

Today potatoes are mostly boiled at home, but chips are very popular for meals in restaurants, fast food outlets and takeaways. The traditional Halloween dish, colcannon, is made from boiled mashed potatoes mixed with finely cut and boiled kale.

Technique: A number of varieties are

important, and two of these, Cara and Rooster, have been bred in Ireland by Teagasc, Oakpark, Co. Carlow. As this is a fresh product, the following summarises the production process. Nowadays potatoes are grown in deep soils which are stone-free. The soil is ploughed and fertiliser applied before sowing. Seed free from virus, about 28–35 mm or 35–45 mm, is generally used. The seed is planted in drills in March or April, when soil temperatures are over 7°C for at least three successive days. The drills must be broad enough to prevent greening and tuber blight. Blight is prevented by regular spraying. The green tops are burned off before harvesting, which is often mechanised. All potatoes should be harvested before the temperature drops to 7°C in October. They may be bagged and sold immediately or stored. They are covered with straw to exclude light and a temperature of 4–6°C is required for long-term storage.

Producers: Irish potato output is about half a million tonnes annually. Besides Cara and Rooster, other important varieties are Home Guard, British Queen, Kerr's Pink, Record, King Edward, Pentland Dell and Golden Wonder.

Season: Potatoes are harvested from June to November and are used throughout the year.

Packaging: Potatoes for sale must be graded according to the Food Standards (Potatoes Regulations, 1977). These regulations relate to labelling, size, physical defects and variety. Potatoes are packed in boxes, nets, sacks, plastic prepacks and in other containers. The main pack sizes are 20 kg and 25 kg bags and prepack sizes include 5 kg.

Useful addresses: Oakpark Research Centre, Teagasc, Co. Carlow Tel 0503-31425. An Bord Glas, 8–11 Lower Baggot Street, Dublin 2. Tel 01-676-3567.

Apple

There is a long tradition of apple-growing in Ireland. The growing of culinary varieties occurs only in Ireland and Great Britain. Apples vary in size from less than 50 mm to over 70 mm. Skin colour and flesh colour also vary with the variety.

Composition: Apples have a high water content and contain some dietary fibre, as well as vitamins C and E.

History: Of all the fruits, both wild and cultivated, the apple is historically the one most associated with Ireland. The crab apple tree is native to Ireland and there is archaeological evidence for the consumption of apples from the 7000 BC Mesolithic site of Mount Sandel in Co. Derry. It is likely that during the early historic period there were orchards of cultivated apples attached to most of the large monasteries. In a monastic context, the penitent monks, the Culdees, were permitted apples in their otherwise severe penitential diet during the ninth century. The apple tree was legally protected in the seventh- and eighth-century Brehon Laws, and interference with the tree entailed a substantial penalty or fine. The tree was classed as a 'noble of the woods' and had the same status as the oak, hazel, holly, ash, yew and pine, which is clearly an indication of the value of its fruit. Apples are also referred to in the eleventh-century tale *Aislinge meic Conglinne*, where they are listed as suitable items for a feast.

In the wake of the English and Scottish Plantations in the late sixteenth and seventeenth centuries the influx of settlers and large landlords established substantial new orchards on their lands. Nelson states that in 1635, for example, Sir William Brereton visited a number of eastern towns; at Carrickfergus he noted of Lord Chichester's house:

a graceful terrace and walk before the house . . . a fine garden and mighty spacious orchards, and they say they bear good store of fruit.

These new settlers also diversified the range of apple varieties in Ireland. This new emphasis on apple-growing encouraged and facilitated the growth of the cider industry, and for the general population apples remained a regular item in the diet. Indeed, the Reverend John Keogh recommended their medical properties in his 1735 *Botanalogia Universalis Hibernica*:

Apples comfort and cool the heat of the stomach, especially those that are somewhat sour.

Throughout the nineteenth century the folklore record indicates that apple-eating was particularly associated with the festival and celebrations of Halloween.

Use: Dessert apples are eaten fresh. Both dessert and culinary apples can be used in many dishes such as apple pies. They can also be baked or stewed on their own. In Irish folk belief, a poultice of crab apples was considered a cure for blisters.

Technique: Traditionally apples were grown on large trees with about 200 trees to a hectare. In the early 1970s the system of growing with dwarf rootstocks was introduced and the number of trees planted per hectare increased to about 1,250. As dessert apples are subject to russeting they must be grown in warmer areas where there are deep loam soils. Trees must be stacked and treated regularly to prevent apple scab. If necessary, treatment for other pests and diseases is given. Yields are between 850 and 1,500 cartons of 18 kg (40 lb) per hectare. Apples are hand picked and stored under cool conditions, preferably in controlled atmosphere stores.

Producers: Bramley's Seedling is the most important culinary variety. They are available all year if there is sufficient production for storage. There are no Irish-bred varieties and those grown for dessert include Discovery, Katy and Spartan. Dublin, Cork and Kilkenny in the south and Armagh in the north are the most important apple-growing areas. In total between 8,000 and 10,000 tonnes of apples are produced each year in the Republic of Ireland, but about 50,000 tonnes are imported.

Season: Locally grown dessert varieties are available from July to April, but quantities are small, particularly after Christmas.

Packaging: Dessert apples are packed in 8–18 kg boxes and culinary apples in 13.6–18 kg boxes. They are graded to meet EU grading regulations.

Useful addresses: An Bord Glas, 8–11 Lower Baggot Street, Dublin 2. Tel 01-676-3567. Teagasc, Kildalton College, Piltown, Co. Kilkenny. Tel 051-643-105.

Cabbage

Also Kale

A green-leaved vegetable of the brassica family, the cabbage, along with the potato, is particularly associated with Ireland—corned beef and cabbage is a traditional dish. Heads are about 20 cm in diameter, and appearance varies with variety. Some are light green, some dark green, and heads may be loose or firm. Varieties grown today in Ireland are non-native and were bred in England, the Netherlands and other countries.

Composition: Cabbage is low in energy and fat and has some fibre and iron.

History: It is clear that a variety of brassicas were consumed in early medieval Ireland. Kale is frequently mentioned in the ninth-century *Félire Oengusso Céli Dé* as a foodstuff permissible in the otherwise penitential diet of the Irish monks. The excavations of medieval Dublin revealed that a large variety of brassicas were being consumed at that time. However, the vegetable, as it is known today, was not introduced into Ireland until the early seventeenth century.

By the late seventeenth century the vegetable was gaining popularity, as is clear from a reference from 1683: Nelson points out that Mr John Cole supplied Trinity College gardens with 500 cabbage plants for cultivation within the college gardens.

By this period the cabbage had also won favour with the Irish peasantry.

John Dunton observes in Ballymoney in 1698:

> Behind one of their cabins lyes the garden, a piece of ground sometimes of half an acre . . . and in this is the turfstack, their corn, perhaps two or three hundred sheaves of oats and as much peas. The rest of the ground is full of their dearly beloved potatoes, and a few cabbages which the solitary calf of the family that is here pent from its dam never suffers to come to perfection.

Cabbage, in particular white cabbage, was regularly consumed by Amhlaoibh Uí Shúileabháin of Callan in Co. Kilkenny. In his diary entry of 28 September 1828 he records his dinner at the home of Father James Henebry:

> we had bacon with cow's kidney and white cabbage.

Because cabbage is a relatively reliable crop, it was used extensively as an emergency food in the Famine years 1845–8. For example, in Castleisland in Co. Kerry a particularly hard month during the Famine years was known as 'July of the Cabbage'.

Use: As part of a main meal. Cabbage also appears in two of Ireland's traditional dishes, bacon and cabbage and colcannon. The leaves are separated and cooked, whole or chopped, in boiling water for a few minutes. Cabbage is served as a main vegetable with any meal, but is particularly associated with bacon. In this case the cabbage is usually cooked in the water used for the bacon. White storage cabbage is used for coleslaw.

Technique: As cabbage is a fresh veg-table, this section deals with field production. The cabbage used today originally came from the wild or sea cabbage, which is a native of Europe. Until about twenty years ago the types used were open pollinated. Cow cabbage types included Savoys, January King, Winningstadt and York. Irish strains of these were developed and selected to suit Irish conditions. Farmyard manure was generally used and all cultivation activities were manually done. There were no herbicides and the season was limited.

Today hybrids are used. These are produced abroad by a few large companies and supplied to markets in many countries, including Ireland. Plants are planted mechanically. Young plants about 10 cm high with a few leaves are planted in rows or drills. Between 35,000 and 40,000 are planted to a hectare. There are winter, spring, summer and autumn cabbages and cabbages are therefore sown at almost any time of the year. For most cultivars there is an optimum harvesting period and both sowing and transplanting dates are chosen taking this into account. Fertilisers are applied and sprays are used for weed, pest and disease control. Yields vary from between 1500 x 12 to 3000 x 12 per hectare.

Producers: Between 45,000 and 60,000 tonnes of cabbage are produced from between 1,500 and 2,000 hectares in Ireland annually.

Season: Different types are available for each season, for example spring cabbage is available from February to May and autumn cabbage from September to November.

Packaging: Boxes for the market may contain 10–17 heads. White storage cabbage is packed in 25 kg bags. Cabbages are sold loose unpacked or in a cellophane wrap to the consumer.

Useful addresses: An Bord Glas, 8–11 Lower Baggot Street, Dublin 2. Tel 01-676-3567. Teagasc, Research Centre, Kinsealy, Co. Dublin. Tel 01-846-0644.

Onion

Also Shallot, sets

A bulbous-shaped vegetable, 40–100 mm diameter, with a strong flavour and aroma when cut. The skin colour varies from off-white to various shades of brown. The onion has a particularly strong flavour when cut. The skin colour varies from off-white to various shades of brown. The onion has a particularly strong historical association with Ireland and remains a widely used vegetable today.

Composition: Onions have moderate energy from carbohydrate. They also contain small amounts of vitamin C, niacin and dietary fibre.

History: Onions are amongst Ireland's oldest cultivated vegetables. The seventh- and eighth-century Brehon Laws stipulate that onions must be included as part of the food rents from client to lord. They were also recommended as suitable food for the sick. The same source also refers to the presence of pickled onions in early medieval Ireland. Onions are mentioned frequently in the eleventh-century middle Irish tale *Aislinge meic Conglinne*:

> *with his hood of flummery about him,*
> *with a seven filleted crown of butter on*
> *his head, in each fillet of which was the*
> *produce of seven ridges of pure leeks*
> *[onions].*

While the type of onion mentioned in early medieval texts is difficult to ascertain, various candidates have been put forward, including shallots and Welsh onions.

From at least the early seventeenth century onwards, onions were regularly cultivated in the gardens of Trinity College Dublin for serving at the Fellows' table. Later in the seventeenth century, Dean Jonathan Swift recorded in verse the practicality of boiling onions:

> *There is in every cook's opinion*
> *No savoury dish without an onion*
> *But lest your kissing should be spoil'd*
> *The onion must be thoroughly boil'd.*

In the early nineteenth century Amhlaoibh Uí Shúileabháin notes the common use of onions in his diary entry for 15 June 1832:

> *A beautiful, delightful, blueskied, sunny,*
> *calm day . . . oinions, scallions and other*
> *vegetables will be copious and cheap.*

Use: Traditionally the onion was used as an addition to many dishes. It was also a basic ingredient in many white sauces that accompanied otherwise bland foods such as tripe. In Irish folk custom, stewed onions eaten at night were used as a cure for constipation. Steak and onions is a typical dish in Ireland today.

Technique: As this is a fresh vegetable this section summarises the field production process (see 'Cabbage' for the traditional approach). They are mostly spring-sown but may also be autumn-sown. Onions may be transplanted or direct sown. Small onions known as sets are also grown. Direct drilled onions are a marginal crop, particularly if a wet spring is followed by below-average summer temperatures. Multi-seeded modular transplant systems can give good crops, even in poor growing seasons.

Spraying is needed for weed, disease and pest control. Weed control is easier in transplanted crops than in direct drilled. Early harvesting is usual, when the onions are still green. The tops are removed by a flail-type harvester. Output is usually between 35 and 50 tonnes a hectare and after harvesting onions must be dried and stored. There are three stages to storing. Surface moisture is removed first, followed by neck moisture. A good skin colour is produced, and gradually the stack is cooled off. Different temperatures, air flows and relative humidities are required for each stage. For the third stage the general aim is to maintain a temperature of 4–5°C in the stack. They are graded and topped for selling into 40–60 mm, 60–80 mm, 80 mm+ and 90–105 mm sizes.

Producers: Between 4,000 and 7,000 tonnes are produced annually. As supply is insufficient to meet demand, considerable volumes are imported.

Season: Onions are harvested in late summer and autumn. As they are stored they are available throughout the year, but the supply of local onions is usually finished early in the New Year, after which time the market is supplied by imports.

Packaging: Normally packed in net bags of 19–25 kg for the market, but sold loosely or in net or plastic prepacks at retail outlets. Net prepacks may contain 10–12 onions while plastic prepacks may have 6–8 onions. Onions for sale must be graded to meet EU regulations.

Useful addresses: An Bord Glas, 8–11 Lower Baggot Street, Dublin 2. Tel 01-676-3567. Teagasc, Research Centre, Kinsealy, Co. Dublin. Tel 01-846-0644.

Fraughans (Pies and Jams)

Also Bilberries, fraochán, whortleberry (bilberry/blaeberry, fraughan/whortleberry)

A wild product gathered for centuries and still collected today, bilberries are strong-flavoured and grow on acid soils in the vicinity of heather in the hills and mountains. They are dark blue in colour, and very juicy.

History: Traditionally bilberries were one of the most popular of all the wild fruits. There exists a substantial body of historical evidence relating to the fruit from the early medieval period onwards. The folklore records of the nineteenth and early twentieth centuries highlight the fruit's association with the festivities of Garland Sunday, the first Sunday in August.

One of the earliest historical references to the fruit appears in the ninth-century poem 'Marbán agus Gúaire':

> *a clutch of eggs, honey and heathpease,*
> *sweet apples . . . whortleberries.*

The excavations of Viking Dublin also indicate that bilberries were a relatively common feature of the diet during the tenth century.

Apart from their dietary importance, John Keogh also details their medicinal qualities in his 1735 publication *Botanalogia Universalis Hibernica*:

> *The bilberry bush has long crenated leaves and black fruit . . . It grows on mountains and bogs. The berries are very cool-*

ing, good against burning fevers, inflam-
mation of the liver and scurvy. They also
arrest diarrhoea and vomiting.

In the diaries of Amhlaoibh Uí
Shúileabháin, the diarist refers to the
fruit in an entry for 18 April 1835.

In Ireland, fraughans are inextricably
linked with the festival of *Lughnasadh* (31
July/1 August) and celebrations on the
last Sunday of July. The general festivities of this time were sometimes transplanted to the nearest Sunday in August
and became known as 'Garland Sunday'
and 'Fraughan Sunday'. During the festival it was customary for communities
to gather on nearby hilltops and lake
shores where they partook in many activities, including sporting and picnick-
ing. It was a time for serious courting
among teenagers, as is clear from the
well-known maxim 'Many a lad met his
wife on Blaeberry Sunday.' The gathering of fraughans was an established and
usual activity for the day and they were
often mashed and eaten with sugar and
cream.

The folklore record also indicates that
in Kilkenny it was customary for a
young boy to present his girlfriend with
the gathered fruit. Once the girl returned
home, she made a fraughan cake which
was enjoyed by herself and her boy-
friend at the bonfire dance on Garland
Sunday night.

Use: Traditionally eaten with pies or
mashed with sugar. Also made into jam.

Technique: Picked and made into pies
or jams, which are sometimes sold locally.

Producers: As these are mountain berries, the amounts harvested are not
known, but thought to be relatively
small.

Packaging: Loosely for pies and glass
jars for jams.

Marmalade

Also Orange preserve. Old Time Irish marmalade is taken as an example.

Marmalade is an orange-based breakfast spread, with the thickness of the cut and the fruit content varying between brands. The spreading of an orange-based preserve on bread at breakfast is a tradition found mainly in Ireland and Britain.

Composition: Sugar, water and oranges. Other ingredients vary. The ingredient list on Old Time Irish lists sugar, oranges, glucose syrup, gelling agent (pectin), citric acid and acidity regulator (sodium citrate). It is prepared with 23 g fruit per 100 g, with total sugar of 67 g per 100 g. Another commercial product contains sugar, oranges, citric acid, gelling agent, pectin, antioxidant (ascorbic acid), preservatives (potassium sorbate, sodium benzoate), stabiliser (gear gum), artificial sweetener (saccharin), acidity regulator (sodium citrate), firming agent (calcium chloride) and colourant (caramel). Lower sugar and higher fruit products are now widely available.

History: It is probable that marmalade first made its appearance in the homes of the wealthy Anglo-Irish gentry from the eighteenth century onwards. In the eighteenth century the *Shapland Carew Papers*, which detail the day-to-day running of the Carew estates in Co. Waterford and Wexford, record regular purchases of substantial quantities of oranges.

Marmalade probably first made its appearance in the homes of the Anglo-Irish gentry in the eighteenth century.

On 3 February 1773 the family purchased a consignment of Seville oranges, while on 3 January 1780 China oranges were bought for the estate. It seems reasonable to assume that orange marmalade preserve was made with at least some of these fruits.

From the early nineteenth century onwards recipes for marmalade appear with increasing frequency in domestic Irish recipe books. For example, an 1801 Co. Waterford manuscript recipe book includes a recipe for China orange jelly. Similarly, marmalade recipes are found in an 1850 Cork manuscript book and another from Co. Limerick dated to 1851. Once marmalade was commercially produced in the early twentieth century, it became available to the general population and quickly became established as an accompaniment to breakfast. In the early twentieth century marmalade was also a popular ingredient used in the preparation of marmalade cakes and puddings.

Wilfred H. Lamb established a new jam factory in Inchicore, Dublin, in 1917. He introduced Old Time Irish marmalade in 1920. This was to be the marmalade brand of Lamb Brothers for a number of years. His recipe is said to be based on traditional Quaker recipes from the Armagh area. The fireside scene on the label was introduced in 1946/7. The coarse cut product was very popular and Mr Lamb called it 'bitter sweet', and said that there was no substitute 'for the joy of that first bite on your morning toast'. For a number of years many marmalade varieties were available from Lambs, including fine cut orange, orange strand, lemon strand and ginger. In 1980 the Willwood Group took over the Old Time Irish and Fruitfield brands. They transferred production to their own modern plant at Tallaght, Dublin. Willwood were taken over by Nestlé Ireland in 1984.

Use: Marmalade is used almost exclusively as a breakfast spread. Industry sources feel this market is growing slowly. The product shelf life is about eight months at room temperature.

Technique: Standard processes of jam-making are used by large manufacturers. In recent years smaller producers such as Ownabee Preserves started making small quantities in a kitchen operation, using traditional recipes over a hundred years old.

Old Time Irish is a coarse-cut marmalade manufactured in a process that has remained virtually unchanged since the 1930s. This coarse-cut marmalade had two components, bitter oranges from Seville and sugar. During production the peel of the orange was separated from the juice and both were processed separately. Besides Old Time Irish Orange coarse cut, a number of other related marmalades are produced today, including Old Time Irish Orange fine cut and Varsity Irish Vintage.

Producers: Old Time, Little Chip and Fruitfield, all from Nestlé, are the main brands. Chivers is the other main local brand, but there are also a number of smaller suppliers as well as imported marmalade from the UK available on the market. The marmalade market is valued at about IR£14 million.

Season: Marmalade is produced and used throughout the year.

Packaging: Glass jars, white and transparent, are generally used. Standard sizes are 454 g and 400 g, but smaller jars are also available. The Old Time Irish label is pasted on the jar and shows a traditional fireside scene. The main colour used on the label is orange. The cap on the jar is also orange-coloured.

References: Paul Kelly and Jack McGouran, Nestlé and Quest, personal communications and information leaflets.

Useful addresses: Nestlé Ireland Ltd, Blessington Road, Tallaght, Dublin 24. Tel 01-451-2244. Chivers and Sons Ltd, Coolock, Dublin 5. Tel 01-848-4044.

Honey

Honey is a thick sweet liquid. It is made by honey bees from the nectar they collect from blossoms or from secretions of or on living parts of plants. They collect, transform and combine the nectar. The wide and varied flora from which bees gather nectar, including white clover and blackberry, give Irish honey a distinct flavour, and it has a special image throughout the country as a quality product with limited availability. Generally honey is used in liquid form, but it can be partly or wholly crystalline. Pieces of the honeycomb, called comb honey, are also sold commercially. The colour varies from light amber to dark brown and the flavour also varies depending on the source of nectar.

Composition: Honey contains about 75% sugar and 20% water. It also contains protein, amino acids, enzymes, organic acids and mineral substances, as well as traces of fungi, algae, yeasts and other solid particles resulting from the process of obtaining honey. The main sugars are glucose and fructose.

History: An aetiological narrative from the ninth-century *Félire Oengusso Céli Dé*, tells that a saint called Modomnoc introduced bees and honey to Ireland:

Modomnoc brought bee; he brought the fill of his bell.

It is likely that bees were in Ireland before the arrival of Christianity and the legend may suggest an increase in bee-keeping and honey production in the post-fifth-century period. The value of honey in early Ireland is clearly evident in the elaborate and comprehensive seventh-century law text *Bechbretha*, which is dedicated exclusively to the rules and good practices of bee-keeping. Honey was used as a sweetening agent for food and drinks: the seventh- and eighth-century vernacular law of fosterage details how honey was used as a sweetener for porridge, while the penitential monastic communities of the ninth century drank honey-sweetened milk on the eves of Christmas and Easter. Honey was also used in the manufacture of alcoholic drinks such as mead and bragget. The abundant availability of honey is noted by Giraldus Cambrensis in the twelfth century:

the island is rich in . . . milk and honey and wine.

By the fifteenth century the home market seemed unable to supply the demand for honey and throughout the century quantities were imported from abroad. An account for 1449/50, for example, indicates that a consignment was imported into Limerick by Breton merchant Maurice de la Noe.

The practice of bee-keeping and honey production continued on Irish farms well into the nineteenth and twentieth centuries, despite the availability of sugar in urban centres and rural village shops. The folklore record for this period indicates that honey was widely used as a sweetener and medical cure. A honey and garlic drink was recommended as a cure for sore throats.

Use: Honey is used in various ways, sometimes eaten pure by the spoonful, sometimes in tea. It is often used as a spread on buttered or unbuttered toast and bread. It can be used in many recipes. As a source of quick energy it is used by athletes. Honey will keep for a few years.

Technique: Worker bees collect the nectar from a wide range of flora. White clover and blackberry are the dominant sources of Irish honey, but hawthorn and chestnut are also important. The main honey flow is from 20 June to the end of July and long-term records from Clonroche in Wexford show that there are only about 15 days in that period when the bees are able to work. They release enzymes which act on the sugar in the nectar, producing simple sugars. When they return to the hive they place the honey in the cells of the comb. After some water has evaporated they seal off the cells with beeswax, where it remains until harvested. Liquid honey is prepared by placing the honeycombs in a centrifugal extractor, which removes the honey. It is then strained to remove solid particles and packed for sale. Comb honey is sold in section form or as cut comb honey. The European regional standard for honey operates in Ireland and only products conforming to the standard may be designated 'honey'.

Producers: There are about 2,000 producers, with 22,000 colonies of bees. They tend to sell individually to local markets and craft shops. The average yield of honey is about 12 kg per hive. As production is insufficient to meet demand, most honey used in Ireland today is imported.

Season: Honey is harvested in late summer and autumn. It is used throughout the year.

Packaging: Honey is usually packed in glass jars. One supplier uses eight-sided white transparent 250 g glass jars.

References: Patsy Bennet, Clonroche Research Station, Teagasc, personal communication.

Useful address: Peter O'Reilly, Secretary, Federation of Irish Beekeepers, Our Lady's Place, Naas, Co. Kildare. Tel 045-97568.

Relish

Also Ballymaloe Relish

A local East Cork product made to an original Ballymaloe recipe. The relish is free from all artificial additives. Ballymaloe Relish has a deep and rich red colour. It has a thick tomato consistency.

Composition: Tomatoes, vinegar, sugar, onions, sultanas, spices and sea salt.

History: Myrtle Allen created the original relish recipe. In the 1930s and 1940s she experimented with different tomato relish recipes and, with tips from friends and acquaintances, the Ballymaloe recipe was eventually perfected. The relish was routinely made every year in midsummer when the tomatoes were at their ripest. Once the relish was potted it was stored for use through the year and quickly became a regular item in the Allen household. In 1990 Myrtle's daughter, Yasmin Hyde, began commercial production of the relish. Since its appearance on shop shelves in 1990 the product has gained in popularity. Yasmin Hyde is in the process of expanding the product into the European market.

Use: The relish is an accompaniment to all foods. It is used particularly with cheese and cold meats, grills, pasta, fish and curries. It can also be used as a flavouring ingredient in the preparation of pasta sauces.

Technique: When commercial production of the product began in 1990 Yasmin Hyde acquired a cooker designed specifically to resemble a kitchen pot. In this cooker/pot the tomatoes are brought to the boil with the other ingredients. Once boiled, the ingredients are reduced slowly over a period of five hours. Subsequently the relish is potted hot.

Producers: Yasmin Hyde is the only commercial producer of the product. Ballymaloe Relish is a registered brand name.

Packaging: The product is sold in 11 oz/ 310 g glass jars. The jar's label is a colourful illustration of the Anglo-Norman Ballymaloe towerhouse which today adjoins the main house and restaurant.

Reference: Myrtle Allen and Yasmin Hyde, personal communication.

Useful addresses: Hyde Ltd, Courtstown Industrial Park, Little Island, Co. Cork. Tel 021-354-810. Myrtle Allen, Ballymaloe House, Shanagarry, Midleton, Co. Cork. Tel 021-652-531.

Dairy Products

Checking the day's output of buttermilk and country butter

Buttered Hens' Eggs

A traditional method of preserving eggs for long-time storage, the process is associated with the Cork region. Buttered eggs come in varying sizes. There is no standard buttered egg size because the eggs are chosen at random for buttering as soon as they have been laid. The eggs have a characteristic shiny, polished appearance, while the cooked egg has a distinctive buttery flavour.

Composition: Hens' eggs and fresh butter.

History: Eggs have always featured strongly in the Irish diet. They are mentioned frequently in the seventh- and eighth-century Brehon Laws, while the ninth-century poem 'Marbán and Gúaire' includes a complimentary reference to the foodstuff:

delightful feasts come . . .
A clutch of eggs, honey, mast
. . . sweet apples

Undoubtedly eggs endured as a popular food and in the late seventeenth century John Dunton, writing in his 1698 *Letters from Ireland*, recounts an enjoyable dinner he was served in Dublin:

salt fish and eggs, hen and bacon and rabbits.

Yet despite the abundance of references to eggs the historical sources are silent as to the origin or prevalence of buttered eggs. However, the practice of buttering eggs for preservation purposes must be one of considerable antiquity, designed to ensure a winter supply of eggs when the hens' laying potential was at their lowest. In addition, the religious custom of abstaining from eating eggs during Lent and the associated practice of saving them for the Easter Sunday egg feast must have encouraged this process of preservation. It is also likely that the process was employed widely through-out the nineteenth century. At this time Ireland was exporting large amounts of eggs to Britain, where there was a great demand. In 1850, for example, Ireland exported 11 million eggs per annum and this figure rose to 40 million by 1900. It is probable, therefore, that many of the eggs destined for export were buttered in an attempt to preserve their freshness.

In the first half of the twentieth century the domestic market demand for buttered eggs was particularly high during the two world wars, when fresh eggs were rationed and only buttered ones were widely available. Today buttered eggs are consumed because of their distinctive rich buttery flavour.

Use: Buttered eggs are used for cooking and baking purposes and they are chosen in preference to standard fresh eggs because of their distinctive flavour.

Technique: The process of buttering eggs for preservation purposes is a very simple one, but its effectiveness is dependent on the freshness of the egg at the time of buttering. Therefore eggs should be buttered immediately after they have been laid, but in general the eggs are buttered any time within 30 to 60 minutes after laying.

At the poultry farms the freshly laid

eggs are gathered. Workers wearing plastic gloves coat their hands in a thin film of fresh butter and the eggs are then rolled individually in the palms of their hands. The butter is absorbed quickly into the hot porous egg shell. After the egg has cooled, the hardened buttered shell acts as a barrier against the absorption of air into the egg cavity. The sealed and clogged shell will keep the egg fresh for up to six months. Eggs treated in this manner have been known to remain fresh for up to twelve months.

Producers: A number of egg distributors produce buttered eggs in the Cork region. One of the biggest suppliers is Riverview Eggs in Co. Cork.

Packaging: The buttered surface of the eggs makes packaging or boxing difficult and messy; instead the eggs are sold loosely in shops and market stalls.

Reference: Dick Collins, Riverview Eggs, personal communication.

Useful address: Dick Collins, Riverview Eggs, Ballyvolane, Co. Cork. Tel 021-501-497.

Country Butter

Also Farmhouse butter

The size and shape of farmhouse butter vary. One producer has a flatter bar (2.8 cm by 16 cm by 8 cm) than standard butter. The bar weighs 340 g. The butter is yellower than creamery butter, with some butters darker than others. The butters are all lightly salted. There are variations—some are stronger tasting than others with specific cultures added and higher acid production. The inclusion of salt is the other key factor that distinguishes Irish country butter from similar butters in other countries.

Composition: Pure cream, salt.

History: It is reasonable to suppose that butter has been produced in Ireland from the Neolithic period onwards (4000 BC), where the simple agitation of milk and cream in a covered vessel would have rendered butterfat and buttermilk. However, while the origins of the product remain unclear, it is evident that by the early historic period (fifth to eleventh centuries) butter had become a well-established food in the diet of the Irish. From this period onwards there is unbroken historical evidence illustrating its immense dietary and economic importance. In addition, the corpus of folk belief relating to butter-making is a testament to its popularity and commonality in Ireland. It must be stressed that butter was not merely a casual condiment in the diet. In fact butter and the range of dairy produce collectively termed 'white meats' formed the staple foodstuffs of the diet for much of the year. Until the close of the seventeenth century white meats dominated the diet. However, while cheese production waned in this period, the butter industry thrived and supplied both the home and foreign markets.

There are continuous references to butter in the seventh- and eighth-century Brehon Laws. In these laws butter is considered a superior condiment for bread and porridge. It is also used in the payment of taxes and penalty fines for petty crime. Butter is also mentioned frequently in the eleventh-century middle Irish tale *Aislinge meic Conglinne*: In the visionary land of plenty a boat with a butter stern is described:

with its prow of lard, with its stern of butter, with its thole-pins of marrow.

Butter was mostly consumed as a necessary condiment to harsh oaten breads. It was also used in the preparation of meal paste. For example, Edmund Campion in his *History of Ireland* (1570) writes:

oatmeal and butter they crame together They drink whey milk and beef broth.

With the introduction of the potato in the late sixteenth century butter also served as a tasty condiment to boiled potatoes. Arthur Young in *A Tour of Ireland* (1780) writes of Farnham in Co. Cavan:

potatoes and milk and butter are his food or oaten bread when the potatoes are not in season.

The partnership of melting butter and hot potatoes is also recorded by Fleming Tait and Hill Williams in their 1831 *Ord-*

nance Survey Memoir of the parish of Tidstraw in Co. Tyrone:

potatoes and milk are the general food . . . during 9 months of the year . . . sometimes butter and oaten bread, eggs are added to the potatoes for dinner.

Traditionally great quantities of fresh butter were consumed during the summer and autumn months. Henry Piers in *A Chorographical Description of the County of West Meath* (1682) details the changing dietary patterns from May Day onwards:

from then milk became plenty, and butter, new cheese and curds and Samrocks, are the food of the meaner sort all this season.

When fresh butter was rare, salted butter and bog-preserved butter were consumed. Butter has been salted in Ireland since at least the seventh century. Old and heavily salted butter is mentioned frequently in the Brehon Laws. The practice of burying butter in bogs for preservation and palatability was common in Ireland from the seventeenth century at least. One of the earliest historical references to the custom was that of Dineley, who, after his travels through Ireland in 1681, wrote:

butter laid up in baskets, mixed with a sort of garlic, and buried for some time in a bog to make a provision for a high taste for lent.

Dating the cessation of the practice in Ireland cannot be accurately ascertained, though some scholars have suggested that it was discontinued late in the eighteenth century.

Until the close of the nineteenth century butter-making was exclusively women's work. The actual churning process gave rise to a considerable corpus of folk belief and superstition—for example no singing, talking or quarrelling were allowed.

Country or farmhouse butter was widely available until the 1940s and, after a period of decline when creamery butter grew in importance, it is now becoming widely available again, although demand is limited. Irish creamery butter is the equivalent industrial product.

Use: On bread and for cooking.

Technique: Before creameries were set up each farmhouse had its own churn and other butter-making equipment such as skimmer, ladle, butter scoops and pats. Mahon describes butter-making in Donegal:

> Skim milk was put into the churn along with the risen cream, . . . the staff was worked up and down for an hour . . . butter was lifted out of churn.

One modern producer in Mayo has a 1.5–1.8 m vat where cream is brought to the top, then churned. Some 2% salt is included. This means the fat content is lower at 80% than the 82% in other butters. This producer also has a wrapping line and a cold room.

Producers: There are a number of farmhouse producers in Ireland. In Mayo producers include Irish Farmhouse Creamery Ltd and producers are selling into larger retail outlets such as Quinnsworth, Supervalu and Dunnes. Today most butter produced is creamery butter and large volumes are sold on the domestic and export markets.

Packaging: A Mayo producer uses a cream label showing a lady with a churn on the pack and a field with dairy cows as background.

Reference: C. Hickey, Irish Farmhouse Pantry, Co. Mayo, personal communication.

Useful address: Tom Butler, Irish Farmhouse Creamery Ltd, Shraheens, Balla, Co. Mayo. Tel 094-31425.

Buttermilk

The next morning a greate pott full of new milk was sett over the fire, and when it was hott they pour'd into it a pale full of butter milk, which made a mighty dish of tough curds in the middle of which they placed a pound worth of butter.

Original buttermilk is the liquid which drains away when butter is made. Most buttermilk today is a cultured milk, generally a liquid product, with an off-white colour. A cultured milk product, and typical of Ireland in the past, it is still available in modified form.

Composition: Pasteurised skim milk and lactic cultures.

History: In the medieval period Ireland's extensive pastoral economy ensured that dairy produce (collectively termed 'white meats') dominated the diet during the summer and autumn months. Within this milk-based economy buttermilk was valued as a refreshment and an ingredient used in the production of soured buttermilk cheese. Buttermilk is mentioned frequently in the Brehon Laws as a foodstuff and a food rent exchanged between clients and lords. Irish penitential literature of the ninth century also refers to buttermilk as one of the few foodstuffs permissible in the diet of the austere monastic communities. In the later medieval period buttermilk is mentioned as a desirable foodstuff in the eleventh-century tale *Aislinge meic Conglinne*.

The continued use of buttermilk in the domestic preparation of soft cheeses is referred to by John Dunton in the late seventeenth century. Writing in his 1698 *Letters from Ireland*, he describes the process as he witnessed it at first hand in a cottage in the west of Ireland:

James Boyle, writing in the *Ordnance Survey Memoirs of County Antrim*, describes the diet of the Irish:

their dinner of potatoes, buttermilk, salt herrings, sometimes a little broth . . . and their supper of potatoes and milk.

From the nineteenth century onwards, buttermilk also became an indispensable ingredient used in the preparation of home-made soda bread. Until well into the twentieth century buttermilk was considered an excellent thirst quencher, particularly during the summer months, and every household held a vat of buttermilk for drinking. It was a refreshment especially associated with the communal tasks of harvesting, haymaking and turf cutting, where it was usual for both men and women to mark a break in the work by drinking a jug of cooled buttermilk. Today buttermilk is rarely consumed as a refreshment and is used mainly in baking. Nonetheless, its popularity is still noteworthy, as is clear from the fact that in 1990 Irish consumption per capita of skimmed milk and buttermilk was 15.7 kg, double the EU average.

Use: Buttermilk has traditionally been used as a refreshment and as an ingredient in cheese-making. In the past people believed that buttermilk was an effective cure for hangovers and it was also used by young girls to improve their complexions. Nowadays it is used mainly as an ingredient in baking breads such as brown bread, soda bread and scones, both at home and commercially.

Technique: Cultured buttermilk was originally manufactured from fresh buttermilk, a by-product of butter manufacture. Buttermilk produced by Caroline Meegan is a natural product and the more liquid part separates out at the top. The pasteurised milk is cream churned, semi-manually, and the buttermilk is released and packaged. About 90 litres are produced at a time. Difficulties in maintaining a consistent supply of high-quality raw material have led to skimmed milk being used by other manufacturers. The skimmed milk is pasteurised and lactic cultures are added. Today's cultured product is kept refrigerated at 6°C or less and has to be shaken well before use.

Producers: Caroline Meegan in Dundalk produces fresh country buttermilk, which has a shelf life of six weeks. It is sold to local bakeries and to national supermarket groups. Irish Farmhouse Creamery is another small producer. The buttermilk produced by most dairies is sold mainly through retail outlets, but is also available through doorstep delivery. Shelf life is about 21 days when kept refrigerated at 6°C or less.

Season: Sales tend to be higher in the winter months when more home baking is done.

Packaging: The Meegans use a 1 litre plastic container and bulk containers of 90 litres. Nowadays creamery buttermilk is generally sold in tetra pak paper cartons, the usual sizes being 500 ml and 1 litre, though they are also available in 22.7 litre catering packs. Premier use a tetra pak laminated board carton. The 500 ml and 1 litre packs are widely available.

References: Premier Dairies, personal communication. Caroline Meegan, personal communication.

Useful addresses: Premier Dairies, PO Box 105, Rathfarnham, Dublin 14. Tel 01-298-3033. Cavistons Delicatessen, 59 Glasthule Road, Co Dublin. Tel 01-280-9120.

Cottage Cheese/Curds

Soft unripened low-fat acid cheese cut in small pieces. It was called cottage cheese because it was commonly made in the small cottages of the poor. Cottage cheese is basically produced by the same process as is used to produce curds, one of the most important foodstuffs for centuries in Ireland.

Composition: Fermented skimmed or partly skimmed milk, cream, lactic cultures, salt, rennet. Modern products contain preservative such as potassium sorbate. The fat content is low, at about 4.7 g per 100 g.

History: Early medieval records abound with references to curd cheese. The seventh- and eighth-century Brehon Laws indicate that curds, together with butter and milk, dominated the summer and autumn diet of the Irish population. It is evident from the ninth-century *Life of St Patrick* that tithes and taxes were commonly paid in the form of curds. The cheese is listed frequently as a desirable and tasty foodstuff in the eleventh-century tale *Aislinge meic Conglinne*. Curds continued to be consumed as a common summer food of the ordinary classes until the early modern period. An anonymous antiquarian visitor to Ireland in 1673 writes:

The Common sort of People in Ireland do feed generally upon Milk, Butter, Curds and Whey.

In 1755 a recipe for curd or cheese cakes appears in the manuscript book of Catherine Hughes of Killinaule, Co. Tipperary.

It is generally accepted that the introduction of the potato into Ireland in the late sixteenth century and the widespread displacement of Gaelic landowners in the late sixteenth and seventeenth centuries marked the decline and eventual abandonment of cheese manufacture in Ireland.

Today a simple curd or cottage cheese is commercially manufactured by many dairies.

Use: Curd cheese is used with salads. It may also be used to make cheesecakes or as a filling for baked potatoes. It has a shelf life of two to three weeks at 5°C.

Technique: Traditionally the most basic form of curd cheese was produced by souring fresh or skimmed milk or with buttermilk. Ó Sé lists the varieties of basic curd cheese which were current in early medieval Ireland: these include 'lath', a sour milk curd, and 'millsen', a fresh milk curd with rennet. Originally milk stored in animal pouches formed a curd. When it was cleaned out, enzymes were left. Some older curd was thrown into the newer material (called 'seeding'), and coagulation produced flavour from lactic acid bacteria. Today different bacteria are used but the process is the same. Setting can be short or long. Rennet is added, and when the clear whey is pH 4.6 the curd is cut with knives. The size of the cut varies according to requirements. The cut curd is cooked at a temperature of 46–49°C for about 100 minutes. It is gently stirred. The starter organisms are killed off in this process. The whey drainage process involves drainage and the addition of tap water, stirring and repeating the process four times. Drainage is continued until the surface of the curd particles are clearly visible. Salting follows. The addition of cream is optional.

Producers: Cottage cheese is produced today by many dairy businesses in Ireland and is widely available in food stores.

Season: Produced and sold throughout the year.

Packaging: It is usually sold in plastic tubs. The 225 g (8 oz) tub is common. Tubs are round or square with a flat lid.

References: CMP, Cork, personal communication.

Useful address: CMP (Cork Milk Producers), Tramore Road, Cork. Tel 021-964-000.

Irish Cheddar

Cheddar is the most widely produced cheese in Ireland. Although English in origin, it is now so well established in Ireland that it is regarded as a typical Irish product. A hard, close-textured bacterial ripened cheese, blocks for sale are usually rectangular in shape, with a typical piece being 5 cm long by 3 cm wide and 2 cm high.

Composition: Whole milk, starter and rennet.

History: By the turn of the twentieth century, attempts were under way to establish a commercial cheese-making industry in Ireland. Experiments in cheese-making were conducted by the Department of Agriculture and Technical Instruction, a government department founded in 1900. They rented a dairy farm for extended trials in cheese-making in 1900–1. This farm, which was in Co. Cork, was fitted with appliances for the manufacture of cheddar-type cheese. Trials were transferred to Ballyhaise in Co. Cavan in 1907, where the cheese-makers were trained by an experienced manufacturer from England. By 1915 a number of factories were making cheddar, selling their produce in Ireland and Scotland. Exports of cheeses (cheddar and other cheeses) increased from a few hundred to over 14,000 tonnes between 1913 and 1919. By 1918 there were 199 factories producing cheese in Ireland and their output of approximately 7,000 tonnes of hard cheese was mostly exported to Britain. Due to decontrolling of prices there was a huge reduction in price and production in the early 1920s.

Mitchelstown Co-op started cheese production in 1933. Production was variable up to 1948. Cheddar continued to be produced and improved systems for production were gradually introduced in the early 1960s, when rindless cheddar was commercially produced. Trade restrictions limited exports in the second half of the 1960s, but EU membership in the 1970s led to a number of new cheddar cheese plants being set up. Today Irish cheddar cheese is produced by most of the large dairy businesses in Ireland.

Use: Irish cheddar is widely used in salads and sandwiches and in various recipes.

Technique: The standard cheese-making unit in the 1950s was a 2,250 litre rectangular vat (McCarthy), which did not have mechanical stirring. Cheese moulds were one-piece galvanised steel; all manufacturing was of raw milk and storage of the cheese was at ambient temperatures. Quality was therefore variable. Heat treatment of cheese milk became standard about 1953. Gradually equipment was improved and the British two-stage system was introduced. A mechanised large vat was used for curd production and cheddaring, and milling, salting and mellowing took place in the secondary vat/curd cooler.

The manufacturing process described here was documented by Teagasc in 1979. Standardised whole milk is inoculated and renneted at 30–1°C. The curd is cut when it is sufficiently firm. The temperature is raised to 39–40°C over a forty-minute period. Stirring is continued for at least an hour after cooking temperature is reached. The whey is then drained. Traditionally this is done through an orifice in the vat. Acid development and cheddaring occurs after 15 minutes, when the curd is cut into blocks and turned at 15-minute intervals until an acidity of 0.045% is reached. The blocks are piled two to three high and, when acidity reaches 0.65–0.7%, the curd is milled and salted. It is filled into moulds and pressed overnight, then packaged and placed in a room at 4°C to mature for a period, which can be six months or longer.

Producers: Cheddar cheese is widely produced.

Season: It is available and consumed throughout the year.

Packaging: In the past it was cut from the block to customer requirements, but is now sold in flat rectangular pieces between 0.2 kg and 1 kg, with pieces 0.2–0.25 kg most common. It is usually sold to consumers in vacuum-packed transparent plastic packaging.

Useful address: Dairy Products Research Centre, Teagasc, Fermoy, Co. Cork. Tel 026-31422.

Ring Cheese

Waterford

Ring cheese is white in colour, and comes in a round 4 kg block. It has a full flavour and firm texture, with high acidity, and tastes somewhat similar to cheddar. The fermenting and maturing processes have not changed in over a century. Fermentation is totally natural, and no additives are used.

Composition: This is a cow's milk cheese, a natural product, made from unpasteurised milk and rennet.

History: Produced for at least three generations on the farm of Thomas and Eileen Harty in the Irish-speaking area of Co. Waterford, Ring cheese was developed by family members at the end of the last century. The recipe used today is the same recipe.

Use: Its melting qualities mean it is particularly suitable for use in sauces and recipes. It has a shelf life of three months after maturity.

Technique: The milk is taken straight from the cow into a vat. All utensils used are sterile. Any surplus milk is sent to the local creamery. The cheese is hand made, and fermentation is natural. It is hand stirred with a steel stirrer. The exact process is secret but is similar to that described for cheddar, including raising the temperature, stirring and draining the whey. It is turned a number of times two hours after renneting. The curd is not cut and milled like cheddar but left to rest to allow the acidity to come up. It is put into a mould for 24 hours, then taken out and put into brine for 48 hours. After brining it is coated in a plastic coat. It is stored for three months to mature.

Producer: Annual production varies from 7,500 kg to 13,500 kg. The scale of production is small, with one farmer, and demand exceeds supply. About 2,270 litres of milk are used at a time to produce 225 kg. The product is available in many delicatessens and supermarkets. It is one of the Irish Farmhouse cheeses distributed by the Traditional Cheese Company. It is also marketed through Horgans and Gleneely Foods.

Season: All year round.

Packaging: Orange-coated truckle.

Reference: Thomas and Eileen Harty, Ring, Co. Waterford, personal communication.

Useful addresses: Cáis, Irish Farmhouse Cheesemakers Association, c/o National Dairy Council, Grattan House, Lower Mount Street, Dublin 2. Tel 01-661-9599. Thomas and Eileen Harty, Ring, Co. Waterford. Tel 058-46142.

Ardrahan Farmhouse Cheese

Cork

A type of semi-soft cheese with a pungent aroma, Ardrahan cheese has a buttery textured honey-coloured centre with a complex delicate flavour. It has a washed rind which grows into a golden colour, and its size and weight tend to vary slightly due to the fact that it is a hand-made product. In general the large wheel weighs about 1 kg. There is also a small consumer wheel which weighs 300g. It is yellow-coloured.

Composition: The ingredients which go into making Ardrahan are milk, which is produced on the farm and is unpasteurised, natural culture, known as a starter, and vegetarian rennet, which is used instead of animal rennet.

History: During the Famine Ardrahan was owned by a local landlord. When the potato crop started to fail he set about organising his tenants to bring their milk to his yard. There he established a dairy house where they made cheese from the milk. The Ardrahan of those days remained the staple diet of all the tenants and neighbouring tenants throughout the Famine. In later years, however, the cheese-making craft died out and Ardrahan cheese was forgotten until the recipe was rediscovered by the present owners of Ardrahan. Nowadays, the cheese is matured in the original (now upgraded) maturing room.

Cottage cheese, Ardrahan and Ring, with country relish

Use: Ardrahan can be used in many different ways. It can be eaten in cubes while sipping whiskey or red wine. It is also used to make toasted cheese sandwiches. It may be used in cooking as it blends well. Ardrahan is also used with baked potatoes.

Technique: The exact recipe is secret. The culture is added to milk at 31°C and, when the milk has ripened, the rennet is added, which sets the cheese. When set, the cheese is cut by hand. The cuttings separate the whey from the curds, which are then put in moulds. When set, the cheeses are brined in a bath of salt water and matured.

Packaging: The 1 kg wheels are wrapped in white paper and boxed individually. Baby Ardrahans are wrapped in white paper and boxed in six packs.

Producer: Ardrahan Farmhouse is produced only by Eugene and Mary Burns at Ardrahan, Co. Cork. The cheese sold first in the Rungis Market in France and subsequently in the UK and Ireland. Ardrahan is now widely available all around Ireland.

References: Eugene and Mary Burns, personal communication.

Useful addresses: Ardrahan Farmhouse Cheese, Kanturk, Co. Cork. Tel 029-78099. Cáis, Irish Farmhouse Cheesemakers Association, c/o National Dairy Council, Grattan House, Lower Mount Street, Dublin 2. Tel 01-661-9599.

Irish Farmhouse Cheeses

Also Farm-made cheeses from Ireland

Emerging local products, Irish farmhouse cheeses are hand made by individual producers, with the milk coming from the maker's own herd. Most makers point to the distinctive flavour and texture of their product. There are numerous farmhouse cheeses: cow's milk cheeses, sheep's milk cheeses and goat's milk cheeses. Generally produced as wheels of varying sizes, small wheels are 1–3 kg, medium wheels are up to 10 kg, and large wheels are 25 kg or more. Colours vary from cream to dark yellow. Some are soft cheeses, others are hard.

Composition: Composed of cow's, goat's or sheep's milk. In many cases unpasteurised milk is used. Other ingredients include starter culture, natural rennet, salt and various herbs. In most cases no artificial colours, flavours or preservatives are used.

History: The historical record reveals that a significant farmhouse cheesemaking tradition existed in Ireland until well into the sixteenth and seventeenth centuries. However, by the seventeenth century the cheese-making tradition declined due to changing economic developments.

There is no historical link between these old cheeses and the new farmhouse cheeses. In the 1980s Ireland witnessed an explosion in small-scale farmhouse cheese-making. The oldest of these was Milleens, set up in 1968, at

Eyeries in West Cork. Today over thirty farmhouse cheesemakers are in operation producing cow's, goat's and sheep's milk cheese varieties. However, none of them can trace their origin to old Irish cheeses and, although some have local origins, most are based on British or Continental (French, Dutch, Swiss) recipes. They are thus combined for this record as emerging local products and separate details on each particular cheese are not given. The products, although new, have established themselves as local farmhouse produce.

The cow cheeses include Glen-o-Sheen and Bandon Vale (Cheddar types), Coolaneen (Kerry farmhouse), Carrigaline, Coolea and Round Tower (Gouda types), blue cheeses such as Cashel Irish Blue, Abbey Blue Brie and Chetwynd Blue, and other cheeses such as Gubbeen, Knockanore, St Killian, St Brendan Brie, Boilie, Lavistown, Mizen, Durrus, Milleens, Liathmore, Cooleeney, St Martins, Baylough, Gabriel and Desmond. Sheep cheeses include Cratloe Hills and Knockalora and Orla. Goat cheeses include Croghan, Corleggy and St Tola, Lough Caum and Ardsallagh. (Two cheeses, Ring and Ardrahan, which have a longer ancestry in Ireland, have been described separately.)

Use: The cheeseboard at the end of any meal is suited for many of these cheeses, but they can also be used with salads and sandwiches. Some are used in recipes (pizza, lasagne, quiche, desserts, starters) and as cheese sauces with fish, lasagne, cauliflower or baked potato, or toasted on French or brown bread or with crackers.

Technique: The cheeses are made by hand in the traditional time-consuming way. There may be seasonal variation, as it is a farmhouse process and produced on a small scale. Each person has their own recipe and approach and each cheese may be made individually, hand turned as it cures. Some are waxed. They are allowed to mature until the flavour is fully developed, which can take several months. Most need to be stored in a cool place and brought to room temperature before serving.

Producers: There is only one producer of each cheese, and only small amounts are produced of each. The products are sold locally and through distributors/agents, and many are available in supermarkets and delicatessens. Many are exported to the UK, the Continent and, in some cases, to the US. The shelf life varies, but can be a number of months if stored at suitable temperature and humidity.

Season: Some are produced throughout the year, others seasonally.

Packaging: Some are sold as waxed wheels unpacked, others are in greaseproof wrapping paper or aluminium foil and packed in cardboard/wooden boxes or cartons. Some are vacuum packed, and most have their own logo and design. They are sold as wheels or in boxes or baskets to shops.

References: Jerry Beechinor and various individual cheesemakers, personal communications.

Useful address: Cáis, Irish Farmhouse Cheesemakers Association, c/o National Dairy Council, Grattan House, Lower Mount Street, Dublin 2. Tel 01-661-9599.

Bakery Products

In Waterford, blaas are popular for breakfast.

Oven-bottom Yeast Breads

Also Variety of oven-bottom breads produced, including plain and small loaves (also called Wellington boots and grinders), batch or brick loaves (turnover loaf), ducks, cottage loaves and skulls

Special feature: A plain loaf (Wellington or grinder) is made of an upright oblong piece of dough which protrudes at the bottom, giving the loaf the appearance of a Wellington boot. The most distinguishing feature of oven-bottom bread is the overall crusty nature of the loaf. All types of Irish batch loaf are different to most British loaves as they have no crust on the sides, only on the top and bottom. The dough sides are greased and placed, sides touching, on high-edged trays in the ovens. The loaves can be peeled apart by hand after baking. In Britain the loaves are separated before baking, although bread with no crust on the side, called plain bread is common in the north of Scotland.

Composition: Batch loaves come in varying sizes (standard and baby), and may be sliced or unsliced, with a rectangular or square slice shape.

A duck loaf is oblong in shape, resembling a duck's body with two pointed ends, and is cut across the top. Duck bread is produced on the oven bottom, and is laid out in the oven where it is free to develop its duck shape.

A skull (Coburg in Britain) is a variant of a round loaf but the top of the dough is scored in the shape of a cross;

when baked the loaf has four peaks on top, reminiscent of a cardinal's hat.

A cottage loaf is two loaves baked on top of each other, the loaf on top always smaller than the bottom one. The circumference of the top loaf is scored all round before baking.

A batch or brick is composed of three or four 'bricks' or rectangular pieces of dough, joined together and baked as a single loaf, which can be cut into separate loaves after baking. The unsliced batch is sometimes called a plain loaf. The grinder, a Kilkenny variant which looks like three pieces of bread held together, is crusted all over. The saltie is a basic bread washed with salt, and is similar to the grinder.

Most oven-bottom loaves come in two standard sizes, 400 g and 800 g, sliced or unsliced depending on the packaging arrangements of the individual bakeries. For details of shape see the Special feature section above. Ingredients are wheaten flour, water, salt, yeast and artificial additives and improvers.

History: It is probable that oven-bottomed leavened loaves were produced in early medieval Ireland. At this period the most widely available leavens were ale barm and liquid yeast, both by products of the brewing industry. In addition, the sourdough system could also have been employed. However, large-scale production of leavened breads in Ireland is attributed to the influence of the Anglo-Normans, who colonised the island in the twelfth and thirteenth centuries. These settlers brought the techniques of yeast bread production with them. Swift says that from the twelfth century onwards

the making of bread appeared as a spe-

Large-scale production of leavened breads in Ireland is attributed to the influence of the Anglo-Normans.

cialised trade operated by tradesmen whose sole business was to make and sell bread.

However, these bakeries, operating common brick ovens fired with wood or turf, would have been confined to urban areas. In rural Ireland flat cakes of oats and barley were the commonly consumed bread varieties until well into the nineteenth century. From this period onwards the establishment of large-scale commercial bakeries brought 'white baker's bread' to the vast majority of Irish rural and urban communities for the first time. This development is evident in the diaries of Amhlaoibh Uí Shúileabháin from Callan in Co. Kilkenny; in his diary entry for 21 November 1830, he states:

> *country people have three kinds of bread namely ["raised"] leavened bread, barmbrack fruit bread, . . . and seed bread.*

In particular the latter half of the nineteenth century saw the widespread ac-

ceptance of yeast breads amongst rural communities. This gradual turn to white bread also marked a decline in the domestic production of flat breads, which were now looked on as inferior to shop-bought varieties. Many commercial bakeries were established at the end of the last century.

Use: Normal breads for breakfast, lunches and sandwiches.

Technique: Using traditional methods of preparation, a three-hour yeast fermentation was required and some bakeries were using traditional processes up to a few years ago. In modern bakeries the dough is chemically and mechanically matured.

A fermentation of less than an hour is used today in St Catherine's Bakery in Dublin, which is over a hundred years old and uses traditional methods of yeast fermentation without chemicals and shapes the dough by hand. The First Modern Bakery was making it in the traditional way up to a few years ago. They along with other bakeries such as Pat the Baker, now use modern technology.

In the larger commercial bakeries the ingredients are mixed together in high-speed mixers for three minutes. After mixing, the dough is automatically cut and weighted ('scaled') by a weighting machine called a scaler. The cut dough pieces are lifted into a dry proofer. They remain there for up to forty minutes where the system of dry heating softens and improves the dough. After proving the dough pieces are dropped on to a 'handling' board. The pieces are rolled ('handed') and shaped ('moulded') and are then returned to a steam proofer for a further fifteen minutes. Finally the bread is baked in reel or rack ovens for forty minutes. Today the above process of dough-making takes place in fully automatic plants and, apart from the rolling and moulding stages, the dough is untouched by human hand. However, in Schull in Co. Cork one bakery continues to produce authentic hand-made oven-bottom and tin-shaped breads. The Courtyard Bakery has a Perkins coal-burning brick oven installed in 1919 which turns out over two hundred pieces a day. The traditional two-hour fermentation process is still employed and the dough is hand scaled and moulded.

Producers: The batch loaf is produced by a number of the larger commercial bakeries including Pat the Baker and the Modern Bakery. The turnover is produced by smaller bakeries, such as St Catherine's Bakery in Dublin and the Courtyard in Schull, Co. Cork. The grinder is produced by local bakeries in Kilkenny. Milford bakeries produce an 800 g white sliced batch loaf. Donnelly's Bakery and O'Keeffe's Bakery in Cork produce a number of oven-bottom breads. The Gingerbread House Bakery and Confectionery also produce a variety of breads, including cottage loaves.

Packaging: Wrapped and loose. The product is sold as traditional sliced batch under various labels.

References: A. Morrissey, The National Food Centre, personal communication. D. O'Brien and R. Humphries, National Bakery School, Dublin Institute of Technology, personal communication. Oliver Sexton (retired baker), personal communication.

Useful addresses: Derek O'Brien, National Bakery School, Dublin Institute of Technology, Kevin Street, Dublin 8. Tel 01-402-3000. Donnelly's Bakery, 102 Shandon Street, Cork. Tel 021-304-068. O'Keeffe's Bakery, Lehenaghbeg, Pouladuff, Cork. Tel 021-962-265.

Tin-shaped Yeast Breads

Also A variety of tin-shaped yeast breads is available including ball pans, high pans, twist pans, ridge pans, lodger loaves (barrels) and baskets

Special feature: Rectangular-shaped pans baked in ordinary tin loaf shapes are most common and variant pans include:

high pan: higher than normal pans

twist pan: the dough is twisted before being placed in the loaf tin

ridge pan: the dough is baked in a four-sided ridged tin

Other varieties include:

lodger loaf (barrel loaf); cylindrical in shape with a ridged surface. It is baked in a double cylindrical mould. The name is said to derive from the practice of slicing a ridge per lodger in lodging houses. This loaf is very similar to the British crinkled or musket loaf. The barrel, popular in Northern Ireland, is about 23 cm long and 10 cm in diameter and

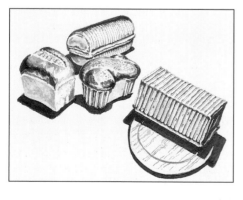

Tin-shaped breads

weighs 400 g.

basket loaf: shaped like an oblong basket. The dough is baked in a fluted tin which is not unlike a brioche mould but is lower in height and longer in length. The dough is also rolled inwards from both ends before being placed in the tin giving an attractive curled shape on top when baked.

Composition: Most tin-shaped loaves come in two standard sizes, 400 g and 800 g loaves. These can be sliced or unsliced, depending on the packaging arrangements of the individual bakeries. For details of shape see the Special feature section above. Ingredients are wheaten flour, water, salt, yeast, and artificial additives and improvers.

History: Baking yeast bread in tins is a relatively late development in Ireland and the practice probably came from Britain. Britain and Holland are the only two other European countries that produce tin-shaped bread. In historical terms the popularity of tin-shaped bread can be attributed to two main factors. The most obvious one is that tin-shaped bread, with its variety of shapes, was a fancy alternative to oven-bottom loaves. Secondly, the production of tin-shaped bread was economically advantageous to commercial bakeries. Tin-shaped bread is manufactured from a lighter dough than oven-bottom loaves, so the greater volume of water used in their manufacture ensures a better yield.

Use: Normal bread for breakfast, lunches and sandwiches.

Technique: See the Technique section in Oven-bottom Yeast Breads. The essential difference between oven-bottom and tin-shaped bread is that, at the rollng and moulding stage, the dough pieces are placed by hand in prepared tins and placed in ovens. With fully automated plants the dough pieces are dropped directly in the tins. The tins used to shape the barrel bread made in commercial bakeries are called tank tins.

Producers: Donnelly's Bakery and O'Keeffe's Bakery in Cork produce a number of tin-shaped breads. A wide variety is also produced by smaller bakeries, including the Courtyard Bakery in Schull in Co. Cork. Baskets are particularly found in Cork City, Bantry and Youghal. Baskets are also produced by Sullivan's Bakery in Killorglin, Co. Kerry. Irwins in Northern Ireland produce the barrel loaf.

Packaging: Wrapped and loose.

References: Oliver Sexton (retired baker), personal communication. D. O'Brien and R. Humphries, National Bakery School, Dublin Institute of Technology, personal communication.

Useful addresses: Donnelly's Bakery, 102 Shandon Street, Cork. Tel 021-304-068. O'Keeffe's Bakery, Lehenaghbeg, Pouladuff, Cork. Tel 021-962-265. Sullivan's Bakery, Killorglin, Co. Kerry. Tel 066-61127.

Soda Bread

Also Soda cake, soda farl, soda square, soda scones. Soda bread is called soda cake in Northern Ireland. Soda farls, which are produced in the northern half of the country, have two quarters. Farls are also produced in Limerick. When a quarter is taken out of the whole piece, it is called a soda square. Soda scones are popular all over Ireland.

Variants: Soda bread with currants was called spotted dog, or sometimes spotted Dick or railway cake. Occasionally soda bread is called treacle cake (when it contains treacle), but this variant is probably not traditionally Irish. Treacle cake is sometimes found in Northern Ireland and Kerry. Some bakers put the emphasis on the use of stoneground wheat and their product is called stoneground wholewheat bread. White bread produced using white flour and soda on an open griddle is called griddle bread.

Bannocks, also called bannock browns, fruit bannock and plain bannock, are a type of soda bread, an aerated wheaten bread, particularly associated with Northern Ireland.

Special feature: Soda rather than yeast is used as a raising agent and buttermilk as an ingredient.

Composition: Typical soda bread is round in shape and usually produced with a cross so can be broken into four quarters. Typically the weight is between 300 and 400 g. It is more raised in the top of the centre. It is brown in col-

Soda bread is made with a cross on the top so it can easily be broken into quarters; soda farls, which are produced in the northern half of the country, have two halves.

our and has a yellow tinge throughout due to the soda. The texture is coarse and the product is firm to the touch. In the north of Ireland soda bread often looks more like a cake. Soda farls are about 2 cm thick and triangular in shape, one side flat and the other humped from the oven. Farls from Sunblest are rectangular and flat on both sides with dimensions of 12 cm long by 9 cm wide by 2 cm high. The product weighs 150 g and is fine and of a soft texture. It is a combination of white, light brown and dark brown in colour. Sliced soda bread is available nowadays in both round and rectangular shapes. There are about eighteen slices in the 300 g Johnston, Mooney & O'Brien product. Griddle bread is also round, 25 cm in diameter and white, with a yellow colour throughout due to the soda. The top is grey-white from the burnt flour dressing.

The bannock is associated with Northern Ireland and a standard bannock is about 600 g. It may be sold in quarters. Mannings sell a farl as one of the quarters of a bannock. They prepare Bannock browns, which are log shape or rectangular and about 0.5 kg in weight. The loaf is 20 cm long, and 10 cm high by 10 cm wide.

The ingredients are wheat flour, bread soda (sodium bicarbonate), buttermilk and salt. Other ingredients can be animal and vegetable fat, sugar and raising agents. White soda bread is also available, produced with white flour. Bewleys' soda bread was richer in the past, for example in the 1930s, as it contained more butterfat. The buttermilk available in the 1930s was so acidic there was no need for baking powder, the bicarbonate of soda being enough. Today buttermilk is more neutral, so baking powder is needed. Bewleys also produce a wheaten soda with a recipe dating back to the nineteenth century. This product has margarine or butter in it, whereas traditional soda bread does not have any additional butter. It is rectangular in shape and baked in a tin.

History: The leavening agent, bicarbonate of soda, was first introduced into Ireland in the first half of the nineteenth century. The National Folklore Archive indicates that its use was commonplace by the 1840s and Cullen says that by the second half of the nineteenth century soda bread had gained widespread popularity throughout the country. This may in part be attributed to the fact that when soda is combined with sour milk or buttermilk it produces a very light and palatable leavened wheat bread that could be successfully produced in a domestic setting. In addition, it was very quickly prepared, in contrast to the more traditional coarse oaten bread. It was also ideally suited to the limited range of baking utensils: the pot oven or 'bastible' and the flat iron griddle. In comparison to the other leavening agents of yeast, barm, sourdough and eggs, soda provided a convenient, storable and predictable leaven that quickly became the standard.

Traditionally a cross was cut into the bread, which helped in the even baking of the bread and assisted in the quartering and cutting of the round loaf afterwards. The custom was specially emphasised on Good Friday in honour of the crucifixion, but the everyday explanation for the practice was 'to let the devil out'.

Jack McKidden's memoirs of his childhood in Dundonald, Co. Down, in the early twentieth century illustrate the commonality of the bread in the diet of the rural Irish:

mother baked soda and wheaten bread . . . if she was baking when we came home from school, we got a piece of warm soda bread and a drink of real buttermilk which satisfied us until tea-time.

In addition, Sean O'Casey, the celebrated Dublin playwright, who grew up in the impoverished, overcrowded tenements of the city, recounts the popularity of bread in one of his autobiographical books, *The Street Sings*:

The carts were big and box-like, filled with double rows of shallow trays on which rested row after row of steaming loaves, tuppence or tuppence-farthing each . . . Underneath a deep drawer going the whole length of the cart, filled with lovely white an' brown squares, soda squares, currant squares, and brown loaves, covered with their shining golden crust.

Farls are produced on a hotplate. Originally they were produced over a fire on the griddle: the housewife would first spread some plain white flour on the griddle and from experience judged its temperature by the changing brown colour of the flour.

Treacle cake probably originated in the north, but is also found in other areas, such as Kerry. Ballymena biscuits were a type of rich soda scone popular in Northern Ireland, but they are no longer produced. The modern version, called a fruit scone, is a type of sweet soda scone.

Florence Irwin includes a number of soda recipes in her 1937 publication *Irish Country Recipes*. Originally widely produced at home, soda bread is made in an oven at bakeries. Kylemore have been producing it since the last century. The Ormeau bakery was started in 1895 and was run by the Wilson family for many years until it was bought by the Belfast flour miller, the Andrews Group, in 1980. The directors acquired the Andrews family interests in 1987. They started making soda bread in 1907 and claim to be one of the first bakeries to do so.

Use: Particularly popular with butter as a snack in restaurants. Also with smoked salmon as a first course. Widely used at breakfast and lunch. Allied Bakeries recommend their soda farls be warmed and buttered.

Technique: A normal raising agent would be made up of two parts acid (acid calcium phosphate), one part alkali (sodium bicarbonate). In soda bread, buttermilk makes up one part acid and one part acid phosphate, and alkali are added. The ingredients are mixed in a standard mixer. Old-style buttermilk is used by some producers. Cutters are used to separate into loaves. In the past each piece was weighed separately, but in modern processes each piece is exactly the same weight, particularly for square-shaped and sliced soda breads. Shaped trays are used and, as the dough comes out of the divider, each piece is dropped automatically on to the tray or tin, after which it is baked in a moving wire oven. The round traditional shaped soda is the batch type, where each unit is attached to the next. It is produced on a solid base in a closed oven. Baking takes about half an hour; for example, it takes 35 minutes for one producer at 225°C in a stone base oven. This holds the heat and gives a better crust in terms of more starch caramelisation and consequent flavour.

Soda farls are produced on a hotplate or griddle. The whole farl piece is cut into four for baking. Ormeau Bakery claims to be the first bakery to invent and patent (in 1928) a travelling hotplate for making soda and potato farls in 1928. Sometimes in the south the term farl is used for oven-baked products rather than a hotplate product and this is a source of confusion. Griddle bread is cooked on an open griddle.

Chemically aerated like other soda breads, the bannock is formed initially into a round shape. Before baking it is crossed into four pieces and the opposite pieces are stuck together, flat sides touching, to give the round version of the bannock. There is also a winged version. Bannocks, which are made less and less often nowadays, are oven baked either in a tin or a baking tray. Irwins say the dough is moulded by hand into a circle, tinned and broken into four pieces by a piece of equipment, but it is the whole piece rather than the quarter that is called the bannock. They produce both wheaten and white soda bannocks.

Producers: Soda bread is produced by a number of bakeries in Ireland, both north and south. Kylemore is one of the oldest producers in Dublin. Others include Lyons (Johnston, Mooney & O'Brien label) and Brennans. Ormeau Bakery (Ormo) in Belfast and Allied (Sunblest) produce soda farls. Frank Gallagher of Gallagher's, Ardara, Co Donegal, supplies Harrods with plain soda bread and fruit soda. Bannocks are produced by Irwins.

Season: The product is made and sold throughout the year. It is widely available in all types of shops.

Packaging: Loose or light transparent cellophane foil with label. Ormeau was the first bakery to wrap soda and potato farls. Allied (Sunblest) do two farls to a cellophane pack with a yellow-orange stick-on label. The logo and writing are dark brown.

References: Emmanuel McCann, School of Hospitality, Catering and Food, Belfast Institute of Further and Higher Education, personal communication. Gerry Murphy, Arthur McCann, Newry, personal communication. Gerard Fox, Kylemore Bakery, personal communication.

Useful addresses: Kylemore Bakery, Finglas, Dublin 11. Tel 01-834-2032. G. McVeigh, Brunswick Street, Belfast. Tel 01232-245-891.

Boxty

Also Traditionally called stampy. Called dippity in the past, if served with milk and salt instead of oatbread. Similar products found in Sweden, Poland and Holland.

Special feature: Boxty is regarded as a typical potato dish in the northern counties of Ireland. Grated raw potato is used, and cooked potatoes are reboiled.

Composition: Commercial products contain cooked mashed potato, raw potatoes peeled and grated, salt and flour. Recipes vary and milk is often an ingredient. One producer sells a flat potato product containing three pieces in a 390–400 g pack. Another has a 350 g pack with four pieces. The pieces are half-moon shape, 22 cm long, with a radius of 13 cm and a thickness of about 0.4 cm. The texture is slightly rubbery. Boxty is white with brown speckles.

History: Given the dominance of potatoes in the diet of the Irish from the late seventeenth century onwards, boxty became an important potato dish. Traditionally, it seems to have a particular association with a number of midland and northern counties, especially Cavan, Tyrone, Fermanagh and Derry. This is supported by the *Ordnance Survey Memoirs* for these counties. For example, in the early nineteenth century the *Ordnance Survey Memoirs* for Urney and Ardstraw in Co. Tyrone record that

'boxty bread', made with potatoes and potato starch is commonplace.

The nature of the dish does not lend itself to historical recording and there is a marked paucity of historical reference to it. Nevertheless, the general folklore record does supply frequent reference to the dish and traditional lore and rhymes establish it as a major item in the Irish diet. The following extract from a traditional song is a clear illustration of its popularity and palatability:

Oh did you ever take potato cake
Or boxty to the school
Tucked underneath your oxter,
With your book, your slate and rule
And when teacher wasn't lookin'
A big bite you did take
Of the floury, mealy, juicy
Sweet potato cake

There was also variation in the types of boxty consumed. Common dishes included boxty bread, boxty pancakes and boxty dumplings, the consumption of which was held to augment a girl's marriage prospects:

Boxty on the griddle,
Boxty on the pan,
If you don't eat your boxty,
You'll never get a man!

Throughout the late eighteenth century and in the early part of the nineteenth century, when the Irish potato harvest was of very poor quality, the rotten potatoes, useless for boiling, were used in the preparation of boxty. The watery and sometimes rotting potato pulp was placed in a cloth and squeezed to remove as much water and starch as possible. The pulp was then shaped into cakes and baked on a heated flagstone or griddle.

Today boxty is still very much a northern and western dish and it is commercially produced in these areas.

Use: Traditionally boxty was prepared as part of the Halloween (31 October) and New Year's Day festive fare. It was also eaten throughout the year and often replaced bread at the midday meal or evening supper. A more substantial form of boxty consisting of milk, salt and potatoes was known as dippity. Another variant dish, stampy, was a type of sweet potato bread prepared from a mixture of raw potato and flour and other flavourings. In the south-western region the end of the potato harvest was marked with a 'Stampy Party', when the harvest workers and helpers were treated with copious amounts of stampy bread.

Technique: It may appear in many forms—bread, griddle cakes, dumplings, pancakes and puddings. Raw potatoes are peeled and grated. Starchy liquid is squeezed out from the potatoes. A similar amount of cooked mashed potatoes is placed over the grated potatoes. Starch is allowed to drop to the bottom and the clear liquid is poured off. A pliable dough is made by adding flour and other ingredients and the dough is rolled to 6 mm thickness. In the most traditional form the combination of boiled and raw potatoes is boiled to produce a grey-looking product which is sliced and fried. Traditionally boxty was cooked on a griddle or pan. In one small commercial unit it is cooked in a 25 cm pan and the 23 cm round diameter product is cut in half. Three pieces are put in each pack.

Producers: There are a number of small commercial producers in Co. Mayo, in Bangor Erris, Belmullet, Charlestown and Foxford. The producer located in Bangor Erris in Co. Mayo markets her product as Mrs King's Boxty. The product is sold in local shops. Mrs King's Boxty is also marketed in a wider area by Irish Farmhouse Pantry. McNiffe's from Leitrim sell to a number of shops in the midlands, north and west of Ireland. Some hotels and restaurants also serve boxty. Boxty has a few days' shelf life in the chill cabinet.

Season: All year.

Packaging: Plastic bag with label. A white paper base is used by McNiffe's with a transparent plastic top and small stick-on label.

References: C. Hickey, Irish Farmhouse Pantry, Co. Mayo, personal communication.

Useful addresses: Irish Farmhouse Pantry, Co. Mayo. Tel 094-81494. McNiffe's Home Bakery, Aughnasheelin, Co. Leitrim. Tel 078-44625.

Potato Bread

Also Potato cakes, tatties, tatie scones, parleys. In some areas of Northern Ireland, particularly in the region of east Ulster, known as 'fadge'. Also referred to as potato farl.

Special feature: Bread made from potato and flour. It is a hotplate product because of the way it is manufactured.

Composition: These are not sweet cakes but more like soda bread. The size and shape vary, but they are mostly flat and round, though they can be triangular (farl). Potato bread can also be scone-shaped and triangles sold in shops are often called tatie 'squares' in Northern Ireland. They may be cut in squares to facilitate packaging. Potato farls from Allied Bakeries are 5 by 5 cm square and 0.5 cm thick. They are white and brown flecked. Potato cake contains potato, flour and butter. Potato bread has no butter. Sometimes the cakes are sprinkled with caraway seed and sometimes milk to make a soft slack dough. In old country recipes eggs may be included as well as chopped mixed peel or finely sliced onion. Some modern recipes contain baking powder and margarine. Most of the commercial recipes have a high proportion of flour. Today some of the bakeries, particularly large bakeries, use potato flakes with cake margarine or vegetable oil.

History: By the late seventeenth century the potato had gained widespread acceptance as a staple food in Ireland. From this period until the eve of the Great Famine in 1845 the potato became the staple and sometimes sole food in the diet of the Irish peasantry, and as a result of this monotonous diet a variety of potato dishes was created. A popular and common dish was potato bread. One of the earliest references to the potato appears in John Worlidge's 1688 edition of *Systema Agriculturae*, which states:

> *Potatoes are much used in Ireland, as in America, as Bread, and are themselves also an unusual food.*

It has been suggested that the preparation of potato bread originated in periods of wheat shortage, when potatoes were used to supplement and stretch the limited stock of white flour. The bread has been traditionally associated with the northern counties: this regional association is clear in the *Ordnance Survey Memoirs for the Parishes of Co. Antrim*, in which James Boyle records the following in relation to the diet of the inhabitants of the parish of Ballymartin, Co. Antrim, in 1838:

> *"fadge", a very good kind of bread made of potatoes and flour and baked on a griddle in large cakes or "scones", is generally used.*

By the end of the nineteenth century potato bread had also gained favour with the prosperous Irish gentry. An enriched potato bread is described in *Some Experiences of an Irish R.M.* (1899) by Somerville and Ross:

> *While I live I shall not forget her potato cakes. They came in hot and hot from the pot-oven, they were speckled from caraway seeds, they swam in salt and butter, and we ate them shamelessly and greas-*

ily and washed them down with hot whis-
key and water. I knew to a nicety how ill
I should be next day, and I heeded not.

Today both the domestic and commercial production of potato bread are important in Northern Ireland, where fried potato bread is an integral component of the 'Ulster Fry'.

Use: Cooked on a griddle or pan and served hot with butter or sugar. After cooking it may also be fried and served with a traditional Irish breakfast or Ulster fry with an egg in it.

Technique: Made from mashed potato, preferably hot, there are several regional variations. The main difference is in texture. This depends on the amount of flour and the shape. More flour ensures a firmer cake that keeps longer but is not as light. A cast iron griddle, which is a flat circular plate about 46 cm in diameter, with two ears, from which it hung from the fire, was used for baking potato cakes as well as other flat breads. North of a line from Drogheda to Sligo people tended to make potato bread. The ingredients are mixed in a mixing bowl. It is often shaped by hand in the case of the farl and then put on a hotplate. Potato farls are left for only a short time on the hotplate. They are almost fully cooked but need a little further cooking from the consumer.

At one bakery today ingredients are weighed and added to a mixing bowl to form the batter. Fixed amounts are dropped straight on to the hotplate. The flow on the plate defines the shape. They are turned and then taken off and allowed to cool before packaging.

Packaging: They are sold in cellophane-type packs with stick-on labels. Allied Bakeries (Sunblest) packs contain four or eight potato farls.

Producers: Produced by many bakeries in Ireland and widely available at retail outlets, including butchers' shops. In Northern Ireland Ormeau Bakery in Belfast is a major manufacturer and they supply many retail outlets. Allied Bakeries produce the Sunblest label in Belfast. Irwins are also big producers.

Season: All year.

References: C. Hickey, Irish Farmhouse Pantry, Co. Mayo, personal communication. D. O'Brien and R. Humphries, National Bakery School, Dublin Institute of Technology, personal communication. G. McVeigh, Belfast Institute of Further and Higher Education, personal communication. Billy Reed and Niall Irwin, Irwins, Portadown, Northern Ireland, personal communication. Michael Connolly, Allied Bakeries, Dublin, personal communication. Ormeau Bakery Ltd, Belfast, personal communication.

Useful addresses: Ormeau Bakery Ltd, 307 Ormeau Road, Belfast BT7 3GN. Allied Bakeries, Orby Link, Belfast and Unit 1, Feltrim Industrial Park, Swords, Co. Dublin. Tel 01-840-9342. W. D. Irwin and Sons, Portadown, Northern Ireland. Tel 01762-332-421.

Pinhead Oatmeal

Also Porridge, stirabout, steel cut oats, cut groats

Variant: Porridge oatflakes

Special feature: Pinhead oatmeal has been a traditional Irish product since earliest times. Pinhead oatmeal takes longer to make into porridge than oatflakes, but the porridge has a unique texture and flavour. As distinct from pinhead oatmeal, porridge oatflakes have been rolled to speed the cooking process.

Composition: Pinhead-size pieces of oatmeal. Off-white brown colour. Porridge oatflakes are milled from oatgrain and are round flat pieces. Pinhead oatmeal is composed of oats from which the inedible outer husk has been removed. The remaining oats are cleaned, passed through steel cutters, and cut into three or four pieces.

History: The cultivation of oats is particularly suited to Ireland's pedological and climatic conditions and therefore oatmeal became a staple food of the Irish from prehistoric times until the seventeenth century. Vast quantities of oatmeal were consumed in the form of porridge or stirabout (a thick mixture). However, the prevalence of oatmeal earned it a very definite low status value. In the Brehon Laws of the seventh and eighth centuries oatmeal porridge is cited as a foodstuff suitable only for the poor (while barley porridge was reserved for landowners and wheat was the preserve of the aristocracy). Porridge was consumed in a variety of forms, ranging from thick creamy stirabout to thin watery gruel. In the ninth century watery oatmeal gruel is recommended for consumption by the penitential Irish monks, while a more substantial thick stirabout is listed in the eleventh-century *Aislinge meic Conglinne.*

With the introduction of the potato in the late sixteenth century, the prevalence of oatmeal porridge declined as potatoes superseded oats as the staple and only in times of poor potato harvest did it temporarily regain its pre-potato status. However, despite the prevalence of the potato, oats maintained a strong foothold in the peasant diet until well into the late nineteenth century and possibly beyond. In particular, oats were heavily relied upon when potato stocks were used up and food was scarce until the late summer early potato harvest. Most households also held stores of oatmeal for the production of porridge, bread and—importantly—as a bulk ingredient for the manufacture of pork puddings.

In the nineteenth and twentieth centuries oatmeal enjoyed some popularity when it was mixed with whiskey as a cure for the common cold. In this period porridge increasingly became a breakfast dish and this was promoted by the establishment of the commercial oatmeal producers, Flahavans, in the eighteenth century. Despite the establishment of bacon and eggs as the 'traditional Irish breakfast' in the nineteenth century, porridge still retained its place as a regular breakfast dish. The popularity of breakfast oatmeal porridge is well illustrated in the culinary advice offered by George Bernard Shaw in his

1904 publication *John Bull's Other Island*:

> *Boil oatmeal porridge for 20 minutes; and if you think the result mere oatmeal and water, try boiling it for two hours. (If you still think it as unpalatable as dry bread, treat it as you treat the bread; stir up a bounteous lump of butter in it, and do not forget the salt.) In eating wheatmeal porridge, remember that there's nothing so becomes a man as moderation and an admixture of stewed fruit.*

Pinhead oatmeal is the original form of oatmeal and flaked quick cooking products were developed in modern times. Porridge still remains important today and both pinhead and rolled oatmeal are widely available. The usual seasonings and additions for the dish include butter, salt, honey, milk, fruit and nuts. Flahavans have been milling oats for the past two hundred years. Odlums have been producing pinhead oatmeal since 1845. Whites was set up in 1841. The mill, on the original site, has now been modernised.

Use: Served as a hot cereal. Preparation involves boiling one measure of oatmeal with four measures of water and a pinch of salt. Once boiled, it is allowed to simmer for 25 minutes with occasional stirring. Oatmeal can also be used in cooking and baking various products such as brown soda breads, and can also be used in black pudding. Stored in a cool dry place, the shelf life is about nine months for the uncooked product. Nowadays oatflakes sold as quick cook are used by many and served with cream or milk and sugar or honey. Oatlets are also used in making muesli.

Season: Used all year round with higher consumption in the winter.

Technique: Oat grain consists of the outer husk and the inner grain. The traditional way of milling the oats is used, which involves taking out the oat, removing the outer layer and cutting the remainder into three small pieces. The product is totally natural and not processed with other ingredients. Further processing involves steaming and rolling, resulting in quick-cooking oatflakes.

Producers: There are three major producers in Ireland—Odlums, Flahavans, Whites (Northern Ireland)—all over a hundred years old. More recent producers include Kelkin and some local firms.

Packaging: Pinhead oatmeal is sold in 500 g and 1 kg packs. The product is described as traditional on the pack. Flahavans pinhead oatmeal is also available in 25 kg bulk bags. Porridge oatflakes are milled from oatgrain and are available in similar size packs to pinhead oatmeal with an additional 1.5 kg size. The Odlum pack is in orange-coloured foil. Three-ply cellophane bags and three-ply paper bags are used. Flahavans use a blue paper pack. Flahavans' oatflake pack is a soft two-wall pack with paper on the inside and poly on the outside. Whites' 1.5 kg pack is yellow and red. The current pack of 'Traditional' Speedicook oatflakes has a photograph of families at Whites Oat Mill in 1910.

References: E. Flahavan and Sons Ltd, personal communication. Stephen Odlum, Odlum Group Ltd, personal communication.

Useful addresses: E. Flahavan and Sons Ltd, Kilmacthomas, Co. Waterford.

Odlum Group Ltd, Alexandra Road, Dublin 1. Tel 01-874-1741. Flake Oatmeal Millers Association, c/o Coyle & Coyle, 30 Lower Leeson Street, Dublin 2. Tel 01-676-3201. Whites Speedicook Ltd, Fane Valley, Scarva Road, Tandragee, Co. Armagh BT62 2BY. Tel 01-762-840-592.

Macroom Oatmeal

Special feature: Additive-free wholefood. Special toasted flavour due to traditional kiln roasting. Stone grinding also gives an original texture.

Composition: Oatmeal packed in 1 kg bags. Finely ground roasted oats with distinctive fresh smell. Whole oats are roasted, shelled and stone ground.

History: Macroom Oatmeal has been milled in Macroom since 1832 when the present mill, Walton's Mills, was built. During the Famine years oatmeal took the place of the potato and many emigrants survived on a supply of oatmeal on the ships carrying them to the New World (see also history of pinhead oatmeal).

Use: Mainly used as a breakfast cereal but also as an addition to soups, brown bread, muffins and biscuits. The older generation speak of having it in tea.

Technique: Whole oats are roasted in a kiln. They are then shelled and stone ground and packed in 1 kg bags. Otherwise the process is the same as outlined for pinhead oatmeal.

Producer: It is believed that the Macroom Oatmeal Mill is one of the last surviving traditional mills in production in Ireland.

Season: Sold all year round, with bigger sales from September to March.

Packaging: Yellow and red printed paper bags.

Oatcake

References: D. Creedon, Macroom Oatmeal Mills, Massytown, Macroom, Co. Cork, personal communication.

Useful address: Macroom Oatmeal Mills, Massytown, Macroom, Co. Cork. Tel 026-41800.

Also Oatmeal bread, *arán coirce*

Special feature: A traditional Irish product, made of oats since at least the early historic period. Oatcakes were a basic item of the diet for centuries. Almost non-existent today in the south of Ireland, oatcake is a typical and local product in Northern Ireland, although no longer a basic part of the diet.

Composition: Flat-shaped round bread, light brown colour, with varying size. Although called oatcake, it is a savoury rather than a sweet product. Ormeau oatcakes are a biscuit-type oatcake and are round or square. The round product is about 10 cm in diameter. The domestic baked oaten cake varied in size, some reaching up to 60 cm in diameter, with thickness varying between biscuit size between 2.5 to 5.0 cm. The circular cake was cut into triangular farls. Typical oatcakes at country markets today are only 2.5 cm in diameter. Oatcake ingredients are oatmeal, water and salt.

History: Traditionally, and up to the advent of modern agricultural techniques, oats have been the most commonly cultivated cereal in Ireland. Prior to the introduction of the potato in the late sixteenth century, it was one of the staples of the Irish diet.

Oaten bread is mentioned throughout the entire corpus of early Irish literature: for example, oaten bread is rendered as a penalty fine in the seventh- and eighth-century law text *Bretha Comaithches*a. It is also mentioned in the eleventh-century *Aislinge meic Conglinne*. In the visionary land of plenty, Aníer encounters a doorkeeper who is described as follows:

> *his steed of bacon under him, with its four legs of custard, with its four hoofs of coarse oaten bread under it.*

An indication of its prevalence can be gleaned from a Catalan pilgrim's observation that oaten bread was served at the banquet of the Great O'Neill of Tír Eoghain in 1397:

> *as a present he sent me two little cakes as thin as wafers and they bent like raw dough and they were of oats and earth as black as coals, although they were very tasty.*

In 1560 the food rents presented to Shane O'Neill of Ulster consisted in part of

> *cakes of oaten bread.*

In the early modern period a host of foreign visitors to Ireland (Cuellar 1588, Moryson 1605–17, Boullaye le Gouz 1644) confirm that oaten bread was the bread of the Irish (Lucas). One anonymous English traveller, writing between 1672 and 1674, recounts:

> *their bread was broad oat-cakes baked on a flat stone, made of stuff much like that which the Welsh call haver-meal.*

Despite the introduction of the potato in the late sixteenth century, oaten bread still retained its important position in the diet of the Irish. Thomas Dineley, writing in Ireland in 1681, illustrates this point in describing the diet of the Irish population, as potatoes, new milk,

Oatcakes

whey, curds and a large brown oatcake, a foot and a half broad, baked before an open fire.

However, throughout the eighteenth and nineteenth centuries the potato came to dominate the diet and the consumption of oaten bread became increasingly associated with the spring and summer months. The seasonal variation in the diet is echoed in the *Ordnance Survey Memoirs* of James Boyle, who, describing the parish of Carnmoney in Co. Antrim in 1839, states:

> *During summer, when potatoes are old and scarce, [oat] meal made into stirabout and into cakes is in common use.*

The preparation of oaten bread continued throughout the nineteenth century but the scale of production declined in the face of the increased popularity of soda bread and white baker's bread. The substitution of oaten bread by baker's bread is also referred to by James Boyle in his description of the parish of Ballymartin in Co. Antrim in 1838:

Oaten bread is still made, but has in great measure been superseded by baker's bread which is cheap and easily purchased from the bread carts, which now almost daily transverse the country.

Of those manufacturing oatcakes to-day, Ormeau has been producing since the turn of the century. The Ormeau Bakery was founded by Robert Wilson in 1875 in Cromac Street, Belfast. It moved to Ormeau Road in 1890.

Use: Apart from its use as a main meal, oaten bread, because it was easily portable, was the food of military hustings, the itinerant worker and the traveller. For example, in the Limerick region, Gerald Griffin's novel *The Collegians* makes reference to an oatmeal 'griddle bread, done in the morning long before you and you goin' a long road'. Similarly, William Tighe in 1802 refers to the Co. Kilkenny practice of workmen taking an oaten cake 'to a distance where potatoes could not be brought hot'. In the folklore record the preparation of oatenbread was associated with the celebration of St Brigid's Day on 1 February. On this day a 'strone' or large cake of oaten bread was baked in the shape of a cross. The bread was placed on the kitchen floor on a bed of rushes. The household knelt in prayer around the cake and after the prayer a piece of the 'strone' was taken off by each of the participants and eaten. The ritual continued until all the cake was eaten.

Throughout the nineteenth and early twentieth centuries oaten bread also featured in a folk custom known as the 'cake dance'. In rural areas it was customary to celebrate Easter Sunday with a communal dance. The prize for the best dancer was often a large oaten cake which rested on top of a churn for the duration of the competition.

Nowadays it is used as a snack. Ormeau recommend their oatcakes be served with butter, cheese, preserves or savouries. Kept in a cool dry place, the shelf life can be up to nine months for the modern manufactured product.

Technique: Traditionally coarse oatmeal was mixed into a dough with water, salt and sometimes a little lard or butter. The oatcakes were baked on an iron griddle over an open fire or on a warmed flagstone. They were then transferred to a wood or metal stand called a 'hardening' or 'harnen', resting in front of the fire, where they dried out. The usual accompanying condiments were salted butter, fatty bacon and a cup of buttermilk.

A more rudimentary method is described by Mahon, who observes that in some rural areas, as late as the 1920s, oatcakes were wrapped in cabbage leaves and baked on a bed of hot ashes with more hot ashes piled on top, to effect an all-round baking. Cakes were usually made with coarse oatmeal moistened with water and flavoured with salt. Richer mixtures included buttermilk, milk, butter, and at times a sweetening agent.

At Ormeau the dough is rolled out and a cutter used to shape and size the product. Ormeau have been using the same cutter machine since 1907. This machine will probably be replaced in the near future, as it is now difficult to maintain. They are the only automated producer; all the others are thought to be cutting by hand. After cutting, the oatcakes go on a plate into the oven for baking.

Producers: Oatmeal biscuits are produced in Northern Ireland by Ormeau Bakery, Belfast, and A. Hyndman & Son in Co. Derry. Ormeau are probably the largest manufacturers of oatcakes in the world. They sell throughout the north and the world through a mail order system. Oatcakes are also produced in Donegal and exported to Britain. While oatcakes are available in many retail outlets in Northern Ireland, in the south Irish-produced oatcakes tend to be available only in up-market outlets. Oatcakes are also available at country markets.

Season: Although there may be periods when they are not produced at Ormeau, oatcakes are generally produced and consumed throughout the year.

Packaging: Loose or in various types of packs. The Ormeau pack is cellophane with cream colours and weighs 200 g. They also produce a 300 g carton. Oatcakes are sold in cellophane wrap at country markets.

References: Tom Simpson, Ormeau Bakery Ltd, Belfast, personal communication. D. O'Brien and R. Humphries, National Bakery School, Dublin Institute of Technology, personal communication.

Useful addresses: Hyndman & Son, Bakers Ltd, 21 Coleraine Street, Magheragh, Co. Derry BT46 5BN. Tel 01648-42605. Ormeau Bakery Ltd, 307 Ormeau Road, Belfast BT7 3GN. Tel 01-232-491-001.

Blaa

Also Blah and blaa, also spelled bla (original name blaad)

Special feature: Local to Waterford, the blaa is a type of ordinary batch bread dough made into specially shaped small round pieces. White flour, sprinkled on top before baking, gives it a distinctive appearance.

Composition: Bigger and lighter than a bap, the baked product is round to oval-shaped. It is very soft and is about 3.5 cm high with a diameter of about 10 cm. It is white on top due to the covering of flour. The weight is about 42 to 57 g. The exact dimensions vary from bakery to bakery. The main ingredients of the blaa are flour, water, salt, yeast and bread improvers.

History: Waterford bakers believe that the blaa was introduced by the Huguenots, who came to Waterford from France in the late seventeenth or early eighteenth century. They set up an industrial area called New Geneva, and it is thought that blaa is derived from the croissants they brought with them. It was called blaad and was originally made from the leftover pieces of dough before baking. Wymberry in *Well, Recollections of Waterford* includes a poem about blaa:

> *A Blaa with two a's is made with fresh dough,*
> *about the size of a saucer, that's the right size you know, . . .*
> *But where did they come from, did they*

happen by chance,
No, the Huguenots brought them from
*   far, the shores of France.*
They called them French Croissants and
*   said u la la,*
We mixed up the translation, and called
*   it a Blaa . . .*
That Waterford people once they have
*   mentioned their Ma,*
Will pop the next question,
Well, did you bring over a Blaa?

Brother Edmund Ignatius Rice used to feed the poor of Waterford with blaa. Long-established bakeries in Waterford have always produced it. For example, Hickey's, formerly Phelans, have produced it for at least eighty years, as have more recently established bakeries such as M&D, which is owned by a family who have been in the baking business in Waterford for many years. The phrase 'baker's dozen' is associated with blaas in Waterford. As they are so small it was common to throw an extra one in a bag for a buyer.

Use: Blaas are a very popular breakfast product in Waterford. The early morning demand means that they must be available in the shops before 8 am. They are used with butter before breakfast, at breakfast, at morning breaks and at lunch. They must be eaten fresh as they have poor keeping qualities and contain no preservative. They can be cut and a sandwich made with dillisk filling; also popular are blaa butties—blaa with chips or a filling of luncheon sausage. As the poem says:

But the real delicacy are Blaas, fresh from
*   the oven,*
Smathered in butter, you'd ate half a
*   dozen . . .*

You can fill them with ham or a slice of
*   red lead,*
In the Summer you could try some dillisk
*   instead, . . .*
They were best eaten fresh and washed
*   down with strong tay.*

Technique: In the past conventional doughs were used as there were no bread improvers. Blaas were baked in drawplate or peel ovens (a type of closed oven with small door, about 2.5 m long, 1.5 m wide and 1.8 m high). The drawplates were huge ovens, fired by coke or coal at the back. The trays were pulled out on tracks about 4.5–6 m in length. The blaas were put in the oven with peels, long pieces of wood with square ends, and left in for 40–50 minutes. Any one of three mixing methods can be used—high-speed, spiral mixing or conventional. High-speed takes two and a half to three minutes, conventional twenty minutes and spiral ten minutes. Spiral mixing of the ingredients includes two minutes' slow mixing and eight minutes fast mixing. Bigger bakeries use high-speed mixing.

At one bakery in Waterford the dough is made and left for five to six minutes. It is put into a scaler, a machine that divides the dough into a number of 1.5–1.8 kg pieces ('heads'). The heads are moulded, put on to a table or in boxes and covered (to prevent skinning) and left for six or seven minutes to relax. They are then flattened out and put through a bun divider moulder. The bun moulder has a plate with thirty separate moulds. The blade cuts the head into thirty round little pieces. In the past they were then rolled by a hand rolling pin to a flat size. Today they are put through a pinner which automatically flattens them, then put on baking trays and dressed with white flour. Rice flour is often used to line the trays.

Larger bakeries have a roll plant. After mixing, the dough is fed on a belt into a cutter and automatically moulded; then it comes out and is fed on to a belt into boxes to go into the pinner for flattening. The blaas are floured and put on racks, proved for about 40 minutes, by which time they have doubled in size, and baked in a rack oven, either single chamber or double rack. Baking time varies from 40 to 50 minutes, depending on the amount of crust wanted.

Producers: Produced by a number of bakeries in Waterford, including Harney's Bakery, John Hickey & Son Ltd and M&D Sunshine Bakery. M&D Sunshine Bakery is run by Walsh's, whose family had a bakery business in Waterford which made blaas since early in the century. As the poem says:

The Summerland and Walsh's made
Blaas for the real,
And the ones sold by Harney's made a
great breakfast meal,
But the Blaas that separated the boys from
the men
Were made by Roche's down in the Glen.

Production is sufficient to meet local demand, but the product is sold only locally.

Season: Blaas are produced and consumed throughout the year.

Packaging: Blaas are sold loose.

References: Michael Walsh, M&D Sunshine Bakery, Waterford, personal communication.

Useful address: M&D Sunshine Bakery, 34 Mount Sion Avenue, Waterford. Tel 051-78080.

Muffin

Muffin or soft roll

(formerly called Ballymena bun)
Also Salad bap, Irish bap, soft roll

Special feature: The original product is from Northern Ireland. It was a solid bread but some modern derivatives are soft-textured bread and may have a flour covering.

Composition: The original product Ballymena Bun was round and bap-like. Today's equivalent is 12 cm in diameter, 4 cm high, flat on both sides and weighs 50 g. Superquinn, a Dublin-based supermarket group, produced an oblong-shaped Irish bap until recently when they reverted to producing the round product. It is a small white bread 11 cm long, 6 cm wide, 3 cm high and raised in the centre. The product weighs 75 g and is dusted with flour before baking; the flour retains its colour. The bap has a very soft texture and contains less sugar than a hamburger bun.

The northern product contains enriched muffin dough. Ingredients include bakers' blended flour, skim milk powder, white fat, caster sugar, yeast, eggs, water and salt. The southern product contains bakers' flour, bread improver, vegetable fat, sugar, yeast, water and salt.

History: In Northern Ireland the product was called a Ballymena bun until recent years. Due to various regulations the name cannot now be used and it is called a muffin. It is very popular and made by many home bakeries. Superquinn probably brought the idea

from the north. The baps are round, but oblong baps were produced to fit the baker's tray and to give a separate identity from a bap.

Use: The muffins or salad baps can be used for any meal. They can be cut in two and toasted and spread with butter as a snack or eaten fresh with or without butter.

Technique: The ingredients are mixed in a standard mixer. In Northern Ireland the muffin dough is enriched with egg, more fat and sugar. About 36 pieces of the rich dough are put in a drawplate oven. Traditionally it is not egg washed but may be done so by some bakers today. After 6–7 minutes, when half baked, they are turned so the final product is baked on both sides and is therefore flat. They may also be baked on a greased hotplate. Rice flour was used in the past. They are not sprinkled with flour.

In southern Ireland they are boxed in 2 kg pieces and left for 20 minutes. They are then cut into round pieces. They are left proving for about 45 minutes, after which they are sprinkled with white flour. They are baked in a hot stationary-type oven (sole oven) for about 25 minutes, and come out linked together at the sides and ends although they are cut through before baking.

Producers: The round product is produced by many bakeries in Northern Ireland. It has also been produced by some Superquinn in-store bakeries for about ten years. There are a number of daily bakings throughout the year.

Packaging: Baps are sold loose in Northern Ireland and in some Superquinn supermarket group stores in the Republic.

References: Eddie Maguire, formerly Superquinn, Sutton and Paul Murphy, Superquinn, Lucan, Co. Dublin, personal communications. Emmanuel McCann, School of Hospitality, Catering and Food, Belfast Institute of Further and Higher Education, personal communication. Gerry Murphy, Arthur McCann Ltd., Newry, personal communication.

Useful addresses: Belfast Institute of Further and Higher Education, School of Hospitality, Catering and Food, Brunswick Street Building, Brunswick Street, Belfast BT2 7GX. Tel 01232-265-167/265-000. Superquinn Ltd, Lucan, Co. Dublin. Tel 01-624-0277.

Ginger Cake

Also Ginger bread

Special feature: The use of ginger as a distinguishing feature in bread.

Composition: Loaf sizes vary, and the following is mainly based on one recently established small bakery, the Gingerbread House in Cork. Their loaf is 20 cm in length, 10.2 cm in width and 7.6 cm in depth. Each loaf weighs 600 g. The baked loaf is a dark brown/rust colour.

Ginger cake is made with white and wholemeal flour, baking soda, mixed spice, freshly chopped ginger and muscovado sugar. The wet ingredients are butter, milk, eggs, black treacle and golden syrup.

History: Ginger probably made its first appearance in Ireland in the wake of the Anglo-Norman invasion of 1169. It is listed as a food in the early fourteenth-century poem 'The Land of Cokaygne', which was probably written in the east of the country.

Specific references to ginger cake do not appear in abundance until the nineteenth century. An early nineteenth-century recipe for the bread occurs in a manuscript recipe or 'receipt' book from Co. Waterford. A later manuscript book, compiled in Limerick in 1852, also includes separate entries for ginger cake and breads.

Apart from domestic production, ginger cake was also sold at markets and fairs throughout the nineteenth century. For example, in the diaries of

Amhlaoibh Uí Shúileabháin, Amhlaoibh travels to Callan in Co. Wexford to celebrate the feast of St James on 26 July 1829. At this festive fair he notes:

There were gooseberries and currants and cherries for children; gingerbread for grown girls: strong beer, and maddening whiskey for wranglers and busybodies.

The *Ordnance Survey Memoirs for the Parishes of Co. Antrim* state that gingerbread was one of the commodities for sale at Lisburn Market in Co. Antrim in May 1837. In all, the evidence suggests that gingerbread was a popular and commonplace sweet cake by at least the early nineteenth century.

Use: Ginger cake is used as a tea-time or dessert confectionery.

Technique: At one bakery ginger cake is made as follows: the muscovado sugar, butter, black treacle and sugar are melted together. The milk and eggs are whisked and added to the melted ingredients. Finally, the flours, baking soda and mixed spice are sifted into the wet solution and chopped ginger is added. All are mixed together to produce a wet dark mixture. The bread is baked for 45 minutes at 150°C.

Nowadays ginger cake mixes are available from bakery suppliers. They supply a number of small bakeries around the country.

Producers: A number of small bakeries around the country regularly make ginger cake.

Season: It is produced and sold throughout the year.

Packaging: Sold loose or in transparent packaging at retail outlets.

References: Barnaby Blacker, The Gingerbread House, Paul Street, Cork, personal communication.

Useful address: The Gingerbread House, Paul Street, Cork. Tel 021-276-411.

Yellowmeal Bread

Also Historically called Indian meal bread, also maize, yellameal, Indian corn, yellow Indian, yellow duck

Special feature: Bread made with American or English corn meal (maize) with resulting yellow colour. Indian meal was used during the Irish Famine in the middle of the last century.

Composition: Yellowmeal bread is a type of soda bread which contains maize meal. It is a round loaf with a cross, similar in shape to soda bread. Its weight is similar to soda bread. The ingredients are baker's white flour, maize meal, buttermilk, sodium bicarbonate and baking powder.

History: Maize was first introduced into Ireland by the British government in the early nineteenth century, when it was distributed as an emergency relief food to alleviate the consequences of potato failures and malnutrition amongst the Irish peasantry. Amhlaoibh Uí Shúileabháin, a Co. Kilkenny schoolmaster and draper, recorded its significance in his diary on 7 August 1829:

> *two pence halfpenny a pottle for "yellow meal" or American maize meal: it was four pence a fortnight ago: only for it, there would be stark famine in this land of Ireland.*

In Ireland yellowmeal is intrinsically linked with the Great Famine of 1845–8. After the first attack of potato blight, *Phytophthora infestans*, on the potato crop in the autumn of 1845, Sir Robert Peel ordered the purchase of £100,000 worth of maize from America in an attempt to relieve the masses.

Although the nutritional value of the corn was acknowledged by many, it was also viewed with disdain and suspicion. In many parts of the country it was known as 'Peel's brimstone'. The objections were not ill founded as much of the corn had not been properly ground and many people died of dysentery, having eaten it without cooking it sufficiently. Consequently government pamphlets were issued to warn against this and advise on proper cooking techniques. In many cases the lumps of poorly ground maize necessitated long boiling.

Nonetheless, maize gained a foothold in the diet of the Irish and the folklore record indicates that by the late nineteenth century it was being consumed in the form of porridge, bread and dumplings.

In many rural areas the preparation of yellowmeal bread continued well into the twentieth century. For example, Maura Laverty, in her 1985 publication *Never No More*, recalls the memory of her grandmother baking yellowmeal scones in her home near the Bog of Allen in the 1920s:

> *She scalded the Indian meal with salted boiling water, made it into a dough, rolled it thinly and cut it into little scones. A bed was made on the hearth by raking amongst the ashes on all sides. Each scone was rolled in a cabbage leaf and placed on the bed with hot ashes piled on top and left until cooked. The scorched leaf was then turned back to disclose fragrant little cakes which were delicious with*

rasher gravy and egg yolk.

Barry's in Tralee, Co. Kerry, have been making yellowmeal bread for over fifty years and Nelligans of Castleisland, Co. Kerry, for a similar period. It is still found as a local product in some parts of Ireland, such as Kerry.

Use: Typical bread product. Used as part of any meal occasion in parts of Kerry, particularly southern Kerry.

Technique: Originally a domestic product in the nineteenth century, it gradually became commercialised. It is manufactured by normal bread-making processes. It is a type of soda bread and no yeast is used; maize meal is used instead of wholemeal brown flour. Some white flour is used as well. Barry's mix the ingredients and shape the bread in the form of a big cake, about a 36 cm diameter round piece. It is crossed before baking into four pieces—these are called squares although they are triangular in shape. The full cake weighs about 2 kg and each triangle about 0.5 kg.

Nelligans in Castleisland use only a portion of yellowmeal to give it colour. In the past maize meal was between 50% and 75% of the flour. Nowadays the proportions are about two to one of baker's flour to maize meal. The mixing and cutting are done by machine, and the individual loaves are shaped by hand. A knife is used to make the cross. They bake the yellowmeal bread in an old-style brick oven for 30–40 minutes.

Producers: Produced by some regional bakeries such as Nelligans Bakery in Castleisland and Barry's of Tralee, yellowmeal bread is for sale in many shops in Kerry. The maize meal is sold by Whites of Tandragee in Northern Ireland. The bread is also produced by at least one bakery in Ballymena, Northern Ireland. Today yellowmeal bread has also gained something of a reputation as a 'health food' and it is made and sold in a number of health food shops throughout the country—for example the Quay Co-op, Sullivan's Quay, Cork, bakes a mid-week batch of yellowmeal bread and sells the bread in its shop.

Season: Baked and consumed throughout the year.

Packaging: Sold loose and unwrapped but also sold wrapped in transparent plastic-type wrap.

References: Jimmy Barry, Barry's Bakery, personal communication.

Useful addresses: Nelligans Bakery, Castleisland, Co. Kerry. Tel 066-41237. Barry's Bakery, Tralee, Co. Kerry. Tel 066-25107.

Cakes, Pancakes and Biscuits

Fruit slice (gurcake) is a great favourite with city children.

Mikado Mallow

Special feature: Original mallow biscuit recognised as a typical and local Irish biscuit.

Composition: Rectangular flat biscuit base with a pink mallow top; the top is in two sections separated by jam. Each biscuit is about 6 cm long and 2.5 cm wide. Mallow ingredients are wheat flour, sugar, glucose syrup, coconut, marine and vegetable shortening, apple pulp, gelling agent, pectin, gelatine, salt, raising agents (sodium and ammonium bicarbonates) and carmoisine (colouring agent).

History: The Jacob family first came to Ireland in the 1670s, fleeing from the persecution of the Quakers in England. Their first biscuits were made by William and Robert Jacob in Waterford in 1851. In 1852 they established a factory in Dublin's Liberties in a vacant coach factory. The firm became a limited liability company in 1883. In 1957 Bolands Biscuits was set up and in 1966 Jacob's acquired Bolands' biscuit interests and Irish Biscuits was established. A modern factory was built and the company moved to Tallaght in the 1970s. Irish Biscuits is now owned by the French Company, Groupe Danone.

Mikado Mallow was developed by W. R. Jacob to celebrate Gilbert & Sullivan's famous operetta, *The Mikado*, and was launched in 1888. It is one of the best-known biscuits in Ireland.

Use: At tea and coffee breaks and after a main meal.

Technique: According to company literature:

Generally for all the biscuits the major ingredients, including flour, fat, sugar, glucose syrup and chocolate are stored in silos adjacent to the factory. These bulk ingredients are treated as fluids and pumped and blown to mixers by an automatic mixing system governed by a master switch panel in the mixing control room. Generally speaking, the dough produced is ready for baking in 20 minutes. It is conveyed from the mixers to the moulding machines which form the biscuit shapes prior to baking in gas fired ovens.

For Mikado a dough recipe which is a basic shortcake recipe is prepared. This is for the flat base and is baked separately the day before or on the day of adding the mallow topping. The bases are baked for about eight minutes and then cooled. The mallow is a sugar syrup aerated as it is pumped on to the biscuit base. Mallow is white, so some colour is added to the syrup so that the output is pink. The jam is manufactured separately and cooled by water circulation tanks.

Originally the mallow was squeezed out of a bag by hand, like icing on a cake, but nowadays high-speed machines are used. The jam was also put on separately in the past, whereas now both mallow and jam are put on automatically in one blob by machine. The syrup is warm (30°C) when pumped.

Immediately after application coconut is shaken on the product. As the jam and mallow are warm and soft, the coconut adheres. The biscuits are then cooled in a cooling tunnel at 12°C for a few minutes. As the biscuits are set by the inclusion of gelatine, they are stable for packing. In the past they were left for a day or so to set properly at ordinary temperatures, 12–13°C, and then packed. As in the case of the other mallow products, Mikado do not lend themselves to machine packing, so packing is labour-intensive.

Producers: Produced by Irish Biscuits in Dublin. Somewhat similar products are made elsewhere. The product is largely sold on the home market.

Season: Produced and consumed throughout the year.

Packaging: Originally packed in returnable metal tins, then in waxed paper, now packed in flow wrap transparent polypropylene with printed labelling. The 250 g pack is standard and contains twenty biscuits.

Reference: Irish Biscuits Ltd, personal communications and company leaflets.

Useful address: Irish Biscuits, Belgard Road, Tallaght, Dublin 24. Tel 01-451-1111.

Kimberley Mallow

Special feature: Unique and original biscuit product, produced only by Irish Biscuits under the Jacob's brand.

Composition: Two round brown ginger-flavoured biscuit pieces with a mallow centre, about 5 cm in diameter. Ingredients are wheat flour, sugar, glucose syrup, marine and vegetable shortening, raising agent (sodium bicarbonate), ginger, gelling agent, gelatine and flavouring.

History: The history of Jacob's and Irish Biscuits is given in the history section for Mikado Mallow. The Kimberley biscuit was developed by Jacob's at the time of the Boer War, when diamond mining in South Africa was in the news, and was named after the Kimberley diamond mines. It was first launched in 1893.

Use: As an accompaniment to tea and coffee.

Technique: The general production process is outlined in the technique section for Mikado. In the case of Kimberley a ginger-flavoured dough, which is a basic shortcake recipe, is prepared for the flat base and top. The bases are baked the day before or on the day of adding the mallow.

The white-coloured mallow is a sugar syrup, aerated as it is pumped on to the biscuit base using high-speed machines. The syrup is warm (30°C) when pumped and the top is pushed on. Immediately after application sugar is dusted on the outside of the product. This sugar represents crystals from the Kimberley diamond mine. It is then cooled in a cooling tunnel at 12°C for a few minutes. The biscuits are set by the inclusion of gelatine, which makes them stable for packing. They are left for a day or so to set properly at ordinary temperatures, 12–13°C, and then packed.

Producers: Produced only by Irish Biscuits.

Season: Kimberley biscuits are produced and consumed throughout the year.

Packaging: Light foil, mostly yellow, with a transparent panel. The 300 g pack is standard but other pack sizes are also available. The 300 g pack contains twenty biscuits.

References: Irish Biscuits Ltd, company information leaflets. Aideen O'Kelly, Irish Biscuits Ltd, personal communication.

Useful address: Irish Biscuits, Belgard Road, Tallaght, Dublin 24. Tel 01-451-1111.

Coconut Cream Mallow

Special feature: Original mallow-type biscuit product introduced by Jacob's of Dublin. Coconut cream mallows are both a typical and local biscuit in Ireland.

Composition: A coconut cream mallow has a flat round base, with a diameter of about 5 cm, which is covered with a half-moon-shaped mallow top. The mallow colour is white or pink. Each biscuit weighs 10 g. Ingredients are wheat flour, sugar, glucose syrup, marine and vegetable shortening, coconut, gelling agent, gelatine, salt, raising agents (sodium and ammonium bicarbonates) and carmoisine (colouring agent).

History: The history of Jacob's and Irish Biscuits is given in the section on Mikado Mallow. Coconut cream was first produced by Jacob's as an Irish biscuit in 1935.

Use: Coconut creams are a popular biscuit accompaniment to tea and coffee.

Technique: The general production process is outlined in the technique section for Mikado. For coconut cream a dough recipe, which is a basic shortcake recipe, is prepared for the flat base. The bases are baked the day before or on the day of adding the mallow.

The mallow is a sugar syrup aerated as it is pumped on to the biscuit base. It is white, so some colour is added to 50% of the syrup so that half the output from the nozzles is pink.

Immediately after application coconut

A cup of tea and a slice of barm brack

Barm/Barn Brack

In Irish bairín breac

Also Bairn brack, brack

Variants: Tea brack, fruit loaf, Selkirk bannock.

Special feature: A barm, which adds valuable flavours, is used. Irwins claim they bake it in the traditional way.

Composition: Traditional brack is round, 4–8 cm high and 12–16 cm diameter. It is brown in colour, and, with its firm texture, looks like a cake. McCanns barm brack is 545 g, Irwins 454g and is round in shape. Breslins of Dublin produce an ordinary brack. Granny Murphy brack is 430 g, and round in shape.

Tea brack is usually rectangular in shape, slightly raised at the centre of the top, with a bread-like texture. Dimensions of about 16 cm long, 8 cm wide and 7–8 cm high are usual, slightly tapered with the top wider than the base. Thunders tea brack is 750 g. It is medium-brown in colour with a lot of currants and a heavy consistency. Nelligans produce an old-style brack which has a lot of fruit and is very solid. They produce square and oblong bracks with weight varying from about 1.5 to 3 kg. A flat teacake-type product about 20 cm in diameter is produced in Northern Ireland. It is called barn brack but has Scottish origins and is really a Selkirk bannock.

The fruit loaf is a type of fruited bread, similar to brack. It is almost like a cake

is shaken on to the product. It is then cooled in a cooling tunnel at 12°C for a few minutes. The biscuits are set by the inclusion of gelatine. They are left for a day or so to set properly at ordinary temperatures (12–13°C) and then packed. As in the case of the other mallow products, coconut cream mallows do not lend themselves to machine packing, so packing is labour-intensive.

Producers: Produced by Irish Biscuits in Dublin. Similar products are now made elsewhere. They are very popular biscuits and are widely available at all food retailing outlets.

Season: Coconut cream mallows are produced and consumed throughout the year.

Packaging: Originally packed in tins, then in waxed paper, coconut creams are now packed in transparent polypropylene, coloured pink, with printed labelling. About half the biscuits in any pack are pink mallows and the other half are white. Packs weigh 200 g or 250 g and contain 20 or 25 biscuits.

Reference: Aideen O'Kelly, Irish Biscuits Ltd, personal communication.

Useful address: Irish Biscuits, Belgard Road, Tallaght, Dublin 24. Tel 01-451-1111.

as it is very rich with fruit and is probably richer than a brack. It is about 20 cm long and 8 cm wide and high. It is produced by Allied and Irwins and other bakeries in Northern Ireland. Irwins also produce a whiskey fruit loaf.

Barm/barn brack ingredients are flour, dried fruit (usually sultanas but sometimes a combination of sultanas, raisins and currants), butter, mixed peel, salt, mixed spice, caster sugar, eggs, yeast and water. The traditional Dublin product had fruit peel. In other parts the product is spiced or has cherries. Danaher indicates that caraway seeds were traditionally used in baking at Halloween and Elizabeth David's recipe for Irish barm brack also includes them. Some domestic recipes include a little brandy.

Irwin's brack contains wheat flour, currants, citrus peel, vegetable and animal fat, sugar, yeast, modified starch, emulsifier, dextrose, salt, glucose syrup, colour, preservative and antioxidants. Other ingredients in the modern brack can be egg, wheat protein and soya flour. The fruit loaf contains wheat flour, water and lots of fruit. The Selkirk bannock is a lot less enriched and is similar to a muffin dough with approximately 25% fruit (sultanas, cherries and mixed peel) added.

Bewleys' current recipe is almost identical to that used in the 1920s, but changes in the wheat characteristics have been taken into account in the baking process.

History: There is a distinct paucity of references to barm/barn brack before the nineteenth century. Nevertheless its association with the Celtic festival of Samhain (Halloween, 31 October/ 1 November) suggests that it has a long historical pedigree.

The name of the cake is an ambiguous area: Dinneen's Irish–English Dictionary states that 'barn brack' is an anglicisation of the Irish *bairgain breac* (speckled cake). A more widely accepted term, 'barm brack' also derives from the Irish *bairín breac* and may possibly refer to the use of barm in its preparation. Barm is the yeast which is drawn off fermenting malt.

The classical commentator Pliny refers to the use of barm by the Celts in their preparation of light raised breads.

In the nineteenth century the baking of barm/barn bracks in celebration of Halloween is well documented. They were consumed on the eve of the festival with other festive foods such as colcannon, pancakes, blackberry pies, apples and nuts. The festival of Halloween marked the end of the year's fertility and the beginning of the infertile and harsh winter months. Barm/barn bracks were also used as a vehicle of divination, particularly the divination of marriage, and charms baked in the cake foretold future events. Those who found the ring in their slice would be married within the year. The rag symbolised poverty, the stick a forecast of a future beating by one's spouse, the bean riches, the pea poverty, and a thimble, if discovered by an unmarried girl, indicated a life as a spinster.

Other nineteenth-century accounts indicate that barm/barn bracks were also used on New Year's Eve in an attempt to banish poverty from the house for the forthcoming year. One such account from Co. Kildare runs as follows:

It was customary on New Year's Eve to bake a large barm brack, which the man of the house after taking three large bites out of it dashes against the principal door of the dwelling, in the name of the Trinity, at the same time expressing that starvation might be banished from Ireland and go to the King of the Turks. The fragments of the cake were then gathered and eaten by all the family.

In the early twentieth century barm/barn brack was a favourite of Lady Gregory, who distributed it regularly to Abbey Theatre actors and actresses (O'Mara and O'Reilly). By the nineteenth century it was customary to use yeast and dried mixed fruit in the preparation of the cake.

The brack is traditional in the south of Ireland, whereas the fruit loaf is more a Northern Irish product. Bewleys have been making bracks since the last century, and Irwins have been producing them since 1912. Kylemore have also produced barm/barn brack for many years.

Use: Brack products are sold all year with big sales at Halloween of barm/barn brack. They are sliced and spread with butter. Irwins' brack can be toasted. Barm/barn bracks will keep for a few weeks. Nelligans' traditional brack will keep for six months. Allied's fruit loaf will keep for six months. The tea brack keeps for about a week at ambient temperatures.

Technique: Before commercial yeast became widely available barm was fermented as a valuable leavening agent. Airborne yeast spores fermented a sugar solution. It was traditional to add flour, whisk it and allow the barm to develop. A barm would be kept for years in the bakery. Sometimes the fermentation was unsuccessful and the process had to be restarted.

Once commercial yeast became available in the eighteenth century, this traditional process required only a three-hour fermentation. Today the modern production process uses a one-hour fermentation as invert sugars and modern yeasts are used. Brown flour (baker's) is used and yeast is added to give the required raise. The ingredients are mixed in a spiral mixer, divided to the required weight and moulded into tins. The dough is proved for about 50 minutes and the product is then glazed and baked in an oven. Baking time is about 40 minutes at 200°C. Both the barm/barn brack and fruit loaf are similarly made. The fermented dough grows in a prover and is then glazed and baked in the oven.

For the tea brack, the fruit ingredients (sultanas and other fruit) are soaked in tea overnight. The next day soft flour, cake margarine, spice and flour are added. Baking powder is used to give a lift. The soft flour gives it a bread-dough-type texture. After mixing, it is tinned in low shaped rectangular tins. Each tea brack is baked separately in a closed oven.

Producers: Made by all bakeries nowadays. Superquinn bake in store. Granny Murphy and bracks from Irwins of Portadown, Northern Ireland, are widely available. Arthur McCanns of Newry are important suppliers in Northern Ireland and their barm/barn brack is found in local and tourist shops. Bewleys produce an ordinary brack. Allied Bakeries in Belfast produce fruit brack. Most sales are in the north. Fruit loaf was originally only produced for Christmas but is now produced throughout the year. Tea bracks are also produced by many bakeries such as Thunders in Dublin.

Season: Bracks are produced throughout the year.

Packaging: Traditionally packed in a round tin, McCanns is packed in a cardboard box, Irwins in thin transparent foil with a white label on top. Many bakeries such as Granny Murphy use a transparent cellophane wrapper with a stick-on label (blue and orange). Bracks are also sold loose (Kylemore) and may be wrapped for the purchaser. Fruit bracks may be sold loose or wrapped in polypropylene.

References: Emmanuel McCann, School of Hospitality, Catering and Food, Belfast Institute of Further and Higher Education, personal communication. D. O'Brien and R. Humphries, National Bakery School, Dublin Institute of Technology, personal communication. Gerry Murphy, Arthur McCann, Newry, Co. Down, personal communication. Alan Stanley, Bewleys Manufacturing, personal communication.

Useful addresses: W. D. Irwin & Sons, Portadown and Craigavon, Northern Ireland. Tel 01762-332-421. Arthur McCann Ltd., Newry, Co. Down. Tel 01693-62076.

Porter Cake

Also Boiled cake

Special feature: Porter cake is an Irish cake with stout.

Composition: A cake made originally with porter, a weak form of stout, but nowadays with Guinness, Murphy's or Beamish stout. Its shape may be round or oblong/rectangular. Its weight also varies. One company makes 500 g and 530 g porter cakes, another bakes a 765 g cake. There are many variations with many family recipes but most recipes contain some of the following: butter or margarine, brown sugar, stout, rind of orange, currants, sultanas, raisins, mixed peel, white flour, bicarbonate of soda, mixed spice or nutmeg and eggs. Some recipes have glacé cherries or walnuts. Commercial recipes contain acidity regulators and modified starch.

History: Porter cake probably originated in the south-west (O'Brien) as a domestic product, but it has been commercialised for some years.

Use: Eaten after lunch, dinner or tea, also as a snack. The porter cake will keep for a number of weeks in a tin.

Technique: The usual mixing and stirring are done as for any cake as ingredients are added. The main differences are the use of stout instead of water and demerara sugar instead of granulated. Fruit is soaked in stout overnight. The other ingredients are added the next day and the mixing is done mechanically. Boiled cake involves boiling the fruit.

Producers: Produced by a number of companies for local markets. These include O'Haras of Foxford, who produce Foxford Porter Cake, available at many retail outlets. Porter cakes from McCambridges, Dublin, and Breslins, Dublin, are also widely available. Kiste produce an 'Irish' Porter cake. Arthur McCanns of Newry produce a porter cake available in most tourist shops. Frank Gallagher of Gallagher's, Ardara, Co. Donegal, supplies Harrods with porter cake. It is also exported to the US.

Season: Porter cake is produced and available throughout the year.

Packaging: The Foxford cardboard package shows the cake and a glass of stout. Photographs conveying an Irish identity are also on the package. The box details the history of the bakery, which is over forty years old, as well as details about porter cake. McCambridges' and Breslins' cakes are sold wrapped in clear polypropylene paper. Cookery experts recommend that porter cake is best left for a week before eating and stored in a tin.

References: D. O'Brien and R. Humphries, National Bakery School, Dublin Institute of Technology, personal communication. J. Thornton, Moy View Bakery, Foxford, Co. Mayo, personal communication.

Useful addresses: Arthur McCann Ltd, Victoria Bakery, Castle Street, Newry, Co. Down. Tel 01693-2076. W. D. Irwin & Sons, Portadown and Craigavon, Northern Ireland. Tel 01762-332-421. O'Haras, Moy View Bakery, Foxford, Co. Mayo. Tel 094-56114. McCambridges Fine Foods, Arkle Road, Sandyford Industrial Estate, Dublin 8. Tel 01-295-8868.

Plum Pudding

Also Christmas pudding

Special feature: Plum pudding is a special type of pudding produced for Christmas. Irish plum pudding usually contains stout, whereas English puddings contain cider.

Composition: Christmas pudding is a rich fruit pudding which is flat at the base and on top. The top may be slightly raised in some puddings. They are round in shape and the base is wider than the top. The base diameter is 12–16 cm, with a height varying from 8 to 12 cm. Weights also vary. Kylemore's pudding weighs 800 g, Allied's weighs 837g. Breslins produce 450 g and 900 g puddings; Chivers produce 454 g and 1.36 kg puddings. Plum pudding is dark brown in colour and has a soft texture. Different flavourings are used by each producer, for example caramel. Ingredients in one commercial product include sultanas, flour, brown sugar, water, stout, margarine, egg, cherry, orange, apple, peel, walnuts, lemon, sorbitol, spice, cinnamon, nutmeg, salt, ginger and baking powder. Other ingredients included in different puddings include breadcrumbs, beef suet, mixed spices, rum essence, caramel, ale and dark rum.

History: There are markedly few references to plum pudding in the Irish historical record. It is possible that the Anglo-Normans introduced a rudimentary version of the dish in the twelfth century, in the form of a highly spiced fruit meal pottage. However, it was during the Tudor and Stuart periods in England that dried plums or prunes were added to the porridge mixture, rendering a dish popularly known as 'plum pottage' or 'plum porridge'. Thus it is probable that the plum pudding was a sixteenth- or seventeenth-century introduction to Ireland, but it is also likely that the dish was confined to the aristocracy until the nineteenth century. There are a number of recipes for plum pudding in Irish nineteenth-century 're-ceipt' books, for example a recipe in an 1801 Co. Waterford manuscript book and another in an 1850 example from Cork.

Towards the end of the nineteenth century plum pudding became an increasingly popular Christmas dish. The folklore record for the period also reveals that a specific variation of plum pudding, 'Cutlin pudding', was prepared in a domestic setting on Christmas Eve throughout Co. Wexford. This pudding consisted of a thick wheaten porridge which was mixed with dry fruit and flavoured with sugar and spices. The mixture was made into a ball and wrapped in a greased calico cloth subsequent to boiling. An important aspect of the Cutlin pudding is that it incorporates features of two distinct culinary traditions: first the spiced porridge is similar to the medieval plum pottage, while the thickened boiled pudding is similar to the solid pudding of the Elizabethan period.

While many are made in the home, plum puddings have been produced commercially for many years. Kylemore Bakeries have been making Christmas puddings since the last century. Breslins use an old recipe from the original bakery Johnston, Mooney & O'Brien, but have been producing puddings themselves for only ten years. Ownabee use a traditional recipe over a hundred years old.

Use: Plum puddings are made at Christmas only. Many commercial plum puddings are almost fully cooked, requiring less than an hour's cooking. The product can be steamed for a while, depending on the extent of cooking by the manufacturers. The Kylemore 800 g pudding is placed in a saucepan of water and simmered for two hours. Alternatively most producers give instructions for cooking in the micro-wave. This usually takes under 10 minutes. Allied Bakeries, in their cooking instructions, say there is no need to boil their pudding, and they recommend oven heating. After cooking the pudding is doused with whiskey which is set alight and then served with cream or brandy sauce.

Technique: Ingredients are weighed, added to a baker's mixing bowl and thoroughly mixed. The product is cooked in a steam oven. After cooking, the puddings are almost ready for the consumer. Nelligans' plum pudding is steamed for four to five hours in a steam oven. Kylemore use a steam tank which contains a large volume of mixture and steam the pudding mix for about six hours. The product is then vac packed in a thick plastic pack so it can be boiled in the bag or microwaved. Puddings can also be produced in half an hour in modern ovens.

Producers: There are many bakeries producing plum puddings, including Kylemore, Breslins and Allied. They are also produced by jam manufacturers such as Chivers and Ownabee Preserves. These products are widely available and are sold at most large food retail shops throughout Ireland.

Season: Produced for Christmas only.

Packaging: The puddings are wrapped in greaseproof paper and outer metallic-type paper by one producer. Other companies use plastic bowls with outer colourful wrappings. The Kylemore pudding is vacuum packed. Both Kylemore and Chivers use cardboard boxes with colourful decorated pudding and Christmas motif designs and pictures.

Reference: E. Manning, Kylemore Bakeries, personal communication.

Useful addresses: Breslins Bakery, Unit F3, Newtown Industrial Estate, Dublin 17. Tel 01-848-0767. Kylemore Bakery, Finglas, Dublin 11. Tel 01-834-2032. Ownabee Preserves, Carrigaline, Cork. Tel 021-372-323.

Pancake

Variant: Beesting, buttermilk, oatmeal and boxty pancakes. Fruit pancake (Northern Ireland).

Special feature: Thin flat product made from a special mixture of eggs, flour and milk.

Composition: The typical Irish pancake is thin, whereas some commercially produced pancakes are thicker. Kylemore produce a traditional round pancake which is 23 cm in diameter and 4 mm thick. It is a flat pancake, like those produced at home on Shrove Tuesday. McCanns is 10 cm diameter and slightly thicker than the traditional domestic pancake. Mannings also produce a pancake similar to the domestic one. It is about 12 cm in diameter and about 0.5 cm thick. Breslins bakery produce a pancake which is raised and round. Allied (Sunblest) pancakes are also round, about 10 cm diameter, 1 cm thick and flat on both sides. They are deep brown in colour with white to slightly yellow margins. Northern Ireland fruit pancakes are aerated. Other pancakes can be yellow-brown in colour. The Allied pancake weighs about 50 g. McCanns also produce a fruit pancake which contains sultanas and cinnamon. Irwins' pancake is 7.5–10 cm in diameter.

The Irish pancake contains flour, egg, salt and milk. Kylemore also use some baking powder. Breslins produce a pancake which is composed of wheat flour, pasteurised eggs, milk powder, vegetable oil, calcium propionate, lemon essence and salt. Allied's pancake contains wheat flour, buttermilk, whole egg, vegetable fat, soya flour and other ingredients such as sugar, golden syrup, raising agents and salt. McCanns include some sugar to sweeten the pancake.

History: Pancakes enjoy a long antiquity in the Irish diet. In the domestic setting, their preparation was facilitated by the popularity of the griddle as one of the main baking utensils in most households. Interestingly, griddles are mentioned in the seventh- and eighth-century Brehon laws and Joyce maintains that beesting pancakes were particularly popular at this time.

An early pancake recipe is included in Selina Newcomen's manuscript book from Co. Longford which is dated to 1717 (Fitzgibbon). This lavish recipe includes the following ingredients: egg yolks and whites, flour, milk, brandy, nutmeg, ginger and butter with sugar and salt to taste. A recipe for pancakes also appears in an 1801 manuscript recipe book from Co. Waterford, whilst a 1917 Dublin publication, *A New Era Cookery Book*, also devotes a section to pancakes. Florence Irwin in her 1937 *Irish Country Recipes* includes a couple of recipes for buttermilk pancakes which were particularly common in rural areas given the unprecedented growth in domestic butter-making throughout the eighteenth and nineteenth centuries.

In Ireland the consumption of pancakes is inextricably linked with Shrove Tuesday. From the early Middle Ages, the Christian church throughout western Europe forbade the consumption of meat during Lent. On Shrove Tuesday, which is the last day before Lent, a feast was held and stocks of butter, milk and eggs were used to make pancakes, which became the central food of the meal. In households today the making, tossing and eating of pancakes remains an important part of Shrove Tuesday.

Commercially produced pancakes have been on the market since the nineteenth century. Kylemore have been producing them since 1850, McCanns since the 1840s, and others since at least the beginning of the century. McCanns also produce a traditional fruit pancake. Although some pancakes have only come on the market in recent years, they are based on old recipes—for example Breslins pancakes.

Use: Usage is associated with Shrove Tuesday, and although pancakes are available throughout the year, they are mainly used in the winter. The batter mixture must be let stand before being cooked on a heavy pan. In the home tossing is a ceremonial part of preparation. The domestic product has only a few hours' shelf life. Pancakes are sprinkled with sugar and lemon juice before eating hot. Breslins recommend heating their product on the pan or microwave and sprinkling with sugar, lemon juice or syrup. Allied (Sunblest) pancakes may be used hot or cold with a topping of the user's choice. Pancakes can also be fried and served with butter. The shelf life of commercial pancakes is a few days at ambient temperatures.

Technique: In the past pancakes were baked on drawplate ovens. These were huge ovens with two plates to an oven. One plate was about 0.3 m off the ground and the other about 1.8 m off the ground. In a typical bakery four of these ovens were placed side by side. These ovens had no sides, just a front and a flat black top. The steel plates, on wheels, could be rolled out 6 m and the dough was dropped on the pulled out plates. The pancake was quickly turned and taken off again. All this was done manually.

Today in commercial bakeries the batter, prepared to enable extended shelf life, is baked on a hotplate. At most bakeries the ingredients are weighed and added to a mixing bowl to form the batter; they may be mixed by a whisk. Fixed amounts are dropped straight on to the hotplate at one bakery, while at another the mix is deposited by hand on the hotplate. They are left for seconds only, turned and then taken off, and allowed to cool before packaging. At another bakery fixed amounts are deposited from a hopper, four at a time on a moving hotplate. They are turned when they are half way along the plate and taken off at the end. The moving hotplate is about 75 cm wide. At yet another bakery the ingredients are mixed by machine and filled into a piping bag. The batter is then piped from the piping bag on to the hotplate. They are allowed to flow freely to form their own round shape, about 10 cm in diameter. Between fifty and sixty are piped out and, when this amount has been piped, it is time to turn them. By the time turning is done they are ready to take off the hotplate.

Producers: Produced by some commercial bakeries, with almost as many recipes as bakeries. These include Kylemore, Mannings and Breslins in Dublin, and Allied Bakeries and Ormeau Bakeries in Belfast. Pancakes are widely available in supermarkets and specialist bakery shops. Some producers only produce for Shrove Tuesday, e. g. Mannings.

Season: Pancakes are mainly used on Shrove Tuesday but are produced and consumed throughout the year.

Packaging: Pancakes are sold loose and in thin transparent cellophane-type packaging. The Breslins pack weighs 200 g. It contains six pancakes and has a yellow and red label stuck on the wrapper. Mannings sell pancakes loose as well as six to a pack. They also sell them hot from hotplates at their shops on Shrove Tuesday. Ormo packs from Belfast also contain six pancakes. Sunblest packs, produced by Allied Bakeries in Belfast, contain four or ten pancakes and the label is yellow.

References: Breslins Bakery, Dublin, personal communication. Mannings Bakery, Dublin, personal communication.

Useful addresses: Allied Bakeries, Orby Link, Belfast BT5 5HW, and Unit 1, Feltrim Industrial Park, Feltrim Road, Swords, Co. Dublin. Tel 01-840-9342. Breslins Bakery, Unit F3, Newtown Industrial Estate, Dublin 17. Tel 01-848-0767.

Irish Crumpet

Crumpet

Also Golden crumpet

Special feature: The Irish crumpet differs from the English crumpet in a number of ways. First, it is a batter crumpet as distinct from a yeast-based crumpet. Second, the Irish crumpet is turned on the plate and baked on both sides, whereas the English crumpet is baked on one side only. Third, it is closed in that it has a smooth top and is not open and sponge-like. Furthermore, a hotter plate is used for English crumpet.

Composition: Crumpets from the Arch Bakery in Dublin are round, 8 cm in diameter and 2–2.5 cm thick. They have a smooth top. A pack of six weighs about 300 g and each crumpet weighs 50 g. The product from Breslins is flat and round, 1.25 cm thick and 6.4 cm diameter, and is a brownish-yellow colour on top and on the base with yellow sides. Inside is slightly yellow in colour. The texture is soft and slightly crumbly and internally it has numerous small holes. Lemon essence gives the crumpet a lemon flavour and yellow colour.

The ingredients in the crumpet from Arch Bakery are wheat flour, sugar, milk powder, baking powder, eggs, vegetable margarine and lemon flavouring. The ingredients in Breslins' crumpet are flour, sugar, eggs, baking powder, milk powder, vegetable oil, lemon flavouring, calcium propionate.

History: Irish crumpets, which originated in Dublin, are demanded by consumers only above a line north of Dublin and Galway. The old Boland's Bakery, which was started in Capel Street in 1823 by John Boland and then moved to Grand Canal Street, used to produce large volumes of these crumpets at the end of the last century and for most of this century. In 1888, Boland's became a limited company. The Grand Canal Street bakery was rebuilt and expanded in the 1950s. Without new investment in the 1980s the plant became uncompetitive and Boland's went into liquidation in 1984. Some employees set up the Arch Bakery and continued to make crumpets. The same recipe was also acquired by Breslins so today's crumpets from Arch Bakery and Breslins are based on the old traditional recipe used by Bolands at the end of the last century and in this century until 1984.

Use: Normally toasted and buttered, the product has a few days' shelf life. Breslins recommend cutting in half and spreading with butter, jam, honey or a topping of cheese.

Technique: Traditionally crumpets were produced on large hotplates. The crumpet was turned on the plate and baked on both sides. At one plant today ingredients are weighed and added manually to a standard 80-quart mixing bowl. Hoops made of stainless steel are placed on the hotplate and a defined amount dropped into each hoop. This defines the size and shape of the crumpet.

At another bakery a unit with 24 adjoining hotplates is used. Each plate is about 1 m by 0.5 m. Five rings are attached to a metal bar and three of these units are placed on each hotplate. Each ring is about 8 cm diameter. Thus fifteen crumpets are produced on each plate. The mix is prepared and is added by hand from a mixing bowl, placed beside the hotplate, to each ring. A hopper above the hotplate can also be used but as this warms up too much it causes more fermentation. A series of static gas jets heat the plates. The plates travel along on a chain about 4.25 m. The speed of movement can be varied and the plates move at the slowest possible rate for crumpets. At 3.5 m the rings are removed to a side table and the crumpet is turned over, the plate moves on and back in the opposite direction to where it started. The crumpets are removed at the start point and new rings are filled to start the next cycle. A full cycle takes about fourteen minutes, the top section taking about five minutes and the bottom about nine. As the baked product takes time to set, it is baked each day for sale the following day.

Producers: Produced by Arch Bakery and by Breslins. Arch sell to agents who distribute to shops throughout the country. Breslins sell to a number of retail outlets.

Season: There are steady sales of crumpets throughout the year.

Packaging: Both the Arch Bakery and Breslins pack six crumpets in a rectangular transparent pack with stick-on labels. There are two layers, with three crumpets on the bottom and three on top. Packaging is done by hand at Arch Bakery.

References: Francis Breslin, Breslins Bakery, personal communication. Edward O'Callaghan, Arch Bakery, personal communication.

Useful addresses: Arch Bakery, North Summer Street, Dublin 1. Tel 01-836-5610. Breslins Bakery, Dublin. Tel 01-848-0767.

Fruit Slice

Also Gurcake, tipsy cake, Chester slice, donkey's wedding cake, donkey's gunge, donkey's gudge

Special feature: Gurcake is unique to Dublin, although similar products are found in other parts of the country. The fruit slice is the modern name for gurcake and the fruit slice's special feature is the incorporation of stale bread and cake. Each producer has their own formulation for fruit slices, but there is only one type of tipsy cake.

Mannings' fruit slice weighs about 150g. It is rectangular—8.75 cm long by 4.5 cm wide by 3 cm high. It is a three-layered cake. The base layer is hard pastry, light brown and nearly 1 cm thick, the middle layer, the main part of the cake, is dark brown and 2 cm thick; the thin top layer is glazed pastry with occasional indentations, light brown and less than 0.5 cm thick. KC fruit slice is 3 cm high. The Chester slice has a thin pastry slice at the base and chocolate icing on top.

Composition: Fruit slice was originally a mixture of stale cakes and poor-quality leftovers, whereas tipsy cake is made from better-quality ingredients. The ingredients in one of today's products, KC fruit slice, are fat (margarine), flour, bread, fruit, sugar, spice, water and colouring. The fruit slice has more fruit than a Chester slice.

History: With the establishment of bakeries and confectioneries on a commercial basis in the nineteenth century, gurcake and fruit slice became a common commodity in many urban areas. In a gesture of economic thriftiness, the factories produced a fruit cake made predominantly from stale and unsold cake and bread products. The fruit slice was considered a somewhat low-status foodstuff but nevertheless enjoyed immense popularity, particularly with city children. Memories of the cake are recalled by Éamonn Mac Thomáis in his book *Gur Cake and Coal Blocks*, which details a Dublin childhood in the early twentieth century:

> *We were just in time to see Miss Noone, the cook, carrying the large tin tray of steaming hot Gur Cake straight from the oven to the shop window. Miss Noone took pride in her Gur Cake and we watched her as she arranged it in the centre of the window and then stood there admiring it and sniffing the steam . . .*
>
> *'Missus Noone, Missus Noone, give us a ha'pert of that. Ah, go wan Missus Noone, a ha'pert of Gur Cake before it gets cold.' . . .*
>
> *'A ha'pert of Gur Cake, Miss.'*
>
> *'You mean fruit cake, We only make fruit cake.'*
>
> *As we came out of the shop we were stuffing ourselves with the Gur Cake. It was only gorgeous, steaming hot, with sugar-coated pastry and the juice oozing out of the large currants and the other soft brown stuff. We could feel our bellies heating up.*

Over time the eating of gurcake became synonymous with poorer Dublin children, so much so that the term 'gurrier' established itself in Dublin dialect, describing *one who eats gurcake; a tough street ur-chin. (OED)*

Its inferior status is also well illustrated by the common appellations given to the preparation in Cork City. The terms 'donkey's wedding cake' or 'donkey's gudge/gunge' (excrement) are clearly derogatory and leave little doubt as to its standing. In recent years the more refined names of 'fruit slice' and 'Chester cake' have been adopted in an attempt to elevate its status and break the connection with its origins.

The fruit slice is related to the old-fashioned home made bread and butter pudding. The main difference is the pastry layer at the top and bottom to hold the fruit slice together.

Use: Eaten cold as a snack between meals or as a cake at the end of a main meal. The product has a very short shelf life. If it is not sold in a day it is disposed of.

Technique: All unused product and over-production are used in fruit slices. More bread than cake may be used at bakeries and more cake at confectioneries. Sponge trimmings and Vienna rolls are much used by some manufacturers. The mix of ingredients is added to the baker's mixing bowl. According to one baker, the fruit slice contains edges of sponge sheets and no bread, whereas the Chester slice contains yesterday's bread and no cake. Whether separately or in various combinations, all the unused bread and cake are added to the bowl. Fruit, such as raisins and water, are added to give a moist texture and taste.

A sheet of pastry (often puff pastry) is prepared and laid out on the baking board as a single sheet and the mix is spread over it. The sheet can be about 60 cm by 40 cm. The mix is covered with another layer of pastry and put into the oven at a temperature of about 190°C for 10–15 minutes. It is then transferred to a second oven at 100–110°C for a further twenty minutes. It is fully baked on removal and allowed to cool before distribution to shops. The shops cut the sheet into a number of small rectangular slices for sale. About sixty slices can be cut from a sheet.

Producers: A number of Dublin bakeries, such as KC Hotshops, Mannings Bakery and Thunders Bakery, produce fruit slices. They are produced daily and are widely available at all types of bread and confectionery shops and in some supermarkets.

Season: Fruit slices are produced throughout the year.

Packaging: Generally fruit slices are displayed loose on the counter. They are wrapped and bagged by the shop for each purchaser.

Reference: Frank Cullen, KC Hotshops, personal communication.

Useful address: KC Hotshops, 11/12 Moore Lane, Dublin 1. Tel 01-873-3298.

Apple Cake

Also Apple pie, apple tart

Special feature: The Irish apple tart and pie are different from the Continental product as the layer of apples is covered with a layer of pastry.

Composition: The apple pie and tart are closed tarts. They are round products, with a pastry base and top, about 17–20 cm diameter with an apple filling. Shortcrust pastry is more traditional but puff pastry is also used. A typical pie weighs 550 g. Typical ingredients are flour, apples, sugar and starch. The ingredients in one modern product are Bramley apples, flour, vegetable fat, butter, sugar, fresh eggs and water.

History: The wild crab apple tree (*Malus sylvestris*) is native to Ireland. Crab apples and cultivated varieties are the most commonly referred to fruits in the corpus of Irish documentary material spanning the sixth to the twelfth centuries. In the later historical period, new apple varieties, e.g. Cockagee, Kerry Pippin, Irish Peach and Ard Cairn Russet, were introduced and prized for baking and preserves. The abundance of the fruit ensured the popularity of apple cake in the diet. One of the earliest references to apple pie is found in *The Kenmare Manuscripts*. Under an entry for 24 December 1718, apple pie or tart is recommended as an aid to proper digestion and good health:

I'm apt to believe that belching and wind you complain of proceeds from emptiness,

and without being a physician I'll venture to tell you that you may eat 'Apply Pye Tarts', roast, stewed and raw apples and 'seagoe' or any other pudding that is not very heavy.

The folklore record indicates that apple pie was an established item in the Irish diet by the nineteenth century. This is confirmed in the diaries of Amhlaoibh Uí Shúileabháin; the diarist, writing on 31 October 1831 in Callan, Co. Kilkenny, states:

I spent the [early] night sociably and comfortably, eating apples, drinking tea, roasting nuts, drinking 'punch' and eating 'apple pie'.

Twenty years later a recipe for apple pie is recorded in a manuscript recipe book from Cork City.

The commercial production of apple cake is also dated to the nineteenth century. Arthur McCanns of Newry was set up in 1837, and have been baking apple tarts and pies since at least the 1860s and probably earlier. As urban living and retail shopping increased, the commercial production of apple pies became commonplace.

Use: Apple pies and tarts enjoy immense popularity in Ireland. They are used as a dessert or snack, usually hot with whipped cream. The shelf life of commercial products is about three days. Traditionally apple cakes were produced as part of Halloween (31 October) festive fare. It was commonplace throughout the nineteenth century to drop charms into the unbaked dough. The charms were connected with marriage divination.

Technique: Throughout the nineteenth century and well into the twentieth century apple cake was baked in an iron pot oven or bastible over the open fire. The dough consisted of flour, baking soda, butter, sugar, eggs and milk and a pinch of salt. Two rounds of dough were shaped and slices of apple, sprinkled with sugar, were placed between the two dough pieces. The bastible pot measured approximately 48 cm in diameter and 10 cm in depth. The cake was of similar dimensions as the dough almost filled the pot.

The factory and domestic processes differ little. Smaller products, about 17.5 cm in diameter, are called apple tarts. A shortbread pastry base is prepared and placed on the base of a plate which is slightly dipped in the middle to facilitate filling. Chunky apple pieces with added sugar and starch are added. Nowadays these are often fresh/raw apples which can be bought in machine-cut. In the past dried apples or canned apples were often used. A top pastry layer which covers the apple filling is added. A little hole is made at the centre of the top pastry layer. The pastry may be brushed with egg before putting the pie in the oven. Larger apple pies 25 cm in diameter may be baked in a ring so that a round shape is obtained. The ring is taken off after baking.

At larger operations pastry is mechanically prepared. However, in smaller bakeries many of the processes are done by hand. McCanns, for example, hand fill the apple filling into the pastry. It is also thumbed around the edges by hand and a hole put in the centre.

Producers: Apple pies are widely produced by both large and small bakeries, including many home bakers, in all parts of Ireland. They are widely available in bakers' shops, supermarkets and general grocery stores as well as newsagents.

Packaging: Apple pies and tarts are sold loose, but usually have a cellophane transparent wrap with a stick-on label.

References: Tony Lonergan, Thunders Home Bakery, personal communication. Gerry Murphy, Arthur McCanns, Newry, personal communication.

Useful addresses: Arthur McCann Ltd, Newry, Co. Down. Tel 01692-62076. Thunders Home Bakery, Drumcondra, Dublin 9. Tel 01-837-1244.

Potato Apple Cake

Also Apple dumpling

Special feature: The potato apple is distinguished by the inclusion of an apple filling in a potato bread and its local association with Northern Ireland.

Composition: Potato apples can be round or triangular. A 10 cm by 10 cm piece is made into a triangle, or two round pieces are put one on top of the other. The ingredients are dried potato, flour, salt, fat, apples and sugar.

History: Given the importance of apples and potatoes in Ireland, it is hardly surprising a dish evolved that combined both ingredients. It is likely that potato apple cake enjoyed seasonal popularity in the autumn months in the wake of the harvest. The cake was probably more usual in the orchard-growing areas of the north and south-east. One of the earliest references to the cake is from the *Irish Farmers' and Gardeners' Magazine* of 1838, which refers to the following culinary practice in the Lagan Valley in Co. Down:

> *The farmer's pudding (which makes a good dinner for a family) is made with apples and potatoes mixed, about equal quantities of each, cut up in slices and tied into a large towel or bag, and let to boil three or four hours, when a little milk mixed with sugar is used along with them by way of a sauce.* (Bourke)

While this refers to a pudding rather than a cake, nonetheless it is most likely that it was equally traditional to bake the mixture on the griddle in the same manner as potato cakes. What is particularly noteworthy is the association with Northern Ireland, as potato apple cake was traditionally and still is a culinary feature of this region. This is also borne out by the inclusion of the potato apple cake recipe in Florence Irwin's 1937 northern-focused publication, *Irish Country Recipes*. In this she speaks of the traditional preparation of potato apple farls baked until golden on the griddle over the open fire. Irwin's Bakery, Portadown, is one of the earliest commercial producers of potato apple cakes; they began production in the early twentieth century.

Use: In Northern Ireland, potato apple was a traditional festive Halloween dish. On the night a ring was placed in the unbaked dough and was used for purposes of marriage divination.

Technique: Traditionally potato cake farls of mashed potato, flour, salt and butter were prepared and rolled out into farls. Slices of apple were placed in one farl slice, another farl was placed on top, sealed and baked on the griddle. Once baked, the top farl was cut open and rolled back. Butter and sugar were spread inside on top of the hot apples; the top farl was then resealed. The farl was reheated on the griddle to ensure the butter and sugar melted to form a rich sauce that soaked through the apples.

Commercially the production process is somewhat similar. Bought-in dried potato product is reconstituted like a mash with the addition of water, improvers and powders. It is put through a machine to produce a consistent product and comes out on to the travelling hotplate. (The potato bread dough is produced as described under potato bread.) The dough is more difficult to pin out than ordinary dough. It is covered with apple filling as described for apple tarts. In Irwins local fresh apples, bought in as pulp, are used. They have been peeled and sliced/diced and juice and sugar added to make the pulp. The pulp is placed in buckets and put out on the potato on the hotplate. It is folded over and then baked on the griddle or travelling hotplate for about 15 minutes.

Producers: Nowadays potato apples are less widely consumed than in the past. They are produced in small quantities by Irwins of Portadown and are prepared to order by McCanns of Newry. Irwins sell through their own bakery outlets and to supermarkets in Northern Ireland.

Season: Potato apple is produced and sold throughout the year.

Packaging: Potato dumplings are sold loose by McCanns of Newry and Irwins of Portadown.

References: F. Irwin, *Irish Country Recipes*, Belfast, 1937. Gerry Murphy, McCanns of Newry, personal communication. Billy Reed, Irwins of Portadown, personal communication.

Useful addresses: Arthur McCann Ltd, Victoria Bakery, Castle Street, Newry, Co. Down. Tel 01693-62076. W. D. Irwins, Portadown. Tel 01762-332421.

Simnel

Special feature: Simnel cake is a fruit cake which has a centre layer of almond.

Composition: Today's simnel cake is a soft moist round fruit cake, about 20 cm in diameter and 20 cm high. The original cake in the last century was 25–30 cm in diameter. Traditionally it contained marzipan, 100% ground almond as a centre layer and toasted marzipan decoration on top. Today peanuts with marzipan flavour may be used. The simnel cake from Ormeau weighs 960 g. Simnel ingredients are flour, fruit (dried sultanas, raisins, currants), sugar, fat, eggs, raising agent, almond (ground/split nuts or flavouring or combination).

History: As with many rich fruit cakes, it is likely that simnel was originally a spiced fruit bread and it is probable that this culinary tradition was introduced into Ireland by the Anglo-Norman settlers in the twelfth and thirteenth centuries. However, the custom of preparing an enriched wheaten cake for Mothering Sunday, the fourth Sunday in Lent, must have been introduced into Ireland by the Elizabethan settlers in the sixteenth and seventeenth centuries. From this time onwards, girls in service in Dublin and in the south-eastern regions baked a rich plum cake decorated with almond paste which they took home to their mothers on Mothering Sunday. If they couldn't go home they liked to send their parents a present at Easter and they made a long-life sturdy cake that could be sent by post. The cake recipe would vary depending on the ingredients that were available in the house, but simnel always had a marzipan centre and top.

A popular Irish ditty which celebrates the custom of young men baking simnel cakes for their sweethearts runs as follows:

And I'll to thee a simnel bring
For when thou goes a Mothering;
So when thy mother blesses thee
Half the blessing thou'll give to me.

James Joyce in his 1922 *Ulysses* also refers to the sale of simnel cakes from open stalls outside Glasnevin cemetery in Dublin.

Today simnel cake is baked by Mannings Bakery for only one retail customer. Mannings have been producing simnel since the 1950s, when the bakery was first established. In Cork, the Old Mill Confectionery produces simnel at Christmas and Easter time. A former city bakery, Thompson and Sons, which closed in the 1980s, had been producing simnel since the nineteenth century and today the Old Mill Confectionery bakes simnel according to this older recipe. Bretzel Bakery in Dublin produces simnel for the Jewish community in the city.

Use: Simnel cake was used at times of celebration, particularly Easter.

Technique: Fruit and flour are mixed as for a wedding cake. The batter is piped into a 20 cm diameter tin. An almond piece or layer (or marzipan) about 0.5 cm thick or slightly more is placed on top of the fruit. It is placed so that it does not quite reach the edge of the batter. The rest of the cake fruit mix is then piped on top, producing a sandwich-

Simnel cake

type product.

The almond is not visible, as the batter fills in around the edges of the two layers. It is baked in the oven and the effect is an almond bake throughout the cake. The almond flavour permeates the cake and, as it is completely covered, a specific topping is prepared to distinguish it from other fruit cakes. Sometimes more almond is put on top as a thin layer which is egg washed but the cake is not iced. This almond-topped cake is flashed in the oven to give a caramelised effect to the almond paste topping. The topping may be different shapes or colours. Usually thirteen small balls of marzipan were placed around the edges of the cake. One of the balls was slightly larger than the others. These balls represented Jesus and the Twelve Apostles at the Last Supper. The side of the cake may be decorated with a light coating of yellow icing.

Producers: At least four bakeries produce simnel cake. Mannings produce it at Easter. The Bretzel Bakery and the Old Mill Confectionery make the cake at both Easter and Christmas. Ormeau produce it at intervals throughout the year.

Season: Simnel is generally made to order only at Easter and Christmas and is not made at other times of the year.

Packaging: Sold loose, packed for each customer. Ormeau also pack in a sealed tin, suitable for posting.

References: Morgan Hack, Bretzel Bakery, personal communication. Eamon Manning, Mannings Bakery, personal communication.

Useful addresses: Bretzel Bakery, Lennox Street, Dublin 8. Tel 01-475-2724. Mannings Bakery, Coolock, Dublin 5. Tel 01-847-7246. Old Mill Confectionery, Watercourse Industrial Estate, Cork. Tel 021-507144.

Seed Cake

Also Caraway bread, caraway seed cake

Special feature: Yeast bread containing caraway seeds.

Composition: Long loaf-shaped unsliced bread which resembles brack more than bread. A butterloaf is a similar product without the caraway seed. Ingredients are flour, water or milk/eggs, yeast, caraway seed, sugar and fat (often cake margarine).

History: In Ireland the practice of flavouring bread and cakes with spices is undoubtedly an Anglo-Norman innovation of the later medieval period. The influx of Elizabethan and Jacobean settlers in the sixteenth and seventeenth centuries popularised the taste for spiced breads, particularly in large towns and cities. Fynes Moryson, in his early-seventeenth-century work, *An Itinerary*, refers to the production of aniseed cakes in the cities of that period:

> In the cities they have such bread as ours, but of sharp savour, and some mingled with anise seeds and baked like cakes, and that only in the houses of the better sorts.

It is likely that flavouring with caraway seeds also enjoyed favour from this period onwards, although such luxuries were probably limited to the tables of the wealthy and aristocratic settlers.

It is evident that seed cake was enjoyed by the general population from the early nineteenth century. In the 1802 *Statistical Survey of County Down*,

Dubourdieu records the following baking technique current in that region:

baked into thin cakes on the griddle, with water and salt; I have never met it baked with barm; sometimes caraway seeds are mixed with it and sometimes it is mixed with butter.

Its popularity is also clear from the inclusion of recipes for caraway seed cake in a number of nineteenth- and early-twentieth-century manuscript books from both urban and rural areas. In country areas the cake was known as 'carvie cake'.

The upsurge in commercial bakeries in the nineteenth century increased the availability of the product on an all-year-round basis. The seed cake features in a sensual reference from James Joyce's *Ulysses* (1922):

Ravished over her I lay, full lips full open, kissed her mouth. Yum. Softly she gave me in my mouth the seed cake warm and chewed. Mawkish pulp her mouth had mumbled sweet and sour with spittle. Joy: I ate it: joy.

Nelligans in Castleisland, Co. Kerry, have been making caraway cake for fifty years.

Use: Traditionally, the cake enjoyed increased popularity on festive occasions, particularly at Easter and Christmas. Today it is more in demand by older people.

Technique: A sweet dough with sugar is prepared in a spiral mix. Each loaf, which is made separately, is shaped like a bread pan by machine, then baked in an old-style brick oven by Nelligans. These brick ovens are over fifty years old. Caraway cake is also produced in modern ovens. Baking time is about an hour.

Producers: Made by some bakeries, including Nelligans Bakery in Castleisland, Co. Kerry.

Season: Caraway cake is made throughout the year.

Packaging: Sold loose.

Reference: T. J. Nelligan, personal communication.

Useful address: Nelligans Bakery, Castleisland, Co. Kerry. Tel 066-41237.

Cream Cracker

Cream crackers and jam

Variants: Snap cracker, wheat snap cracker

Special feature: The original product, from Jacob's, was unique, the first cream crackers produced in the world.

Composition: Flat, ridged, square, hard, crunchy product with small dimpled indentations, light brown toasted colour. The 300 g pack contains about thirty crackers. The snap cracker is the same product and the same size with perforations down the centre so it can snap into two pieces. The wheat snap cracker uses brown dough instead of white. Cream cracker ingredients are wheat flour, hydrogenated vegetable oil, salt, yeast, defatted soya flour and raising agent (sodium bicarbonate).

History: Original cream crackers were first developed by W. R. Jacob and marketed in 1885. An export business was quickly developed and a depot opened in Liverpool. Nowadays cream crackers are marketed by Irish Biscuits as original and best. The product today is almost the same as that produced over a hundred years ago, although there are some variations in ingredients. It is the oldest product in the Jacob's range.

At the modern Jacob's plant today over a million biscuits can be produced in an hour. Raw materials go in at one end and packaged goods come out at the other.

Use: Mainly as a snack product with cheese or other topping at the end of a meal or between meals.

Technique: A yeast dough is made up similar to any other bread dough, yeast being important to the flavour and texture of the cracker. The dough is allowed to ferment for 24 hours with the yeast raising the dough so it is flattened or sheeted out. The sheeted dough, two sheets and a fat layer in between, is laminated and folded and refolded a number of times to give layers. This process is now highly automated. The laminated product is baked in a travelling oven. A fast bake at high temperatures is used. The exact details of time and temperature are confidential. Cream crackers are the fastest baked of all Irish Biscuits products.

Producers: Produced by Irish Biscuits. Similar products are now produced in many countries. Jacob's Cream Crackers are exported to over 35 countries around the world.

Season: Produced and consumed throughout the year.

Packaging: Long, rectangular, flexible,

light plastic-type pack. Jacob's Original is a 200 g pack, but 300 g packs are also available.

References: Marion Rogan and Aideen O'Kelly, Irish Biscuits, personal communications and company information leaflets.

Useful address: Irish Biscuits, Belgard Road, Tallaght, Dublin 24. Tel 01-451-1111.

Fig Rolls

Special feature: Original biscuit, produced by Jacob's, thought to be one of the first extruded products.

Composition: A fig roll is a light brown biscuit with a dark brown filling and weighs over 12 g. It is an extruded biscuit filled with figs. Each fig roll has a flat biscuit base, a filling of fig paste and a biscuit top. It is rectangular in shape, about 6 cm long, 2.5 cm wide and 1.2 cm high. Ingredients are wheat flour, figs, glucose syrup, sugar, marine and vegetable shortening, cornflour, salt and raising agents (sodium bicarbonate and ammonium bicarbonate). Chocolate fig rolls are also available.

History: The history of Jacob's and Irish Biscuits is given in the section on the history of cream crackers. Fig rolls were introduced by Jacob's, now Irish Biscuits, in 1903. Fig rolls are a unique Irish product and are mentioned in James Joyce's 1922 novel *Ulysses*:

> *a bag of fig-rolls lay smugly in Armstrong's satchel. He curled them between his palms at whiles and swallowed them safely. Crumbs adhered to the tissues of his lips. A sweetened boy's breath.*

The formula for getting the figs in the fig roll became the focus of a promotional campaign in the late 1960s and early 1970s.

Use: At tea and coffee breaks and after a main meal.

Technique: The general production

process is outlined in the technique section for Mikado. In the case of fig rolls the outer dough is not flavoured, and the inner is a fig paste. The fig jam, which is paste-like but uncooked, is made at the production plant. Two tube-like components, fig paste in inner and raw dough in the outer, are co-extruded and the dough is cut with a knife to separate each biscuit.

The baking, done in a moving conveyor through a travelling oven, allows for a soft bake so that the fig paste permeates the outer biscuit. This, as well as the more moist dough, makes for a softer biscuit. Fig rolls are the slowest baked of all the biscuits mentioned here. More exact details on the production process are confidential. Packaging is done automatically by machine.

Producers: Fig rolls are produced by Irish Biscuits, the original producers. They are also now produced by other companies in other countries.

Season: They are produced and consumed throughout the year.

Packaging: Fig rolls were originally packed in tins. Partly transparent light polypropylene foil, red with a yellow strip, is used today. At Christmas larger packs with special tins about half the size of the original tins are used. There are 24–28 per 300 g pack. The 28-roll pack weighs 360 g. A 200 g pack is also produced.

References: Irish Biscuits Ltd, information leaflets. Aideen O'Kelly, Irish Biscuits Ltd, personal communication.

Useful address: Irish Biscuits, Belgard Road, Tallaght, Dublin 24. Tel 01-451-1111.

Confectionery

*'Did you treat your Mary Anne
To dulse and yallaman'*

Yellowman

Northern Ireland

Also Yallaman

Produced since the nineteenth century, yellowman is a unique, golden yellow, hard, brittle, boiled toffee, made with soda to achieve an airy texture. It is hammered from a large block into smaller blocks, bars and sticks. Bars or sticks are 2 cm in diameter and about 23 cm long, weighing about 75 g. Blocks weigh about 4.5 kg, and are 85 cm square and 7–8 cm deep. Chips are small pieces of variable size and weight.

Composition: According to Fitzgibbon, the ingredients are butter, baking soda, brown sugar, vinegar and golden or corn syrup. A traditional recipe for yellowman is included in Florence Irwin's 1937 publication, *Irish Country Recipes*: the ingredients are golden syrup, brown sugar, butter, water and baking soda. Ingredients in the product available today are sugar, glucose syrup, flavouring, colour, tartrazine and chocolate brown.

History: Yellowman, or as it is pronounced in Northern Ireland 'yallahman', was popularly sold at Irish fairs. It has a particular association with the Lammas Fair in Ballycastle, Co. Antrim, which is over 350 years old. Ballycastle, which was a sheep and pony fair, is held on the last Tuesday in August. Everyone in the community, young and old, took time off to celebrate and enjoy the fair. Young boys went to great trouble to

sport elaborately and delicately fashioned plaits of corn straw called 'harvest knots', designed to win girls' attention, in their buttonholes. If successful, they might express their affections further by treating their new-found love to some yellowman. A popular traditional ballad recounts:

> At the auld Lammas Fair, were you ever there?
> Were you ever at the fair of Ballycastle, oh?
> Did you treat your Mary Anne to dulce and yallaman
> At the auld Lammas Fair of Ballycastle, oh?

The confection is presented in a large block, which is brittle in nature, and the vendor simply hits the block with a small hammer to produce suitably sized pieces. The most usual and traditional way to hold loose sweets, and presumably yellowman, in Ireland was in a cone of paper known as a 'tomashín'.

Yellowman was sold at stalls in fairs all over the north-east of the country and families became renowned for their recipes and their products. Specific family recipes are said to be very old and the current sweet may well hail from the first introduction of sodium bicarbonate into Ireland in the early nineteenth century.

One renowned maker of yellowman was Dick Murray from Lurgan, Co. Armagh. He sometimes put a halfpenny or two into the preparation while it was in a liquid state, and there was great excitement if you got the halfpenny in your portion. If you got the halfpenny, it automatically meant you purchased more yellowman, which he claimed 'cured all disease'. This type of traditional producer appears to be no longer in business and the main commercial producer of yellowman is a company called Crilco, based in Co. Down, who have been producing yellowman for twenty years.

Use: Its use is tied in with romantic associations, at the old Lammas Fair, as outlined in the famous lines quoted above in the history section.

Technique: The ingredients are melted and boiled at 285°C, when baking soda is added, causing foaming. The mixture is poured on to a greased dish or slab. It is pulled on a machine, where it changes colour from dark yellow to pale yellow, and is then poured on to a cold slab and marked into blocks or slabs or made into sticks.

Producers: According to Fitzgibbon, it used to be made by one family, the Devlins in Co. Antrim, for many years. Another famous maker was Dick Murray of Lurgan. Today it is produced by Crilco Confections Ltd, a Newry-based firm. They produce it from before Easter until the end of September. Local shops and stalls in Ballycastle sell yellowman.

Season: Most consumption takes place at the Lammas Fair in Ballycastle in Co. Antrim, on the last Tuesday of August. In recent years Crilco have developed the market and it has become more widely available throughout Northern Ireland.

Packaging: Mostly sold loose from a block, it is also wrapped in transparent cellophane with the label 'Traditional Yellowman'. Chips are sold in 227 g tins.

Reference: Peter Crilly, Crilco Confections Ltd, personal communication.

Useful address: Crilco Confections Ltd, Newry, Co. Down, Northern Ireland. Tel 01693-64877.

Toffee

A typical confectionery made from a combination of skimmed milk and sugar, toffees vary in size and shape. Small toffees are 2 cm long, 1.3 cm wide and 0.8 cm high.

Composition: Sugar, glucose syrup, water, vegetable fat, sweetened condensed skimmed milk, butter, salt and flavourings such as caramel. There are other ingredients, which vary with toffee varieties. Lecithin may be used as an emulsifier.

History: It is probable that toffee was produced in a domestic setting since at least the nineteenth century, when refined sugar became more widely available. Commercial production goes back to the start of the century at least. Original slab toffee was made by Cleeves in Limerick, which was established about seventy years ago. The Cleeve brand of toffee consisted of large flat slabs and was made for many years; although the brand is owned by Clara Candy, the toffee is no longer manufactured. Milroys, another well-known brand, which started in 1910 under Joseph Milroy, are no longer in business. The name is not used today but is still owned by the family. Exchange Toffee Works, although still in business, no longer produces toffees due to the high cost of ingredients. Many other companies such as NKM and Savoy, who made toffees in the 1930s, are no longer trading. McKinneys, who started in the 1920s, have been producing toffee since 1928 and are the main toffee producer in Ireland today.

Use: Toffee was a very popular sweet with children of all social classes in the past. Nowadays its popularity has declined because of the wide range of alternatives and because it is more expensive. Shelf life is about 12 months from the time of production.

Technique: There are three main stages—emulsification, cooking and cooling. In the past copper pans over coke stoves were used to boil the mixture of sugar, glucose, water, fat and condensed milk. The first boiler was installed in McKinneys in the mid-1930s and since then all cooking has been done by steam. Today modern processes are organised to allow for rapid change in production requirements. Most of the ingredients can be sourced locally, including skim milk powder, fats and sugars. Sweetened skim makes up about 20 per cent of the final toffee. Various types of toffee are produced, such as toffee supreme and dairy cream toffee, but the exact process is not available for reasons of confidentiality. In general the mixture is boiled to form a creamy white milky solution. There is central mixing, two pre-cookers and a holding tank, so that a continuous plant system can operate. The cooking stage follows emulsification, with boiling of the mixture to produce toffee. Fruit, nuts and basic flavourings are added at this stage. The product then goes to a cooling tunnel for rotating cooling. It is forced out through an extruder to make it square. Sometimes the toffee is enrobed—for example the Emerald brand is caramel toffee enrobed in milk chocolate. As each long piece comes out it is cut and

Bulls' Eyes

Bulls-eyes, clove rock and iced caramels

Bulls' eyes were one of the most typical boiled sweets for children in Ireland for many years, particularly in the 1940s, 1950s and 1960s. Bulls' eyes are black and white striped round sweets sold in variable amounts at retail outlets such as newsagents. They are about the size of a marble, with a diameter of 1.75 cm. Each bull's eye weighs about 2.75 g. The finish is shiny and natural glazed. The special features of this product lie in its appearance, with characteristic black and white stripes and a strong peppermint flavour. There are about 20 stripes, 8–10 white and 10–12 black on each sweet.

Composition: The main ingredients are sugar, glucose, flavourings and colouring.

History: The confectionery industry in Ireland started with retailers who made and sold their own sweets. Successful products were sold to other retailers and in time the retailers became manufacturers. Firms producing sugar confectionery became important in the 1920s. Although definite information is not available, bulls' eyes were probably produced by a number of these confectioners.

Bulls' eyes have been produced by Waverley Confections since the firm was set up in 1936, and today's product is little changed from the original. In the 1940s and 1950s a number of sugar confectionery factories were set up by ex-

wrapped to give cut and wrap toffee. It is then further cooled by dry air.

Producer: McKinney's Oatfield brand is the main producer today. Distribution is through national and international distributors, with products widely available.

Packaging: Standard packs are 100 g. Other packaging includes a 200 g pack, a 450 g bag, a 3 kg bag, and a 2.27 kg (5 lb) jar and bag. Toffees are also available in various assortments.

Reference: Michael Purcell, McKinney Ltd & Sons, personal communication.

Useful address: McKinney Ltd & Sons, Oatfield Confectionery Works, Letterkenny, Co. Donegal. Tel 074-22011.

army officers who had been allocated sugar quotas, and these factories probably produced bulls' eyes. However, as UK sugar confectionery production increased, most of these small factories lost their export market and went out of business.

Use: Bulls' eyes have for many years been a typical sweet bought by Irish children in local shops and sucked and savoured at any time of the day. They are stocked by most cash and carrys and wholesalers.

Technique: White granulated sugar is melted in water in a large copper pan, diameter about 60 cm, depth 42 cm. The mixture is boiled and glucose is added. It is then boiled at a temperature of 130–140°C for a specified period. This temperature is sufficiently high to give the desired amount of glazing to the final product. The mix is then spilt out on a large flat slab, about 1.8 m by 0.9 m, which has been cooled with water before the mixture is poured on. The mix forms a glassy effect as it cools. It is divided into three sections, two small and one large. The large section and one of the smaller sections are treated with black colouring.

Two small pieces of white and one piece of black are taken to a hot table and pulled out into a cylindrical shape to form a long strip about 110 cm long. These pieces are cut in two halves with a shears, giving six pieces. The process of pulling out to 110 cm and cutting is repeated to give 12 narrow pieces, which are laid out to form a square on the table. As more black than white is used, the end product has more black than white stripes. Strips of white and black are wrapped around a large, wider, long cylindrical piece of black (a black shell), made from the large pile, and placed in a cylindrical machine casing. Considerable skill is needed to wrap the pieces around the black shell. The rope-like piece is then cut into individual bulls' eyes in the machine casings. In the past brass rollers were used and a handle was turned to form the balls. The individual bulls' eyes are cooled on a roundabout.

Producers: The main producer who has been identified is Frank Edwards, Waverley Confections, Superb Confectionery Ltd, Parnell Street, Dublin. Bulls' eyes are available at many retail outlets throughout the country but not to the same extent as twenty years ago. They are also produced by Exchange Toffee Works in Cork and are available in tourist shops under the 'A Taste of Ireland' label.

Season: Bulls' eyes are produced and sold throughout the year.

Packaging: In the past bulls' eyes were packed in small 250 g and larger glass jars. Today they are sold to retailers in 3.6 kg solid plastic transparent jars, with larger volumes packed in loose plastic bags for agents who deliver to shops. At shop level the sweets are sold in 227g amounts and wrapped in small paper bags for each customer.

Reference: Frank Edwards, Waverley Confections, Dublin, personal communication.

Useful address: Waverley Confections, Superb Confectionery Ltd, 64 Parnell Street, Dublin 1. Tel 01-873-3895.

Peggy's Leg

Peggy's leg and chocolate cream pie

Also Peggy's leg sticks

A sweet with a long tradition in Ireland, Peggy's leg is a long stick of sweet candy, about 10 cm long. Cylindrical in shape, the colour is brownish yellow. Each stick weighs about 50 g.

Composition: Sugar, glucose, vanilla flavouring, colouring and salt.

History: Peggy's leg has been a popular children's candy stick since at least the early decades of the twentieth century. Its name derives from the sweet's characteristic light brown cylindrical shape, which resembles a wooden peg leg. The sweet is mentioned by the popular media personality, Paddy Crosbie, in his evocative account of Dublin life in the early 1920s. In his 1981 work *Your Dinner's Poured Out!* he reminisces:

> *from Mrs Cullen we bought bread, tea, sugar, biscuits and cakes. All of the Haymarket boys bought their sweets from her. Peggy's Leg was one har penny, Sharp's Kreemy Toffee cost one penny, Aniseed Balls were 16 a penny, bulls' eyes 12 a penny, fizz bags cost one har penny, and the popular drink Vimto was two pence.*

Traders selling Peggy's leg at market stalls in Omeath and Dundalk and other areas regularly shouted the following rhyme:

> *Peggy's leg and Nancy's thigh, that never wore a garter.*

Peggy's leg was made for many years from the 1930s onwards under the supervision of Charlie Duffy in the Dublin firm of Williams and Woods. Charlie Duffy later moved to J. W. Dowling in Liffey Street and it was made by Dowlings, who had four sweet factories in the Dublin area, until sometime in the 1950s, when the company closed. It was also produced in the 1950s by George Denham at the firm of Gordon Stewart, sweet manufacturers and wholesalers in George's Street, Dublin. Until a few years ago it was produced in Dublin by Wilton Candy. Today it is still produced by Crilco in Newry, Northern Ireland.

Indeed many Irish people have fond childhood memories of Peggy's leg, which was often eaten while playing street games and pranks. Crilco have been manufacturing Peggy's leg since setting up in business over twenty years ago.

Use: Popular sweet for children. Demand was much greater years ago, when choice of sweets was more limited than today.

Technique: Trade sources provided Crilco with their recipe. Sugar, glucose and water are boiled in a copper pan to a temperature of 280°C. The liquid mixture is poured on to cooling slabs. Colouring, vanilla flavouring and a little salt are added. Part of the mix is cut off and put to one side to make the casing (outer skin) for the bar. The rest is put on a pulling machine to aerate the bar. It is still quite soft when taken off and is worked until firm. It is then filled into the casing to form a large bar, which is put into a batch roller, and spun down long rolling tables. It is rolled into long strings, which are cut into 10 cm lengths to give individual Peggy's legs.

Packaging: There are 100 sticks to a box for retailers and wholesalers and they are also available in standard size sweet jars. Each stick is individually wrapped in cellophane.

Producer: Crilco Confections Ltd, a Newry-based firm, are the only company producing Peggy's leg today. They make small amounts to order for customers all over Ireland.

Season: Peggy's leg sells throughout the year, with greater sales in winter.

References: Peter Crilly, Crilco Confections Ltd, personal communication. Paddy Crosbie, *Your Dinner's Poured Out!*, Dublin, 1991. Leo Cummins, Wilton Candy, personal communication.

Useful address: Crilco Confections Ltd, Newry, Co. Down, Northern Ireland. Tel 01693-64877.

Clove Rock

Cork

Also Clove drops

Clove rock is a hard-boiled sweet in the form of chopped rock in a stick shape. First made in Ireland, it is a hand-made rock with clove flavouring, which gives the sweet its unique taste. It is not known who came up with the idea of clove as a flavouring. Each stick is 1.9 cm in diameter and of similar length. The centre is red and the thin outer case white.

Composition: Sugar, water, glucose, colouring and clove.

History: James Linehan set up Exchange Toffee Works in 1929 in Cork, and started making clove rock in the early 1930s. The product is little changed and is the same as the original. Exchange continue to make clove rock by hand as the market is limited and automation would not be viable. Today it is also made by other manufacturers.

Use: Clove rock is a popular sweet eaten by children and adults.

Technique: At Exchange Toffee Works batches of about 25 kg are made at a time. The mixture of sugar, water and glucose is boiled at 155–157°C. Extract of bought-in natural clove oil is added to the mixture. The exact amount is a company secret, but if too much is used the flavour becomes too strong and the rock loses its appeal for most people. The boiling produces a clear liquid of a sticky or gummy nature. This is then pulled, which means it is stretched out on a dough-type hook over a hot table so that it becomes white and fluffy. The effect of air on the candy turns it white. The outer white part becomes opaque and is softer due to the pulling. This red centre is prepared by hand mixing with added colouring (kneaded like bread). The red centre is not pulled so it forms a solid block. Despite its red colour it is glassy and transparent. The red centre is rolled into a ball and the white outer is wrapped around it. Both parts immediately bind. The piece is about 30 cm long and 35 cm high and produces a rope-like piece when rolled. The rope is about 122 cm long before chopping. This is all done by hand at a temperature of 155°C. When the product is made, the rope is chopped by hand, as a mechanical chopper causes too much damage.

Producers: Producers include Exchange Toffee Works in Cork. Clove rock is sold in Cork and distributed in the Dublin area by Crescent Confectionery. Other producers of clove rock include Shaws Confectionery in Belfast (producing for over forty years) and Crilco in Co. Down. (Clove drops are produced by McKinneys in Donegal.)

Season: Clove rock is produced and consumed throughout the year.

Packaging: Clove rock is packed in plastic jars or packs. Jars take 3.6 kg and 227g packs. Packs must be airtight or the rock absorbs moisture and goes soft.

Reference: Danny Linehan, Exchange Toffee Works, personal communication.

Useful address: Exchange Toffee Works, 37A John Redmond Street, Cork. Tel 021-507-791.

Iced Caramels

Dublin

This product, originally made only in Ireland, is a toffee caramel centre with an iced sugar coating. Each iced caramel is square in shape, about 20 x 20 mm and 12 mm high, with a very slightly raised top. The caramels are coloured pink or white with a grained brown soft toffee centre.

Composition: Sugar, glucose syrup, vegetable oil, dried skimmed milk, gelatine, milk protein, egg albumen, salt, vanillin and colour.

History: Iced caramels were first produced in the old Clarnico Murray plant in Dublin. Clarnico Murray started producing toffee caramels in Ireland in 1926. One of the workers, Dan Monaghan, had the idea of dipping the toffee in icing in the late 1930s or early 1940s and created the iced caramel. The product was so successful that the company considered setting up a plant in England, but the labour-intensive nature of the process and the long and complicated drying procedure persuaded them not to proceed. Trebor, an English-based confectionery company, bought Clarnico in England and acquired the Irish Clarnico business. Trebor continued to make iced caramels and was bought by Cadbury's in 1990. The small scale and complicated process did not suit large-scale manufacturing. Leo Cummins of Wilton Candy acquired the licence and techniques from Cadbury's and took on some workers from Trebor with the requisite skills, and Wilton Candy is now thought to be the sole producer of iced caramels.

Use: Iced sweet popular with both adults and children.

Technique: Exact information is not available and the following gives a general outline and may not be accurate. Caramel and glucose are mixed and a forming machine used to produce the toffee. The caramel toffees are then dipped in icing. Initially each toffee was put on a spoon and dipped in the icing, but by the 1940s or early 1950s a chocolate-type enrober was used for coating the caramels. The caramel centres are fed along a machine and, as they go through it, a curtain of icing comes down around it and along a pre bottom so the bottom of the sweet also picks up a bit of icing. Colouring is used so that half the caramels are white and half pink.

In the past toffees were put through a cooling tunnel 100 metres long and came out the other end ready to be packed or iced. The icing was put on at a high temperature and, because it was wet, moisture was absorbed into the centre, giving a graining process to the toffee so that it went soft over time. The cooling machine had to be adapted as the sweets took so much time to dry.

The iced caramels were then put on a plaque to dry for 24 hours. After this time in the dry rooms, where caramels were stacked on boards 20 boards high, hydraulic trucks took out the boards and the sweets were taken off and wrapped. As this was a very labour-intensive process, dehumidifiers are now used to speed up the drying process. Shelf life is about 10 months.

Producer: Produced by Wilton Candy and distributed by Trebor to a wide range of shops. Wilton produce about 180 tonnes annually. In the past iced caramels were also sold in the UK and the USA.

Season: Produced and consumed throughout the year.

Packaging: Sold under the Trebor label as Clarnico Iced Caramels. Pack size is 90 g or 205 g and contains a number of caramels. Each caramel is separately wrapped in a transparent wrapper, with the Clarnico name.

Reference: Jim Raleigh (former Managing Director Trebor), personal communication.

Useful addresses: Trebor Ireland Ltd, Tallaght, Dublin 24. Wilton Candy, St Ignatius Avenue, Dublin 7. Tel 01-830-3588.

Chocolate Cream Pies

Also Cream pies

A local product, first produced in Ireland, the cream pie consists of an outer flat-bottomed cone biscuit with a filling and flat-topped with chocolate. One producer uses a marshmallow filling, the other an albumen-based filling. This filling has a soft creamy texture. The cone is about 5.7 cm wide at the top, 3.3 cm at the base, and is 6.5–7 cm high. The diameter is the same for the top 2.5 cm and the bottom part then tapers inwards. The bottom part of the cone is patterned with rectangles, each rectangle being 0.5 x 0.75 cm approximately. There are 2 x 16 such rectangles and a further 16 rectangles about half this size.

Composition: Biscuit, mallow or albumen and chocolate. The full ingredient list for one producer is albumen, cocoa powder, flour, glucose, sugar, lecithin, skim milk solids, sodium bicarbonate, salt and vanillin.

History: Dan Linehan started making cream pies at Exchange Toffee Works in Cork in the late 1940s. His son, Danny, and grandsons have continued to make the product. Bertie Dowling set up a confectionery business and also started producing cream pies in Liffey Street in Dublin in the late 1940s or early 1950s. Production was continued by Bill Power and John Broderick of Glendale Products of Castle Street, Dublin. Today's product is basically the same as the original of nearly fifty years ago.

Use: Confectionery product for children. The shelf life is 6–7 weeks.

Technique: The biscuit comes from the Irish Cone Company in Kilmainham in Dublin, who have supplied the cone since the business began. At Exchange a lower boil than for other sweets is used to produce a soft mallow. Gelatine, lecithin and agar are added to get the whipping properties. A fluffiness is attained with the whipping process in producing a solid foam like a whipped cream. The foam is then piped with a piping bag into the cones, after which the mallow is coated with chocolate. The mallow does not dry because of this coating, so the product does not need to be kept airtight.

At Glendale, the filling is a mixture of albumen, glucose and sugar. Considerable skill is needed to get the fluffiness right or the 'cream' will collapse. It is filled into the cups with a knife by hand and the top scraped flat. Chocolate topping, made with skim milk solids and cocoa powder, is also poured on by hand. A small amount may drip over the side of the cone. The pies are put through a drier to dry the chocolate, and are then packed. The shelf life is longer for the mallow than the albumen-filled product.

Producers: Cream pies are produced in Cork by Exchange Toffee Works and in Dublin by Glendale Products. They are supplied to C & Cs (cash and carrys) and wholesalers and distributed reasonably widely to newsagent outlets and small supermarkets. Glendale are temporarily out of production, due to relocation, but will recommence in the near future.

Season: Cream pies are produced and consumed throughout the year.

Packaging: At Exchange, pies are not packed individually, but are loosely packed 36 to a cardboard carton. They are then sold loose at retail outlets. At Glendale they are packed in three layers of 16, 48 to a box. The printed box is specially designed, with four main colours—white, light and dark yellow and brown. A medieval-type shop outline and an empty cream pie are illustrated as well as the company and product name on three sides. The ingredients and manufacturer's name are given on the fourth side.

References: John Broderick, Glendale Products, Dublin, personal communication. Tom Keogan, Crescent Confectionery, personal communication. Danny Linehan, Exchange Toffee Works, personal communication.

Useful addresses: Crescent Confectionery, 46 Broomhill Close, Tallaght, Dublin 24. Tel 01-462-2401. Glendale Confectionery, Ballymount Industrial Estate, Dublin 12. Tel 01-460-1061. Exchange Toffee Works, 37A John Redmond Street, Cork City. Tel 021-507-791.

Drinks

'A pint of plain is your only man.' (Brian O'Nolan)

Irish Whiskey—Pure Pot-stilled (Malt and Grain)

Two brands of pot-stilled Irish whiskey are produced—Jameson Redbreast and Green Spot. Old Comber is not produced, but a small amount is available. Tyrconnell is also a pot-stilled whiskey, but is included under single malts.

Special feature: Originally all Irish whiskies were pure pot-stilled and Redbreast and Green Spot are two of the whiskies that maintain this tradition. In general, different techniques are used in producing Irish whiskey to other whiskeys.

(1) No peat is used to dry the malt and malt for Irish whiskey is dried in a closed kiln, thus tasting more perfumed and rounded.

(2) It is distilled three times in copper pot or grain stills—no other whiskey is distilled more than twice and this contributes to the flavour.

(3) Pot stills used in Ireland are larger than anywhere else.

(4) Whiskey is matured in casks, some bourbon and some sherry.

Composition: Pure Irish pot-still whiskey is a mixture of distilled fermented mash of malted and unmalted barley. It has a light brown colour. The main ingredients are barley, malt, water and yeast. Alcohol content is 40% for Green Spot, Redbreast and Old Comber.

History: Early history is outlined in this section, and more recent history is described in the column and pot-stilled (blend) section. The earliest reliable historical reference to whiskey in Ireland dates to the fifteenth century: the *Annals of Connaught*, the *Annals of Clonmacnoise* and the *Annals of the Four Masters* each record the following incident for the year 1405:

> *Risderd Mag Ragnaill, eligible for chieftainship of Muintir Eolais, entered into rest after drinking Usci Bethad [water of life, whiskey] to excess; it was a deadly water to him.*

Edmund Campion, writing in Ireland in the late sixteenth century, recounts that whiskey-drinking was commonplace among the 'mere Irish' who eat 'raw flesh' that 'bleedeth in their stomachs with aquavita, which they swill in after such a surfeit by quarts and poltes'. Even in this early period the quality of Irish whiskey was well established and recognised by a host of English commentators. Its qualities were highlighted in verse by John Derricke, who travelled to Ireland in 1581. Similar sentiments were expressed by Fynes Moryson, who regarded Irish whiskey as 'the best drink of its kind in the world'. By the end of the sixteenth century, the widespread and commonplace consumption of whiskey was a source of concern for the English authorities. A series of by-laws issued in Galway in 1585 were designed to discourage whiskey-drinking:

> *the aqua vite that is sould in town ought rather to be called aqua mortis to poyson the people than comfort them in any good sorte.* (Murray)

[179]

However, by the seventeenth century the English government had realised the financial potential of Irish whiskey distillation and on Christmas Day 1661 a tax of fourpence was imposed on every gallon of whiskey distilled.

The eighteenth century witnessed the establishment of the major Irish distilleries on a commercial basis. Distilleries included the Kilbeggan Distillery, which was built in 1757, and Jamesons in 1780.

There were two Comber Distilleries which were established in 1825 and closed in 1953. The Jameson Heritage Centre has been established at Midleton as a self-contained eighteenth-century industrial complex. All the major buildings, mills etc. have been refurbished and the largest pot still in the world, with a capacity of more than 30,000 gallons, is on display.

Green Spot pure pot still, bottled by Mitchells, has been produced since the 1920s or earlier. In the past wine merchants filled casks with whiskey from local distilleries. Mitchell & Son of Dublin have been doing this since the early 1920s and are now the only wine merchants doing so. For a period when Redbreast was not available it was the only Irish pure pot still produced. Old Comber, although out of production, was of course still available. Today Green Spot, along with Redbreast, both produced at Midleton, are the main pure Irish pot-still whiskies commercially produced.

Jameson had the second-largest pot still in Ireland in 1810. There was continuous expansion and the company became a public company in 1902. The Redbreast name was first used in 1939 by Jameson in Gilbey casks and there is little of the original remaining. Jim

Murray states:

> *Redbreast was the brand name for Jameson Pure Irish pot still.*

Redbreast in a new form was relaunched in recent years. Comber whiskey was produced at Comber near Belfast until 1953. The remaining stocks were bottled in the 1980s and sold as Old Comber, and there are still a few bottles left in bond.

Use: Used at festive and party occasions but widely drunk in ordinary everyday situations in public houses (see single malts).

Technique: The general procedures used in producing Irish whiskey are set out in the section on single malts. Only pot stills are used for pure pot still.

For Green Spot half the casks used held dark sherries and the other half lighter sherries. After five years they are vatted and blended and then allowed to mature for a further five years. The company has an agreement with Irish Distillers which ensures that Green Spot will continue as pure single pot-still whiskey. At present Green Spot is made from seven- and eight-year-old Midleton pot still, with 25% coming from sherry casks.

When making the original Redbreast, for every two ex-sherry casks one ex-bourbon cask was used. The last bottling of the original was in 1985. The present Redbreast was relaunched with twelve-year-old pure pot still. Murray states, 'Some sherry casks are still used but the bourbon cask character is clearer.'

Producer: Irish Distillers, a wholly owned subsidiary of Pernod Ricard and a limited company, are the producers of both Green Spot and Redbreast.

Season: All year round.

Packaging: Bottled, sizes vary. Green Spot and Redbreast are 700 ml. Bottle shapes and colour vary from white to green to dark brown. The Green Spot label is on a white cream background with green and brown lettering.

References: Leaflets on Jameson Irish Whiskey Heritage Centre and Irish Whiskey Corner.

Useful addresses: Irish Distillers, Irish Whiskey Corner, Smithfield, Dublin 7. Tel 01-872-5566. Jameson Irish Whiskey Heritage Centre, Midleton, Co. Cork. Tel 021-631821.

Irish Whiskey—Column and Pot-stilled (Blend)

There are a number of brands of distilled in-house Irish whiskey blends. The principal brands are: Original Bushmills, Black Bush, Jameson, Jameson Crested 10 and Jameson 1780, Tullamore Dew, Power's Gold Label and Paddy.

Special feature: The most popular brands today are made from a blend of traditional pot still and grain whiskey. Grain whiskey is whiskey produced from column stills, with some malted barley for fermentation purposes. It is the distilling that is considered the important art, rather than the blending, and all the Irish whiskies are distilled in house and never bought in. The general differences in the techniques used in producing Irish whiskey are shown under pure pot-stilled whiskey.

Composition: The main ingredients are barley, malt, grain, water and yeast. The alcohol content is 40% for Powers Gold Label and 43% for Bushmills Black Bush. It is 40% for Jameson and Tullamore Dew Finest Old Irish.

Powers is taken as an example for this group. It is a blend of pot still and grain whiskey, made up of 70% pot still and 30% grain. The pot-still portion is 60% unmalted barley and 40% malted. No single malt is used.

History: The early history of Irish whiskey is outlined in the section on pure pot-stilled whiskey. At the close of the eighteenth century there were in excess of 2,000 whiskey stills in the country, most of which were illegal, illustrating the popularity of whiskey-drinking among all sectors of Irish society. William Makepeace Thackeray during his travels about Ireland in 1842 interviewed a Corkman who drank 'from 18 to 20 glasses of whiskey a day'. He was by no means unique in his drinking habits and the upsurge in whiskey-drinking throughout the eighteenth and nineteenth centuries sprang not only from its intoxicating qualities but also from the belief that it was a wholesome and beneficial medicinal beverage.

Powers was founded by James Power in 1791 in Thomas Street, Dublin. When his son, John, became involved, the business moved to John's Lane. Output in 1823 was 33,000 gallons. The business continued to grow and there was huge expansion, including rebuilding in 1871. While other distillers sold their whiskey in casks, Powers bottled their own.

Jameson, established in 1780, is the most important export brand. For many years the company preferred to sell to merchants. The whiskey was sold in casks and individual companies sold Jameson under their own labels, and despite its huge sales it was not sold in bottled form by Jameson until the 1960s.

Bushmills is the world's oldest licensed distillery. It was formed into a limited company in 1880. Despite difficulties, it eventually prospered in the 1920s and 1930s and, following further ups and downs, was acquired by Irish Distillers in 1972. Bushmills Original and Black Bush are the best-known blends.

The Murphy brothers bought a disused mill building in Midleton in 1825 and set up a distillery called James Murphy & Co. Other Cork distillers and Murphys agreed to merge and the Cork Distillers Company was formed in 1867. As well as having the largest pot still in the world, it also had a Coffey still, which allowed for continuous distilling and blending of pot and grain whiskey. Paddy is the most important blend from the Cork Distillers Company.

The distillery at Tullamore was founded in 1829. Expansion took place under Daniel Williams, who developed Tullamore Dew as a pot-stilled whiskey. The distillery stopped producing in 1954. Irish Distillers acquired Tullamore Dew, their most famous brand, and today it is produced in Midleton, Co. Cork. The brand was sold to Cantrell & Cochrane in 1993.

The distilling industry flourished in the nineteenth century when several export markets were developed. However, a number of unrelated nineteenth- and twentieth-century events delivered a financial blow to the distilling industry. Throughout the 1840s and 1850s the growth of the total abstinence movement resulted in a considerable decrease in whiskey consumption. In addition, the increased preference for blended Scotch whisky on the international market brought further decline. The downward trend continued with the enforcement of prohibition in America in the 1920s and 1930s, and the situation was further exacerbated by the introduction of English trade embargoes after the establishment of the Irish Free State in 1922. Only the most resilient names and brands survived and in 1966 most of the remaining distilleries, Powers, John Jameson and Cork Distillers, merged to create the Irish Distillers Company, which consolidated the industry and established a co-ordinated marketing campaign for Irish whiskey abroad. The manufacture of these whiskies moved to Midleton.

The Coffey still at Midleton was replaced in 1962. A new all-purpose pot and column still was put in when Irish Distillers took over and this came onstream in 1975. The new pot stills are squatter with swan-like necks. The complex at Midleton was set up to produce Irish whiskies similar in character to those produced by Jameson in Bow Street and Powers in John's Lane, as well as Tullamore Dew and the whiskies already produced at Midleton.

Use: Used at festive and party occasions but widely drunk in ordinary everyday situations in public houses (see single malts).

Technique: The general procedures used in producing Irish whiskey are set out in the record for single malts. Both pot stills and continuous stills are used.

Bottling of Powers began in 1894, at which time it was pure pot still. Bottled Powers is called Gold Label or Three Swallows. Powers remained a pot-stilled whiskey until the 1950s, but after that a continuous still was installed to make grain spirit which was blended. Jameson pot grain still content is about 50/50. Crested 10 contains more pot still than grain and Jameson 1780 has about 75% pot still. It is matured for not less than twelve years. While Bushmills Original is now a blend, it is not known if this was always the case. Black Bush is now one of the best-known blends of Irish whiskey. Paddy was originally a pot-stilled whiskey. Today it is a blend of pot still and grain, with the pure malt and pot-still content combined higher than the grain content. Tullamore Dew started as pure pot-stilled whiskey, but is now more grain than pot-stilled.

Producer: Powers and Jameson are made by Irish Distillers at Midleton. Irish Distillers, with a turnover of IR£300 million and huge sales on domestic and international markets, are the main producers of whiskey in Ireland. They also make Bushmills in Co. Antrim. There is one other producer, Cooley Distillery, whose products have started to come on the market in recent years. They have negotiated a deal with Heaven Hill Distilleries of Bardstown, Kentucky, USA, for sale of a new version of some old brands such as Kilbeggan in the US.

Season: All year round.

Packaging: Bottled, sizes vary. The full bottle size is 1 litre. Half-bottles are also available. Bottle shapes and colour vary from white to green to dark brown.

Useful addresses: Irish Distillers, Bow Street Distillery, Smithfield, Dublin 7. Tel 01-872-5566. Jameson Irish Whiskey Heritage Centre, Midleton, Co. Cork. Tel 021-631-821.

Irish Whiskey—Single Malt

There are several brands of single malt Irish whiskey produced. The brands produced today are mainly from Bushmills, including Bushmills 5-Year-Old Single Malt, Bushmills 10-Year-Old Single Malt, Bushmills 14-Year-Old Single Malt and Bushmills 16-Year-Old Single Malt. Tyrconnell Single Malt is produced by Cooley Distillery. Rare Coleraine 34-Year-Old Single Malt is no longer produced, but a small amount is available.

Special feature: A single is a malt whiskey produced at one distillery and not mixed with either grain or pot-stilled whiskey.

The general differences in Irish whiskey production compared to other whiskeys are shown in the section on pure pot-stilled Irish whiskey.

Composition: Irish single malts are made from malted barley. The main ingredients are malt, water and yeast. Alcohol content is 40% volume for Bushmills 5-Year-Old Single Malt, Bushmills 10-Year-Old Single Malt and Tyrconnell Single Malt. It is 60.6% for Bushmills 14-Year-Old Single Malt and 58.4% for Bushmills 16-Year-Old Single Malt. Rare Coleraine is 57.1%.

History: The eighteenth century witnessed the establishment of the major Irish distilleries on a commercial basis. Although Bushmills is the oldest licensed distillery, Bushmills Old Distillery Company was not set up until 1784. In 1891 Bushmills launched a pure malt whiskey. In a successful phase in the 1920s and 1930s they bought the malt distillery at Coleraine. Due to a fire at the Bushmills offices during the Second World War all records were lost, but some believe that Bushmills Original was initially a single malt.

Bushmills 5-Year-Old Single Malt is a recent introduction. Bushmills 10-Year-Old Single Malt was introduced in the early 1980s. The current bottles of Bushmills 14-Year-Old Single Malt and Bushmills 16-Year-Old Single Malt were distilled in 1977.

Cooley acquired the Tyrconnell brand in the 1980s. Tyrconnell was a pure pot-stilled single malt whiskey and one of the main brands made at the Derry Distillery, which closed in 1925. Bottles of the new Tyrconnell, a vatting of three- and four-year-old single malts, are now on the market. Rare Coleraine 34-Year-Old Single Malt comes from some of the last malt whiskey produced in Coleraine. It was casked in 1959 and bottled in 1993.

Malt for most Irish whiskey is supplied today by the Malting Company of Ireland, Ballincollig, Co. Cork, recently purchased from Irish Distillers by the IAWS agribusiness group. They will continue to supply Irish Distillers and breweries in the Republic.

Use: Traditionally every house had a bottle of whiskey for the entertainment of guests. It was considered an indispensable item for the execution of proper hospitality. It was also particularly associated with weddings and wakes. Nowadays, it is used at festive and party occasions but it is more widely drunk every day in pubs. It is also used in baking and in more recent years it has become a popular ingredient in sauces for beef dishes.

Technique: Malt is barley which has been steeped in water to enable germination of the barley. This modifies the starches to sweeter-type carbohydrates. At an appropriate stage the barley is dried to prevent further germination. The malt is ground into grist, mash is made with water heated by steam and mixed with the grist in a metal vessel called a mash tun. Three washes are extracted, the starches are converted to fermentable sugars and the liquid is drained off for fermentation when yeast is added. The wash is triple distilled, evaporated and condensed in pot stills producing low wines. Liquid is boiled in a low wine still and mixed back into the low wine. It is pumped to a filling store where demineralised water is added. It is put into casks and stored.

Packaging: Bottled, sizes vary, but 700 ml is a standard size. Bottle shapes and colour vary.

Producers: Irish Distillers, a wholly owned subsidiary of Pernod-Ricard, are the producers of all the Bushmills brands. Tyrconnell Single Malt is produced by Cooley Distillery.

Season: All year round.

Useful addresses: Irish Distillers, Bow Street Distillery, Smithfield, Dublin 7. Tel 01-872-5566. Jameson Irish Whiskey Heritage Centre, Midleton, Co. Cork. Tel 021-631-821.

Irish Cream Liqueur

Special feature: A special homogenisation process ensures that the whiskey and cream do not separate. The process breaks the fat into tiny molecules which stay suspended in the liquid and bound to the other ingredients. The key to success is the chemical link between caseinates and alcohol to ensure their binding; the cream will not then separate from the liquid. Only products which conform to an official government standard may be called Irish cream liqueur.

Composition: There are a number of Irish cream liqueurs—the two main brands, Baileys and Carolans, are 17% alc/vol. Other brands include Emmett's and St Brendan's. Bottle sizes vary, but 35 cl and 70 or 79 cl are typical. The ingredients are cream, Irish whiskey, neutral spirit, water and stabilisers. Carolans also contains honey.

History: Although only developed about twenty-five years ago, Irish cream liqueurs are strongly associated with Ireland. Baileys was developed in the 1970s. Carolans, named after the seventeenth/eighteenth-century Irish harpist, Turlough Carolan, was developed in 1978. Both the main ingredients are traditional Irish products.

Use: Often given as a gift, Baileys and Carolans are used at the end of a celebratory meal. Irish cream liqueurs can be drunk on the rocks or straight, or they can be used as a substitute for cream in cocktails. They should be kept in storage (5–27°C) and their shelf life is about two years unopened and a year opened.

Technique: The following outlines the process for one manufacturer. For reasons of confidentiality only limited information is available. Combining spirits, double cream and honey, which give it a distinctive flavour, there are four stages in production:

(1) Neutral spirit and whiskey are blended in a vat.

(2) Cream, water and stabilisers are mixed together at high temperatures in large stainless steel tanks, with stabilisers ensuring the product does not curdle.

(3) The cream mixture is fed to a homogeniser and spirits, honey and flavours are added. Homogenisation ensures the cream does not separate and binds all the ingredients together.

(4) The mixture is then cooled and bottled.

Production: The total market for Irish cream liqueurs is about 5 million cases, each with twelve bottles. Baileys is produced by R. A. Bailey & Co. and distributed by Gilbeys. It is the world's fifteenth-largest spirit brand and dominates the cream liqueur sector internationally.

Carolans is produced by T. J. Carolan & Son Ltd, Clonmel, Co. Tipperary, and is marketed by Grants of Ireland. Carolans is the world's second most popular Irish cream liqueur and is marketed in over seventy countries. Emmett's is made by Baileys and St Brendan by Leckpatrick in Northern Ireland.

Packaging: Brown-coloured 700 ml bottle. Baileys' label is mainly green with a pasture scene. Carolans' is mainly cream with a country scene including a small house.

References: Kevin Abrook, Cantrell & Cochrane International Ltd, Dublin, personal communication.

Useful addresses: Gilbeys of Ireland, Gilbey House, Belgard Road, Dublin 24. Tel 01-459-7444. Cantrell & Cochrane International Ltd, Kylemore Park, Dublin 10. Tel 01-623-3133.

Irish Mist

Special feature: Unique Irish liqueur produced to a secret recipe. No other product has this combination of Irish whiskey, honey and herbs. Only three people share the knowledge of the exact combination of ingredients.

Composition: Gold-coloured Irish whiskey-based liqueur, 35% alc/vol. The ingredients are Irish whiskey, honey and herbs.

History: While whiskey has been produced in Ireland since at least 1405, by the seventeenth century the Irish had developed a taste for a more palatable whiskey liqueur flavoured with a variety of ingredients, which included raisins, dates, liquorice, aniseed and herbs. An Irish recipe for whiskey liqueur appeared in the 1602 publication *Delights for Ladies:* this recipe advised the addition of aniseed, molasses, liquorice, raisins and dates to a fine-quality whiskey and the ingredients were allowed to macerate in the spirit for a period of ten days. (Mahon)

In the early seventeenth century Fynes Moryson noted the Irish preference for liqueur. In *An Itinerary* he states:

And the usquebaugh [Irish whiskey] is preferred before our aquavitae because of the mingling of raisins, fennel-seed and other things, mitigating the heat and making the taste pleasant, makes it less inflame, and yet refresh the weak stomach.

In 1620, Luke Gernon also refers to the popularity of whiskey liqueur in Ireland (Myers, 1983). By the seventeenth century a rudimentary form of whiskey liqueur produced in a domestic setting enjoyed considerable popularity amongst more affluent sectors of Irish society. It is against this seventeenth-century background that the present-day product, Irish Mist, has its origins. Irish Mist is based on a recipe taken from a manuscript book belonging to an Irish aristocratic family who fled from Ireland to the Continent in 1691. The recipe in the manuscript is for 'Heather Wine', and its principal ingredients are Irish pot-still whiskey, herbs and heather honey. In the late nineteenth century, the general manager of Tullamore Distillery, Daniel E. Williams, was anxious to renew the tradition of a honey and herb Irish whiskey liqueur. However, it was not until the 1940s that a chance visit to the distillery by an Austrian produced the manuscript book containing the recipe for 'Irish Heather Wine'. The distillery developed the blend and relaunched this traditional beverage under the brand name Irish Mist. The present product was the first liqueur to be produced in Ireland, with its commercial production beginning in 1947 at Tullamore, Co. Offaly. Product ownership changed from the Williams family of Tullamore to the current owners, Cantrell and Cochrane International, in 1985.

Use: Direct, straight or over ice. As a drink with soda, tonic and ginger ale mixers. It can be used in desserts, as a cocktail, or as a special Irish coffee, with hot black coffee and cream.

Technique: Exact processes are secret.

Premium whiskies are matured in oak wood casks for a minimum of five years. Two different whiskies are mixed and left for two weeks and then blended with other whiskies which are allowed to rest for four weeks. The blend is then transferred to storage tanks and sealed. The next stage involves transfer to mixing tanks where herbs, honey, sugar and distilled water are added. Water and caramel are added until the blend has the right alcohol/volume percentage and colour. After a week the blend is transferred to resting tanks for at least four weeks. The product is then filtered and bottled.

Producer: Irish Mist is produced only by the Irish Mist Liqueur Co., Tullamore, Co. Offaly. Blending is in Tullamore and the product is bottled at Clonmel, Co. Tipperary. Distribution in Ireland is by Grants of Ireland and internationally by Cantrell & Cochrane International. The brand was first exported in 1950 and is available in over eighty countries today. The biggest markets are the US, Ireland, Canada and the UK. Worldwide sales are 75,000 cases, each with twelve bottles.

Packaging: Moulded glass bottle, inspired by traditional Irish cut glass crystal, in 500 ml and 250 ml bottles. The label has lots of Celtic emblems and is in the style of a brooch. It is also available in 375 and 700 ml size bottles.

References: K. Abrook, Cantrell & Cochrane International Ltd, Dublin, personal communication.

Useful address: Cantrell & Cochrane International Ltd, Kylemore Park, Dublin 10. Tel 01-623-3133.

Mead

Also Bunratty Mead

Special feature: A fermented honey-based drink of the aristocracy in medieval times. It was also drunk by the poor in earlier historical times in Ireland.

Composition: An alcoholic drink, 14.5% alc/vol, made from honey, very potent when mature. The liquid is clear, transparent and packed in bottles, and is composed of honey, water and aromatic plants (fruit of the vine and selected herbs).

History: A mead-like beverage was a popular drink among the Celts of mainland Europe. The classical writer Diodorus Siculus states that the Celts enjoyed a beverage made from the washings of honeycomb. It is possible that the techniques of mead production came to Ireland as part of the migration of Celtic culture during the Iron Age *c.* 300 BC.

The keeping of bees and the production of honey are major facets of monastic Christianity, which came to Ireland in the fifth century, and there is evidence from the seventh century that mead was a regular item in the diet of Irish monks. One life of Colum Cille, for example, states that 'very little mead sufficed him'. Mead-drinking among the monastic communities is also alluded to in one of the lives of St Brigid, where the saint offers the King of Leinster a cup of mead on his arrival at the monastery of Kildare.

The evidence suggests that mead drinking was predominantly associated with the aristocratic classes. The twelfth-century *Book of Leinster*, referring to the legendary King of Ulster, Conchobhur, states:

Sweet to you the fine mead,
that battle glorious Conchobhur drank.

In addition, mead features as an important item on a list of provisions burnt during Easter week in 1107 at the O'Briain palace in Ceann Coradh. As the preserve of the aristocracy, mead is considered as a luxury drink in the period, as is evident from its description as 'the dainty of the nobles' from the eleventh-century tale *Aislinge meic Conglinne*. Its elevated status is also clear from a number of descriptions of Irish places and regions: for example, the twelfth-century *Metrical Dindsenchas* cites Armagh as a region 'rich in mead'.

Plain mead in the form of the fermented mixture of honey and water is continuously referred to in the literary material of early Ireland. There is also mention of an interesting variant, 'hazel mead' from the fifteenth-century tale *Oidheadh Chlainne Lir — The Tragic Fate of the Children of Lir.*

Despite the large number of references to mead, Lucas maintains that its status and popularity were somewhat limited. In the later medieval period the production and consumption of mead declined greatly in Ireland. Increasing imports of cheap wines from England and Europe in the fifteenth and sixteenth centuries, together with the introduction of techniques of distillation from 1405 onwards, succeeded in displacing the beverage.

There is some evidence to suggest that mead production continued on a small scale until the early nineteenth century. The folklore record indicates that it was customary to toast the departure of the bride and groom at their wedding with a drink of mead.

The age-old tradition of mead production is maintained today by the Bunratty Mead and Liquor Company, which began commercial production of mead in 1979.

Use: In the past a drink for rich and poor as a dinner drink, nowadays it is mainly used at special meals or on special occasions. It may be drunk lightly chilled as an aperitif or at room temperature as a table wine. Mead may also be used in trifles and fruit salads.

Technique: O'Dwyer, quoting Dillon, states that Bunratty Mead is based on 'natural process methods as against the more commercial form where flavourings and certain chemicals are added'. Detailed information is not available for reasons of confidentiality.

Producer: Only one producer, the Bunratty Mead and Liqueur Company in Co. Clare, has been identified. The product is used at medieval banquets in the Limerick and Clare region, and is sold at off-licences, as specialist orders and at tourist and duty-free shops.

Packaging: It is packed in clear glass transparent bottles. The usual sizes are 1 litre, 75 cl and mini-glass bottles. It is also sold in large (70 cl), medium (55 cl) and mini-decanters. There is also a 50 cl honeymoon decanter.

Useful address: Oliver Dillon, Bunratty Mead and Liqueur Company, Bunratty Winery, Bunratty, Co. Clare. Tel 061-362-222.

Gin

Also Cork Dry Gin

Special features: A local gin produced from triple distilled grain spirit. This gives it a distinctive flavour different to other gins.

Composition: An alcoholic drink made from grain spirit. A selection of berries is used for flavouring. Alcohol is 38% volume. The ingredients are grain spirit, a blend of berries, fruit and flavourings.

History: Gin has its origins on the Continent and the gin used today appears to have been first made by a professor at Leyden in the Netherlands. Cork Dry Gin is a well-known local product in Ireland and has a long association with Cork. It is particularly associated with the Cork Distillers (CDC) of the Watercourse. The distillery was founded in 1793 and the grain spirit from it was found to be particularly suitable for gin. The first bottling took place in 1943.

Use: Gin is rarely drunk neat. It is often accompanied by vermouth, tonic water or lime. It is the basis of the original iced and shaken cocktail, and is an essential ingredient in a dry Martini cocktail.

Technique: Some of the following practices may not be used for Cork Dry Gin, as exact processes used by CDG are not available. Cork Dry Gin is made from triple distilled grain spirit. On the base of this is lain a complex blend of juniper, citrus fruit and botanical flavours. The first part of the process is rectifying the pure spirit. The spirit contains im-purities which must be removed to produce a neutral spirit. Impurities known as 'feints' come over at the start of the rectification and only the best in the centre is used for gin. The second stage involves making the gin flavour. The clean spirit is reduced with water and into this still the ingredients used in the flavouring are steeped in the spirit. The exact selection of herbs and botanical species is a trade secret. As much flavour must be extracted, the mixture is left overnight before distillation the next day. The third stage, compounding, blending and redistillation, is to ensure that the gin is free from impurities and very smooth to the taste. The gin is then reduced with distilled water to the strength required and is ready for bottling and use. Gin does not need to be matured as all impurities have been taken out. The spirit does not benefit from ageing and can lose flavour over time.

Producer: Cork Dry Gin is produced only by the Irish Distillers group, now part of Pernod-Ricard. It is the market leader in Ireland in a market which demands over 100,000 cases annually.

Season: It is produced and consumed throughout the year.

Packaging: Bottled in white transparent square glass bottles with red labels and cap. The 700 ml bottle is the standard size.

Reference: Camillus Dwane, personal communication.

Useful address: Irish Distillers, Bow Street Distillery, Smithfield, Dublin 7. Tel 01-872-5566.

Smithwicks Ale

Also Two products are included in this section: Smithwicks No. 1 Ale and Smithwicks Draught

Special feature: Unique ale brew, made in Kilkenny for over two hundred years. The product has been modified and the production method modernised, but the basic brewing process is the same.

Composition: Ale, brown colour, 4% alc/vol. Smithwicks No. 1 Ale is the direct descendant of the original ale. Smithwicks Draught is a dark Scottish-type ale which was introduced in recent years and is now the main product. It is made from barley, water, hops and yeast.

History: From the early medieval period ale is established as one of the most popular beverages in society. The corpus of ninth-century penitential literature indicates that ale was brewed in many of the Irish monasteries. These sources state that ale was a permitted beverage for the penitential Culdee monks, who were committed to a rigid dietary regime. Ale is also mentioned in the eleventh-century text, *Aislinge meic Conglinne*:

> *son of mead, son of wine, son of flesh, son of ale.*

The continued popularity of ale, as opposed to beer, is also clear from Fynes Moryson's observations of Ireland in the early modern period. Writing in the early 1600s he found that the

> *ordinary food of the common sort is of white meats . . . and they drink not English beer made of malt and hops, but ale.*

Similarly, John Dunton, writing in his *Letters from Ireland* (1698), notes the prevalence of ale-drinking in Ireland:

> *Dinner came in, we had salt fish and eggs, . . . the woman of the house or her maid brought a quart of ale to us she poured some into the glass and drank it off.*

The original Smithwick family came from England. Most of the family were wiped out in the 1641 insurrection, with the exception of one young boy. It was one of his descendants, John Smithwick, who moved to Kilkenny in 1710. Richard Cole and John Smithwick leased property in 1710 on the site of the fourteenth-century St Francis Abbey in Kilkenny and started a brewing business. It is the oldest operating brewery in Ireland and remained a small brewery for about a hundred years. Brewing, it is thought, had been carried out since the fourteenth century in the Franciscan abbey—probably a light ale.

Pigots Trade Directory of 1824 makes a specific reference to a distiller located at St Francis Abbey, Kilkenny. In 1827 the property was purchased as a brewery and distillery by Edmund Smithwick (1800–76). It was during the life of Edmund that the brewery began to grow and become an important commercial business. A flourishing export business was built up in the early part of the nineteenth century. In the 1851–73 period several different varieties of ale, porter and beer were brewed, including Extra Stout, Porter, XX Ale, X Ale, Pale Butt,

Beer and India Pale Ale.

The brewery became a private company in 1898. Sullivans, another brewery in Kilkenny, was taken over in 1919. Between 1900 and 1944 business suffered as exports were blocked by the tied house system in Britain. Business was concentrated on the local market around Kilkenny, until national distribution of the No. 1 ale began about 1944 with a switch from rail transport to a lorry fleet. By the mid-1950s Smithwicks had become a national drink, and the old Great Northern Brewery in Dundalk was purchased in 1953. Shares were offered to the public in 1956 and the new company, Smithwicks Brewery (Holdings) Ltd, was formed to control brewing at both Kilkenny and Dundalk. Guinness underwrote the issue and in 1964 took a controlling interest.

The Kilkenny plant was modernised in 1958, the demise of the wooden cask became complete, and chilled and filtered beer was introduced. In 1960 the Dundalk plant was leased and eventually sold to Guinness to brew lager. As drinking tastes changed, the demand for a darker sweeter product became apparent and a new type of chilled and filtered beer, Smithwicks Draught, was launched in 1966. This product is the main Smithwicks ale sold today. The original Smithwicks No. 1 ale is still brewed and bottled at Dundalk but is now a minority product.

Use: Found in most pubs in Ireland, Smithwicks is widely drunk in pubs and at many types of social occasions.

Technique: The ale has been brewed and matured by traditional methods since 1710. The current plant has been modernised, but there has been little change in the brewing methods used This modernisation, associated with expansion, took place between 1964 and 1985 and involved the brewhouse, fermentation plant, maturation vessels, filtration, and the keg and bottling plant. Malting barley is left for at least a month after harvesting. Malt is produced by successive steepings of the barley for two days, to enable enzyme activity to germinate it. The germinating barley starts to sprout and is turned at intervals over a four-day period to prevent the roots from matting. The sprouting barley is dried in a kiln to give the product called malt, which is then milled to a coarse flour, known as grist, and stored in a grist case. It is then passed on to a container called a mash tun. Liquor, i.e. brewing water at a particular temperature, is added to the grist in the mash tun and the starches are converted by natural enzymes into sugars. The mash is filtered through lauter plates which retain the solid and drain off the pure liquid, which is called sweet wort. The wort is boiled in a copper, a very large kettle, for one and a half hours. The hops, which make the wort bitter, are added at this stage. This gives the beer its distinctive flavour. The hopped wort is strained, cooled and pumped into the fermentation vessel. Yeast is added and the fermentation is allowed to continue for four days. As the yeast grows, it converts the barley sugars into alcohol and carbon dioxide. The beer is stored for three weeks, then chilled, filtered and pasteurised and stored again in a beer tank. Finally it is kegged and bottled. The beer is distributed throughout the country by the company's fleet of trucks.

Producer: Produced by E. Smithwick & Sons Ltd, Kilkenny. The company is owned by Guinness and Smithwicks has large volume sales in Ireland. The brewery produces about 8,000 kegs every day and a further half a million bottles are shipped from its Dundalk and Belfast bottling plants for both home and export markets. Smithwicks is the largest-selling ale in Ireland. Export markets include Canada, France, the UK and the Isle of Man.

Season: Smithwicks is produced and drunk throughout the year.

Packaging: Draught and bottles and cans of various sizes. A typical can is 500 ml.

References: Jim Cradock, private communication.

Useful address: E. Smithwick & Sons Ltd, St Francis Abbey Brewery, Kilkenny. Tel 056-21014.

Guinness Stout

Also Two types: Foreign Extra Stout and Irish Draught Stout

Composition: World-renowned Irish drink. Stout, black drink with white head, 4.3% vol. Distinctive malt flavour and bitter taste of hops. Made from malted barley, roast barley, water, hops and yeast. A small amount of yeast is collected from each brew for use in successive brews, so 'today's yeast is a direct descendant of that used by Arthur Guinness'. A percentage of the grist used in making Guinness consists of roasted barley. This gives Guinness its characteristic colour content.

History: Brewed by Arthur Guinness at St James' Gate brewery since the late eighteenth century. A Guinness booklet states:

> *In December 1759 Arthur Guinness rode through the front gates of an old . . . brewery in Dublin's James's Street. He had just signed a lease on the property for 9000 years at a rent of £45 per annum.*

He started brewing ale but soon looked at a drink called Entire, as it was served from a single barrel, a black beer then being imported from London. It was dark due to the addition of roasted barley. Guinness tried to produce it and was so successful that, in 1799, at the age of 74, he decided to stop brewing ale and concentrate on porter. His business grew from strength to strength and today Guinness is the most famous stout in the world. An Enniskillen dragoon at

Waterloo in 1815 said:

I felt the extraordinary desire for a glass of Guinness . . . I am confident that it contributed more than anything else to my recovery.

Robert Louis Stevenson wrote in 1893 in Samoa:

You will see from this heading that I am not dead yet . . . I shall put myself outside a pint of Guinness.

The first export was in 1769, and Guinness became a public company in 1886. A new brewhouse was soon built, as well as a cooperage, a racking shed, an internal railway system and new vathouses. The company's barges brought the porter from the brewery to the port and exports were so huge that the company bought its own ships. For many years the *Lady Patricia* and *Miranda Guinness* carried the Guinness to Liverpool for further shipment. Guinness is now brewed in a number of breweries overseas, either in Guinness-owned breweries or under licence, and over 10 million glasses are produced daily.

Use: Guinness is widely drunk in pubs throughout Ireland, but is also often drunk to complement a meal. It is used in porter cake, casseroles and plum puddings.

Technique: Barley is converted to malt by germination. More barley is steam cooked and rolled to give flakes. Some barley and malt are roasted and this gives Guinness its deep dark colour. The malt, roast and flakes make up the grist and the grist is mixed with hot water, mashed and then run into a kieve where the barley starches are turned into sugar. This dark sweet liquid is called wort. Hops are added to the sweet wort and boiled in the kettle, which gives Guinness its characteristic flavour. Special Guinness yeast is then added to the wort, a process called pitching, and the mixture passes on to the fermenting vessel. Fermenting converts some of the sugars to alcohol and CO_2 and helps forms the Guinness head. The yeast species most suited is *Saccharomyces Cereosial*, or brewer's yeast. Fermentation proceeds for about two days. In the skimmer and centrifuge surplus yeast is removed and the liquid has now become stout. Stout is stored, conditioned and blended in huge vats. Tankers, kegs and bottles are filled for delivery to bars all over Ireland and exported to many countries.

Producer: Brewed at St James Gate Brewery by Arthur Guinness in Dublin. Some 90,000 tonnes of barley are used each year in its production. Production is about 2.3 million litres (4 million pints) per day, and the sales volume in Ireland is large. It is also produced at other Guinness breweries throughout the world.

Season: Produced and consumed throughout the year.

Packaging: Draught from kegs, cans and bottles. Bottles can be 250 ml and can sizes include 330 ml and 500 ml.

Reference: Arthur Guinness & Sons Ltd, Dublin 1991. Guinness Hop Store Brewery Museum leaflet and booklet.

Useful address: Hop Store Museum, Arthur Guinness & Sons Ltd, St James Gate, Dublin 8. Tel 01-453-6700.

Beamish Stout

Special feature: A distinctive-tasting stout produced in Cork for two hundred years.

Composition: Black stout drink with head, 4.3% volume. Bitter taste, but sweeter than other stouts. The raw materials are water, malted barley, hops, roast barley, syrup, wheat and maize.

History: Brewed by Beamish & Crawford in Cork since 1792. Two local merchants, William Beamish & William Crawford, formed a partnership with two ale brewers and started to brew porter at Cramer's Lane, where brewing had been carried out by the Allen family since at least 1715 and probably earlier. In the first half of the nineteenth century it was probably the largest brewery in Ireland. There were a number of acquisitions of other local breweries in the early part of this century, and in 1963 new fermentation and beer storage facilities were built. In 1971 ten new fermenting tanks of 450-barrel capacity were installed. The brewhouse has a capacity of 1,400 barrels every 24 hours. A new kegging line was installed in 1979 and extended to eight lanes in 1986. Canadian breweries in Toronto took over the brewery in 1962. They were in turn taken over by Elders IXL, now Fosters of Australia, in 1987. Fosters sold Beamish to Scottish and Newcastle in May 1995.

Use: Beamish stout is drunk mostly in pubs, and is served lightly chilled.

Technique: Ballincollig malt (malt barley), roast barley and imported malted wheat are used. Continental hops are used to give a bitter taste and syrup is also used. Up to 1960 brewing was done with mash tuns and copper kettles over sixty years old. Modern facilities were installed to brew stout and other products between 1962 and 1972, when open square fermenters were replaced by enclosed cylindrical flat-bottomed tanks.

The various brewing stages are mashing, lautering, kettle/boiling, whirlpool separation, cooling and fermentation. The purpose of mashing is to render soluble as much of the malt as possible. The mixture is heated and held at a selected temperature for a period. The resulting product is called the sweet mash or 'wort' and contains maltose, other sugars, carbohydrates, proteins and other flavour-bearing compounds. The contents are transferred to the 'Lauter Tun' or separation vessel. The perforated bottom acts like a sieve and the liquid wort is drawn through. The wort solution is then boiled for an hour, during which the hops are added. The boiled wort is pumped to the whirlpool, which acts as a crude separator. It leaves the whirlpool at 95°C and is cooled to 10°C before yeast and oxygen are added for fermentation. Before 1981 fermentation was in the open air, but the process has now been modernised. Fermentation lasts 1–2 weeks. It is cooled after fermentation (the green beer is cooled to 0°C) and centrifuged so that the yeast is removed. It then remains in the maturation tanks from two days to three weeks at 0–1°C. The final stages include filtration, carbonation, storage and packaging. Producing Beamish takes about two weeks from brewing to packaging.

Producer: Produced by Beamish & Crawford (owned by Scottish and Newcastle) in Cork. Stout accounts for 60% of output. There are large volume sales in Ireland and the UK. It is also sold in about thirteen other countries.

Packaging: Draught is packed in kegs, and Beamish is also put in cans and bottles. Cans can be 500 ml.

References: Beamish & Crawford, Cork, private communication and company leaflets.

Useful address: Beamish & Crawford, South Main Street, Cork. Tel 021-276-841.

Murphy's Stout

Special feature: Traditional Irish stout brewed in Cork with a distinct flavour.

Composition: Stout is a black drink with a creamy head, 4.0% volume. Its ingredients are malted barley, hops, yeast and water.

History: James J. Murphy and Co. Ltd was founded by the Murphy family in Cork in 1856 at Lady's Well. Initially porter was brewed but over a century ago they switched to stout. As business developed, Murphy's began to export. In the late nineteenth and the early twentieth centuries, Murphys stout was enjoyed by the O'Briens of Lough Gur, as is evident in the following passage from Mary Carbery's *The Farm by Lough Gur*:

> *In a moment, glasses, cups, mugs were whipped from pockets where they had been concealed, and enthusiastic cheering encouraged Tom as he broached the casks of Murphy's stout.*

Since 1975 Murphys have had a licensing agreement to brew Heineken. In 1983 Heineken International purchased the brewery, which was in the hands of a receiver. A major investment programme was undertaken and a new brewery was built on the site. Modern technology was introduced, Murphy's Irish Stout was relaunched and is now sold on both the home and export markets.

Use: At any social occasion. It is best served chilled, and main sales are in public houses and at off-licences.

Technique: The barley is malted, allowing the enzymes which convert starch to sugar to be activated. Pale malt and roasted barley are cleaned, weighed, milled and mixed with hot water in a mash tun, a large mixing vat. The mixture is stirred and the sugars extracted. The liquor is transferred to a copper or boiling vessel and hops are added to give the wort taste and aroma. The brew is transferred to a whirlpool for rotation at high speed. This results in the hop residues in the brew settling in the middle, from where they are drained away. The wort is cooled and transferred to the fermentation tanks, where yeast is added. Fermentation occurs and the sugars turn to alcohol and carbon dioxide. When fermentation is complete, the stout matures and the remaining yeast cells are removed by centrifugation or filtration. Gas levels are adjusted and the product is filled into kegs. All these operations are today managed from a control point by brewers.

Producer: Produced by Murphys of Lady's Well Brewery in Cork. Over 20,000 kegs were sold in 1993. There are large volume sales in Ireland in pubs and retail outlets, particularly in Munster and Cork, and major exports to the UK. It is sold in about forty countries and other major markets include Germany, France, Italy and Spain.

Season: It is brewed and consumed throughout the year.

Packaging: Draught and in cans, such as 330 ml, and bottles. Red and yellow are the main colours on the label, which states 'Extra Quality Murphy's Irish Stout, Lady's Well Brewery, Cork, Ireland'.

Useful address: Murphy's Lady's Well Brewery, Cork. Tel 021-503-371.

Cider

Also Original Vintage Cider

Special feature: Cider is a typical apple-based alcoholic drink with a long tradition in Ireland. Fermentation in oak vats influences the flavour.

Composition: Cider is a light brown colour and carbonated. Bulmer's Original Vintage Cider is 4.5% alc. Cider is fermented apple juice.

History: One school of thought suggests that cider was produced in early medieval Ireland. A number of sources mention a drink called nenadmin, a fermented apple drink made from wild or crab apples. However, it seems more likely that large-scale cider-making in Ireland was influenced by the influx of English settlers in the late sixteenth and early seventeenth centuries. The historical record highlights a clear association between orchards and cider-making with areas of strong English settlement; especially in Antrim, Armagh, Clare, Cork, Down, Limerick, Waterford and Wexford. Luke Gernon, writing in the early 1600s, states that gardens and orchards were attached to many of the large houses in Limerick and Kilkenny:

delightful orchards and gardens, which are somewhat rare in Ireland. (Myers, 1983)

A more specific example of the establishment of orchards for cider-making in the seventeenth century is seen in the activities of George Rawdon, who owned lands around Moira in Co. Down. Nelson refers to a letter, sent to Lord Conway in 1664, where he speaks of his intention to start

an orchard under the new house, and I hope to have it furnished this winter with trees . . . the objection of the orchard is chiefly to make cyder.

By the eighteenth century it seems that cider-drinking was commonplace amongst the general populace. A parliamentary report in 1730 observed its increased consumption:

of late years, more drunk than ever, especially in the southern parts.

Similarly, Arthur Young, writing in his *Tour in Ireland 1776–1779*, comments on the abundance of fine orchards amongst the gentry. Of Drumoland in Co. Clare he notes:

this country is famous for cyder orchards, the cakage especially which is incomparably fine. An acre of trees yields from four to ten hogsheads per annum, average six, and what is very uncommon in the cider countries of England, yield a crop every year.

In the nineteenth century, William Makepeace Thackeray also indicates the prevalence of cider in Irish society. In his 1843 *Irish Sketch Book*, he gives the following account of a meal in Waterford City:

The dinner is plentiful and nasty—raw ducks, raw peas, on a crumpled tablecloth, over which a waiter has just spirited a pint of obstreperous cider.

In 1935, a cider-making business was

set up in Clonmel by William Magner. In 1937 he joined with H. P. Bulmer and they established Bulmer-Magner Ltd. After a number of changes of ownership, the firm is today controlled by the Cantrell & Cochrane group.

Use: Cider is best served chilled or with ice. Most sales are in public houses, although it can also be used in cooking. It is stored under dark cool conditions.

Technique: At Clonmel some 28 varieties of apples are used. After passing through a water bath, they are crushed in the pressing plant. A mechanical worm takes the apples to a rotary mill which grinds them to pulp. Some slicing is used to help juice extraction. A number of layers of this pulp form a 'cheese', which is encased in nylon sheets and subject to a series of pressings by a mechanical presser which extracts all the juice. Building a cheese is a traditional craft and one of the core skills of cider-making. After filtering, the blended juices are fermented in a vat house. Apple varieties used include Tardive Forrester, Brown Snouth, Bulmer's Norman, Medaille d'Or and Yarlington Mill.

Nowadays the manufacturing process is modernised, but the transformation from juice to cider is still a natural process, involving slow fermentation for about eight weeks at a temperature of 18–24°C in huge oak vats. The vat house in Clonmel holds a total of 1.5 million gallons of fermented cider. Juice is fermented for three weeks and is then 'racked' or drawn off from the residue into another vat. After further filtering and chilling, the cider is carbonated and packaged.

Traditional techniques are also used by M. J. Gleeson in the production of Anvil cider.

Producers: Apples are supplied from 250 acres owned by Showerings and from about 400 local producers. Cider is produced by Showerings (Ireland) Ltd, Clonmel, who are part of the Cantrell & Cochrane group. It is also produced under the Anvil label by the Gleeson Group in Tipperary. Cider is available in many shops and pubs, and the market was valued at IR£68 million in 1994.

Season: Cider is produced and consumed throughout the year.

Packaging: In cans and glass and plastic bottles of different sizes such as 500 ml cans or 250 ml brown bottles and long-neck glass bottles. One-litre glass packs and 2 litre PET packs are also available. Cans are brown with a yellow and green logo. Draught cider is also available.

Reference: John Keogh, Bulmers, private communication.

Useful addresses: Bulmers, Showerings Ltd, Annerville, Clonmel, Co. Tipperary. Tel 052-25222. Cider Industry Council, 27 Sydney Parade Avenue, Ballsbridge, Dublin 4. Tel 01-283-0088.

Red Lemonade

Also various brands, e.g. T.K. Red Lemonade, Deasy's Red Lemonade and Cadet Red Lemonade.

Special feature: The addition of colouring to white lemonade to give red lemonade, a drink that was produced only in Ireland for many years.

Composition: Red lemonade is a carbonated water drink with red colouring. Its ingredients are carbonated water, sugar, citric acid, flavourings, artificial sweeteners (aspartame, saccharin), preservative (sodium benzoate) and colours (chocolate brown HT, quinoline yellow).

History: Although it is not known for certain, it is believed that red lemonade has been available in Ireland since the end of the last century. Almost every local town had a red lemonade manufacturer. These included Stafford's in Wexford, Deasy's in Clonakilty (Cork), Nash's in Newcastle West (Limerick) and Williams in Tullamore (Offaly). Red lemonade is more a tradition in the south of Ireland than in the north. Nash's was set up in 1875 by Richard and Joanna Nash. They started with soda water and ginger ale but, after experimenting with different techniques and flavours, came up with Nash's Red Lemonade before the turn of the century. This is an original formula which remains a family secret. Farm workers regularly had a bottle for their lunch. A lady born in the area in the 1930s recalls:

I have fond memories of Nash's and their red lemonade . . . I remember when the hay and corn were saved, the extra men had been sent to help from Nash's, also the jars of porter and the red lemonade . . . fair day in Ardagh was another great occasion for lemonade.

Savage Smyth, one of the larger producers for many years in Dublin, developed red lemonade as a national product under the Cadet label, which was introduced in the 1970s. The company is now owned by United Beverages. At one time in the 1940s red lemonade was the only lemonade available in some parts of southern Ireland, as white lemonade was not always produced. Deasy's, who have been producing white lemonade since the start of the century, only began to produce red lemonade during the early 1940s.

One of the best-known red lemonades was produced by Taylor Keith of Dublin. The company was bought some years ago by Cantrell & Cochrane and Pepsi Cola and they continue to sell red lemonade under the T.K. label.

Use: Drunk at home, at social events and in pubs, both as a mineral and a mixer. Particularly popular with children. In some areas, such as Cork, there is a large demand in the city, but little in the countryside.

Technique: At Nash's the original bottling was a kitchen table operation but in 1905 a separate factory was built and steam power introduced. Electricity was introduced in the 1920s. Today the plant is fully automated.

Red lemonade is produced in a similar way to other lemonades. Sugar and water are the base of the recipe, forming a sugar syrup. At one plant they are added to a tank manually but agitated automatically, and it takes about 2.5–3 hours to prepare a batch of syrup to the right consistency. Flavourings and citric acid are also used. In the past the red colour was achieved with the use of artificial colourings, but natural-based vegetable extracts are used today, such as beta carotene. The lemonade is carbonated and packed in plastic or glass bottles.

Producers: T.K. is produced in Dublin and Cork. Cadet from United Beverages is the other main brand. Nash's is particularly important in some counties such as Limerick and Kerry but is also sold throughout Ireland and more recently in the UK. Red lemonade is also produced by Deasy's in Cork and other mineral water producers in Ireland. Total sales account for an important slice of the soft drinks market.

Season: The product is made all year. Demand is highest in summer and at Christmas, but is steady throughout the year.

Packaging: Plastic bottles are usual for many producers today. The large T.K. size is 2 litres. It is transparent with a green and red label. Other sizes are 250 ml and 1.5 litres. Cadet sizes include 250 ml, 1.5 litres, 2 litres and 3 litres. They are generally plastic. They also have a 750 ml returnable glass bottle for pubs. Deasy's have a range of glass and PET bottles. Nash's use mostly glass bottles but also produce a 1.5 litre plastic bottle.

References: Susanne O'Reilly, Nash's Mineral Waters, personal communication. Michael O'Donovan, Deasy and Co., personal communication. Philip Smyth, United Beverages, personal communication.

Useful addresses: Cantrell & Cochrane (C&C), PO Box 2020, Dublin 10. Tel 01-626-6611. Nash's Mineral Waters, Newcastle West, Co. Limerick. Tel 069-62022. United Beverages, Finches Industrial Park, Longmile Road, Dublin 12. Tel 01-450-2000.

Bewleys Tea

Tea — the cup that cheers

Special feature: Bewleys were the first tea blenders in Ireland. They originally sold China tea but also offer a range of speciality teas.

Composition: Tea leaves. The teas used in Ireland are black tea, as distinct from green tea. Loose tea is generally large-leafed tea as against the small-leafed tea for tea bags. Loose tea generally contains more orthodox tea (rolled leaf) than CTC tea (curl, tears and cut). Tea bags generally contain more CTC. The size of leaf is no indication of quality; small-leaf tea is just as good as large-leaf tea.

History: Tea was first introduced into Ireland in the mid-seventeenth century. During this initial period, availability and consumption were confined to the wealthier sectors of Dublin society. This period is also distinguished by the establishment of a number of 'Coffee Houses' in the larger regional urban centres of Cork, Limerick, Galway, Kilkenny, Wexford and Clonmel, and it is likely that the expensive beverage was first encountered by the fashionable clientele who frequented these establishments.

It is certain that tea had very quickly grown in popularity by the early eighteenth century, for by September 1719 a duty of 12d was imposed on every pound of tea imported from England. The new beverage was known as 'China Drink' or 'China Ale'. As the eighteenth century progressed, tea increasingly became known to rural society. An English lady visitor to Co. Mayo in 1732 took shelter

in the thatched cabin of a man . . . who, nevertheless was refined enough to be able to refresh his unexpected guests with tea. (Lysaght)

In addition, tea features frequently in the list of provisions purchased by the prosperous Carew family of Castleboro estate in Co. Wexford in the 1760s: for example, on 2 May 1769 a pound of breakfast green tea was purchased for 6s 6d. The first half of the nineteenth century witnessed the additional adoption of tea-drinking among farmers and labourers. For example, records for 1819 show that tea-drinking was popular among the farmers of Holywood, Co. Down, while the success of the weaving industry in the north of the country provided labourers with enough cash to purchase small quantities of the beverage. However, tea-drinking was still predominantly for the social elite. The *Parish Reports* of the Commissioners for Enquiry in to the Conditions of the Poorer Classes in Ireland in the 1830s declare that tea-drinking was still a luxury for the labouring classes and an item enjoyed only on the festive occasions of Christmas and Easter. Indeed, tea-drinking at this time was viewed with suspicion; its consumption was considered to promote idleness and it was viewed as an indulgence akin to alcohol consumption.

Bewleys started in the China tea business as wholesale suppliers and they are regarded as an integral part of Dublin city's character. The following section is drawn from *The Legendary Lofty Clattery Café: Bewley's of Dublin*. The family first came to Ireland in 1700 and it was in 1835 that Charles Bewley imported:

2099 chests of tea on the Hellas, *said to be the first ship ever freighted directly from Canton to Dublin. With the breaking of the monopoly of the East India Company in 1833 tea could be imported directly. At that time tea consumption was very low.*

Tea was a key product of Bewleys for many years. Joshua Bewley set up a tea business in the 1840s and tea was very expensive, due to duties. He worked from Sycamore Alley, where he based his China tea company. Teas had various grades with exotic names such as gunpowder, caper, bohea, conjpou, singlo and twankay. The tea-drinking habit spread rapidly after the Famine. A combination of direct deliveries from merchant houses like Bewleys and a system of travelling salesmen spread the new drink. In the 1870s Joshua moved to South Great George's Street in Dublin. In the coming years the Bewley business deteriorated as it specialised in China tea and other companies were marketing branded Indian teas. Bewleys

thus concentrated on the shop side of the business rather than wholesaling. In 1894 Ernest Bewley opened their first Oriental Café in George's Street and another in Westmoreland Street two years later. Tea, coffee and various rolls, buns and cakes were on the menu. By the 1930s tea was still important but it had been overtaken by coffee. In the 1980s the company had trading difficulties and was taken over by Campbell Catering in November 1986. A new subsidiary, Bewley's Tea and Coffee Ltd, was set up in 1988, and this runs the catering and wholesale division. Packaging was revamped and a range of teas was marketed in department stores and speciality shops in Europe and North America. More recently Bewleys commenced distribution of a range of teas at multiple and other retail outlets throughout Ireland.

Use: Water is freshly boiled. The teapot is scalded. The tea bags or leaves are added to the pot and the boiling water is added immediately. The tea is allowed to brew for a few minutes. Before pouring, the tea is stirred in the pot. Tea is a popular drink at all meals and between meals. In fact the Irish are among the highest per capita tea drinkers in the world. Bewleys tea will keep for a few months but after that it will lack freshness.

Technique: Details are shown under Lyons tea and Barry's tea. In the 1930s Bewleys teas were specially blended from several teas, bought from Travers & Co. of London.

Producer: Bewleys are of importance as the first blenders in Ireland and today they are expanding their tea operation.

Season: Tea is popular throughout the year with highest consumption in winter.

Packaging: In the past most tea was packed loosely in light cardboard boxes but today it is mostly packed in muslin-type tea bags, either single serve or multi-cup, with about 80 to a standard box (250 g). The tin of Bewleys Irish Breakfast tea states that Bewleys have been tea blenders since the 1840s and has a picture of the original Bewleys Oriental Café.

Useful address: Bewleys Tea Ltd, Greenhills Industrial Estate, Walkinstown, Dublin 12. Tel 01-450-0643.

Lyons Tea

Special features: Tea as a drink has a unique place and is the most typical non-alcoholic drink in Ireland. Lyons Green Label tea is a household name.

Composition: Tea leaves (see Bewleys).

History: The early history of tea is described in the section on Bewleys tea. Cullen points out that there was an explosive increase in tea-drinking in the quarter century after 1850, when 'the rural community everywhere were engulfed with addiction'. Increased commercialism was manifest with the establishment of grocer shops in most rural towns and villages. These grocers were willing to exchange sugar and tea for farm-produced butter and eggs—indeed insisted on it. The period also saw the advent of tea dealers or 'the tay man'—traders who travelled from house to house selling tea. In rural Ireland tea-drinking was strongly associated with the availability of white baker's bread. The folklore record reveals the ignorance of the rural peasantry in preparing the beverage: sometimes the tea was boiled in water and then the water discarded, while the leaves were mixed with butter and served as a food. In the early twentieth century, bread and tea became the staple fare of the impoverished urban classes. In Paddy Crosby's reminiscences of Dublin life, he recounts that between 1914 and 1918 'bread and tea was the menu for *all* meals' and the popular cant from mothers around the streets of Dublin at this time rang:

Johnny, come in here this minit, your din-ner's poured out!

The consumption of tea is inextrica-bly linked with social occasions and is the chief expression of hospitality, which is rarely refused. Tea often accompanies all meals and is taken on nearly all oc-casions of rest and social interaction.

J. Lyons and Co. Ireland started blend-ing in Ireland in 1902. Before that the teas were blended in England and sent over. Lyons started in High Street, Dub-lin, but later moved to Inchicore. Only Indian teas were used for many years. Because stocks had been built up it was possible to maintain Indian tea supplies even during the war. In the 1950s more Sri Lankan tea was used, as well as some African teas. Lyons Green Label tea has changed little from 1902. It is a blend of Assam, Sri Lankan and Keynan teas.

Use: See Bewleys.

Technique: At Lyons a tea taster and blender decides which types and amounts of each type go into each tea. Before blending started the retail out-lets and customers did their own blend-ing. Agents brought tea to the retail out-lets in chests and a number of opened chests were put on display. The look of the leaf was consistent and was a key factor in deciding which teas to choose, so tastings were not undertaken. In the early part of this century floor blending was used. The teas were spilt out on a floor and were blended by repeated shovelling. Blending drums were in-stalled and Lyons have been using the same two blending drums for sixty years. Each drum holds about 1,500 kg. The tea is fed into the drums manually.

The company staff visit the produc-tion regions and decide which teas are to be packed in chests for transport to Ireland. After arrival the tea is tipped from the chests manually through a sieve on to a closed conveyor and car-ried up from the ground floor to the first floor into the drum. The blender needs seven turns to ensure a proper blend-ing. The whole process from opening a chest to blending takes about 25 min-utes. The blended tea goes from the blender into silo cars which are placed over a packing machine. Modern highly technical equipment is used to put the tea into tea bags. The equipment used by Lyons can fill 2,000 bags a minute.

Tea tasting is the most important skill. The taster decides which teas make up each blend. It takes 10–11 years to fully train as a taster. The more experienced a taster is, the better he or she can dis-cern the qualities of any tea. Blending is necessary for price, flavour, consistent quality and other factors such as strength and body. A blender will do a few hundred tastings every day. The matching of leaf and liquor (liquid) is the key skill of the blender. Tasting is necessary, as quality varies with sources and climate. Two people do all the blending and tasting at Lyons.

Producer: Lyons was owned by Lyons Irish Holdings until a recent takeover by Unilever. Lyons are one of the two main suppliers of tea. Tea bags account for 89% of sales. There are also a number of other blenders.

Packaging: Today Lyons tea is mostly packed in tea bags of custom-made tis-sue paper, either single-serve or multi-cup. The colour of the box is the same as for loose tea. They have three packed blends and five tea bag blends. The use of colours to distinguish different teas is traditional for Lyons. Colour labels include green, mauve and gold. Eighty is the standard number of tea bags to a box. Other numbers are 40, 160 and 500.

Season: Tea is popular throughout the year with highest consumption in winter.

References: Christopher Moloney, J. Lyons & Co., personal communication.

Useful address: J. Lyons & Co. (Ireland) Ltd, Davitt Road, Goldenbridge, Inchicore, Dublin 12. Tel 01-455-6423.

Barry's Tea

Special features: Tea is the most common hot drink in Ireland. Barry's, like Lyons, is a household name.

Composition: Tea leaves (see Bewleys).

History: The early and recent history of tea in general is shown under Bewleys and Lyons.

Barry's of Cork owned a tea, wine and spirits shop and started tea-blending in 1901, but did not begin to specialise in tea until the 1930s and 1940s. The wholesale distribution side of the business was set up in the 1960s and Barry's became national distributors in the 1970s. Originally Indian and Sri Lankan teas were used, but since the Second World War African teas (from Kenya, Uganda, Tanzania and Rwanda) have become more important for Barry's, so that today 90% of their teas are African and only 10% Indian.

Use: See Bewleys for details on preparation.

Technique: In general in the production regions the tea leaves are first dried, but some fermentation is allowed to release enzymes. The leaves are then fully dried or fired by blowing through a large oven-type chamber so that fermentation is totally stopped. The producers offer samples of various leaf sizes to the blenders. Some companies use cutters to give CTC tea, i.e. cut, tear and curl. CTC tea is found in tea bags. Orthodox tea is from smaller leaves and, as it is not cut, it is larger. A circular motion is used to roll it up. CTC tea is claimed to give a quicker infusion (i.e. tea release into the water) than orthodox tea.

The tea arrives packed in chests from designated gardens in the production regions. It is tipped from the chests manually into the blending drum. The blended tea is drawn from the blender into hoppers and packed. Bagging is described under Lyons. At present Barry's blend is usually made up of tea from as many as ten chests but in the future the blend may come from as many as twenty chests.

Barry's have two trained tasters. Tasting is necessary throughout the year as quality varies with the sources, season and climate. For example, Indian tea may be available only between May and September. Some teas may be vacuum packed for blending when fresh tea is not available.

Producer: Barry's are one of the two main suppliers. Tea bags account for 75% of their sales.

Season: Tea is popular throughout the year with highest consumption in winter.

Packaging: Today Barry's tea is mostly packed in muslin-type tea bags, either single-serve or multi-cup, with about 80 to a standard box (250 g). Other sizes are 125 g and 500 g, with 40 bags and 160 bags respectively. Barry's range includes Classic Gold, Red Label and Green Label.

References: Tony Barry, Barry's Tea, Cork, personal communication.

Useful address: Barry's Tea, Kinsale Road, Cork. Tel 021-966-644.

Select Bibliography

Allen, D. *The Festive Food of Ireland* London, 1992

An Bord Glas (Irish Horticultural Development Board) *Fresh Produce Guide* Dublin, 1994

Archer, J. *Statistical Survey of the County of Dublin* Dublin, 1801

Beckett, S. *Molloy* Paris, 1951

Bennet, J. A. and Smitters, G. V. (eds.) 'Land of Cokaygne'. *Early Middle English Verse and Prose* Oxford, 1968

Best, R. I. and Bergin, O. 'Fled Bricrenn' *Lebor na hUidre* Dublin, 1992

Bourke, A. *The Visitation of God: The Potato and the Great Irish Famine* Dublin, 1993

Campion, E. *A History of Ireland Written in the Year 1571* Dublin, 1633

Carbery, M. *The Farm by Lough Gur* Cork, 1986

Connery, C. *In an Irish Country Kitchen* London, 1992

Corkery, D. *The Hidden Ireland* Dublin, 1924

Crosbie, P. *Your Dinner's Poured Out!* Dublin, 1991

Cullen, L. M. *The Emergence of Modern Ireland 1600–1900* London, 1981

Cummins, L. 'Sectoral Analysis of the Irish Chocolate and Sugar Confectionery Industry' unpublished Master of Business Studies Thesis, University College Dublin, 1977

Danaher, K. *In Ireland Long Ago* Cork, 1962

——*The Year in Ireland* Cork, 1972

David, E. *English Bread and Yeast Cookery* London, 1977

Day, A. and McWilliams, P. (eds.) *Ordnance Survey Memoirs of Ireland, Vol. V, Parishes of County Tyrone, 1821, 1823, 1831–36* Dublin, 1990

——*Ordnance Survey Memoirs of Ireland, Vol. II, Parishes of County Antrim 1838–39* Dublin, 1990

Department of Agriculture and Food 'Potato Varieties Irish (recommended list)' Dublin, 1994/1995

Derricke, J. *The Image of Ireland with A Discovery of Woodkarne* London, 1581

Dineley, T. *Observations in a Voyage Through the Kingdom of Ireland in the Year 1681* Dublin, 1870

Dinneen, Rev. P. S. *Foclóir Gaedhilge agus Béarla, An Irish–English Dictionary* Dublin, 1927

Doyle, L. 'Apples Can Give Good Margins' *Today's Farm* Teagasc 5, 1995

Dubourdieu, J. *Statistical Survey of the County of Down* Dublin, 1802

Dunton, J. *Unpublished Letters* (1699) *see* MacLysaght, E.

Edwards, D. R. and Williams, T. D. *The Great Famine. Studies in Irish History 1845–52* Dublin, 1956

Evans, E. E. *Irish Folkways* London, 1988

Falkiner, C. Litton *Illustrations of Irish History and Topography* London, 1904

Farmar, T. *The Legendary Lofty Clattery Café: Bewleys of Ireland* Dublin, 1988

Fitzgibbon, T. *Irish Traditional Food* Dublin, 1991

Gantz, J *Early Irish Myths and Sagas* London 1981

Gmelch, G. and Saddlemyer, A. *J. M. Synge's Ireland: In Wicklow, West Kerry and Connemara* Dublin, 1980

Gogarty, O. St J. *Tumbling in the Hay* London, 1939

Hogan, W. *The Complete Book of Bacon* London, 1978

Hutton, A. W. *Arthur Young's Tour in Ireland 1776–1779* , *Vols 1 and 2*, London, 1892

Irish Manuscripts Commision *The Shapland Carew Papers* Dublin, 1946

Irwin, F. *Irish Country Recipes* Belfast, 1937

Jackson, K. H. *Aislinge meic Conglinne* Dublin, 1990

Johnston, J. *A Hundred Years Eating* Dublin, 1977

Joyce, J. *Dubliners* London, 1914

——*Ulysses* Paris, 1922

Joyce, P. W. *A Social History of Ancient Ireland* Dublin, 1903

Keane, J. B. *Durango* Cork, 1992

Kelly, J. *The Letters of Lord Chief Baron Edward Willes to the Earl of Warwick, 1757–1762. An account of Ireland in the mid-eighteenth century* Aberystwyth, 1990

Keogh, J. *Botanologia Universalis Hibernica* see Scott, M.

Laverty, M. *Never No More* London, 1942

Lucas, A. T. 'Irish Food Before the Potato', *Gwerin 3*, 1960

—— '"When I make Tea, I makes tea . . ." Innovation in Food— the Case of Tea in Ireland' *Ulster Folklife* Vol. 33, 1987

Lysaght, P. (ed) *Milk and Milk Products from Medieval to Modern Times* Edinburgh, 1994

McCarthy, J. 'History and Development of the Irish Cheese Industry' 3rd Cheese Conference, Moorepark, 1993

McGrath, M. (ed.) *Cinnlae Amhlaoibh Uí Shúilleabháin. The Diary of Humphrey O'Sullivan Parts 1–4*, London, reprinted 1989

McKenna, J. and McKenna, S. *Bridgestone Irish Food Guide* Cork, 1993

McKibbin, J. 'Childhood Days in Dundonald' *Ulster Folklife*, Vol. 26, 1980

MacLysaght, E. *Irish Life in the Seventeenth Century* Dublin, 1939

MacThomáis, É. *Gur Cake and Coal Blocks* Dublin, 1978

Mahon, B. *Land of Milk and Honey* Dublin, 1991

Moryson, F. *An Itinerary Containing His Ten Years Travel* Glasgow, 1908

Murphy, G. (ed.) *Early Irish Lyrics: Eighth to Twelfth Century* Oxford, 1956

Murray, J. *Irish Whiskey Almanac* Neil Wilson Publishers, Glasgow, 1994

Myers, J. P. (ed.) *A Selection of Writings by Elizabethan Writers on Ireland* Hampden, Conn. 1983

Nelson, C. '"This Garden to Adorne With All Varietie" The Garden Plants of Ireland in the Centuries Before 1700' *Moorea* 9, 1990

——*The Trees of Ireland* Dublin, 1992

Ní Chinnéide, S. 'A Frenchman's Impressions of County Cork in 1790' *Journal of the Cork Historical and Archaeological Society*, LXXIX, 1974

O'Curry, A. *The Cider Industry of Ireland* Dublin, n. d.

O'Dwyer, G. 'Irish Mead—an Export with Tradition behind it' *Irish Exporter*, March 1984

O'Keefe, A. and Phelan, J. A. *Cheese Varieties* (Handbook Series 14) An Foras Talúntais, Dublin, 1979

O'Mara, V. J. and O'Reilly, F. *An Irish Literary Cookbook* Dublin, 1991

O'Meara, J. *Giraldus Cambrensis: The History and Topography of Ireland* (revised edition) Dublin, 1982

O'Neill, T. *Merchants and Mariners in Medieval Ireland* Dublin, 1987

Ó Sé, M. 'Old Irish Cheeses and Other Milk Products' *Journal of the Cork Historical and Archaeological Society*, 53, 1948

Petty, W. *The Political Anatomy of Ireland* London, 1691

Piers, H. *A Chorographical Description of the County of West Meath. In Collectanea de Rebus Hibernicis* Dublin, 1770

Piggott's Almanack or *Directory* Birr, 1823

Plummer, C. (ed.) *Bethada Náem nÉrenn* Oxford, 1922

Pococke, R. *Pococke's Tour in Ireland in 1752* London, 1891

Pochin-Mould, D. *Discovering Cork* Dingle, 1991

Reade, C. *The Sportsman in Ireland* London, 1897

Ritchie, R. B. 'The Chocolate and Sugar Confectionery Industry in Ireland' unpublished M. Econ. Sc. Thesis, University College Dublin, 1970

Salaman, R. N. *The History and Social Influence of the Potato* Cambridge, 1989

Scott, M. (ed.) *An Irish Herbal: Botanalogia Universalis Hibernica* Dublin, 1986

Sexton, R. 'Cereals and Cereal Foodstuffs in the Early Historic Period' unpublished M.A. Thesis, University College Cork, 1993

——'I'd Ate it Like Chocolate: the Disappearing Offal Food Traditions of Cork City' *Disappearing Foods; Oxford Symposium on Food and Cookery* London 1995

Shaw, G. B. *John Bull's Other Ireland* London, 1904

Shiperbottom, R. 'The Decline of the Tripe Trade' *Disappearing Foods: Oxford Symposium on Food and Cookery* London,1995

Somerville, O.E. and Ross, M. *Some Experiences of an Irish RM* London, 1899

Stokes, G. T. (ed.) *Pococke's Tour in Ireland in 1752* Dublin, 1891

Stokes, W. (ed.) *Lives of Saints from the Book of Lismore* Oxford, 1890*Lives of Saints from the Book of Lismore* Oxford, 1890

——*Acallamh na Sénorach* Irische Texte, ser. 4, Leipzig 1900

——*Lives of Saints from the Book of Lismore* Oxford, 1890*Félire Oengusso Céli Dé* London, 1905

Swift, J. *History of Dublin Bakers and Others* Dublin, 1949

Synge, J. M. *In Wicklow, West Kerry and Connemara* London, 1911

Teagasc *Management Data for Farm Planning* Dublin 1994

—— *Recommendations for Vegetable Production* Co. Dublin, 1991

Thackeray, W. M. *The Irish Sketch Book* London, 1865

Uí Shuilleabháin, Amhlaoibh *see* McGrath, M.

Verdon, M. *Shawlies, Echo Boys, the Marsh and the Lanes: Old Cork Remembered* Dublin, 1993

Vossen, A. F. (ed.) *Two Bokes of the Histories of Ireland by Edmund Campion* Assen, 1963

White-Lennon, B. *Poolbeg Book of Traditional Irish Cooking* Dublin, 1990

Woridge, J. *Systema Agriculturae* 1688

Wymberry, E. *Well, Recollections of Waterford in the 1940's and 1950's* Waterford, n.d.

Young, A. *A Tour In Ireland see* Hutton A. W.

Index